Editing
for the
Digital
Age

SAGE was founded in 1965 by Sara Miller McCune to support the dissemination of usable knowledge by publishing innovative and high-quality research and teaching content. Today, we publish more than 750 journals, including those of more than 300 learned societies, more than 800 new books per year, and a growing range of library products including archives, data, case studies, reports, conference highlights, and video. SAGE remains majority-owned by our founder, and after Sara's lifetime will become owned by a charitable trust that secures our continued independence.

Los Angeles | London | Washington DC | New Delhi | Singapore | Boston

Editing
for the
Digital
Age

Thom Lieb
Towson University

Los Angeles | London | New Delhi
Singapore | Washington DC | Boston

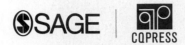

Los Angeles | London | New Delhi
Singapore | Washington DC | Boston

FOR INFORMATION:

CQ Press
An Imprint of SAGE Publications, Inc.
2455 Teller Road
Thousand Oaks, California 91320
E-mail: order@sagepub.com

SAGE Publications Ltd.
1 Oliver's Yard
55 City Road
London EC1Y 1SP
United Kingdom

SAGE Publications India Pvt. Ltd.
B 1/I 1 Mohan Cooperative Industrial Area
Mathura Road, New Delhi 110 044
India

SAGE Publications Asia-Pacific Pte. Ltd.
3 Church Street
#10-04 Samsung Hub
Singapore 049483

Acquisitions Editor: Matthew Byrnie
Digital Content Editor: Gabrielle Piccininni
Editorial Assistant: Janae Masnovi
Production Editor: Jane Haenel
Copy Editor: Mark Bast
Typesetter: C&M Digitals (P) Ltd.
Proofreader: Susan Schon
Indexer: Michael Ferreira
Cover Designer: Scott Van Atta
Marketing Manager: Liz Thornton

Printed in the United States of America

Library of Congress Cataloging-in-Publication Data

Lieb, Thom.

Editing for the digital age / Thom Lieb, Towson University.

pages cm
Includes bibliographical references and index.

ISBN 978-1-4833-0654-4 (spiral : alk. paper)

1. Editing. I. Title.

PN162.L493 2015
808.02′7—dc23   2014043956

This book is printed on acid-free paper.

15 16 17 18 19 10 9 8 7 6 5 4 3 2 1

BRIEF CONTENTS

Preface x

Acknowledgments xi

Chapter 1. You, the Editor 1

Chapter 2. Choosing Content That Clicks: Publishing for Your Audience 9

Chapter 3. Getting the Facts Straight 24

Chapter 4. Polishing Writing 43

Chapter 5. This One Weird Chapter Will Help You Grab Readers 57

Chapter 6. Defamation 71

Chapter 7. Privacy, Copyright, International Regulations and Other Legal Issues 89

Chapter 8. Handling Matters of Ethics, Fairness, Taste and Sensitivity 103

Chapter 9. Managing Engagement 124

Chapter 10. Curation, Aggregation and Creation 138

Chapter 11. Editorial Triage 155

Notes 162

Index 179

About the Author 187

DETAILED CONTENTS

Preface   x

Acknowledgments   xi

Chapter 1: You, the Editor   1
Traditional Editors' Roles   2
New Challenges   3
- Wrapping Up   3
- Key Points   4
- Chapter Exercise   4
- Write Right: Choosing the Correct Word   5
- Editor's Toolkit: Choosing a Dictionary   7

Chapter 2: Choosing Content That Clicks: Publishing for Your Audience   9
What New Publishers Can Learn From Old Media   9
Finding a Niche   10
Defining the Target Audience   11
Creating Useful Surveys and Focus Groups   12
Creating a Mission Statement   13
Deciding What to Publish   14
Case Study: The Scientist Gets a Makeover   15
Worry About This/Don't Worry About That:
   Long-Term Planning vs. Gradual Evolution   18
Letting the Audience Lead You to Ideas   19
Objectivity in the 21st Century   20
- Wrapping Up   20
- Key Points   21
- Chapter Exercise   21
- Write Right: Making Sure Subjects and Verbs Agree   21
- Editor's Toolkit: Using an Editorial Calendar   23

Chapter 3: Getting the Facts Straight   24
Common Factual Errors   25
   Names and Titles   26
   Place Names   26
   Numbers   27
Myths, Hoaxes and Urban Legends   28
Manipulation of Images and Videos   29
Case Study: Fox News Channel Finds Itself Outfoxed   30
Filling Holes   31
Case Study: The Manipulated Image That Wasn't   32
Using Online Resources to Find and Verify Information   35
Corrections   37
- Wrapping Up   37
- Key Points   38
- Chapter Exercise   38
- Write Right: Using Quotations Properly   39
- Editor's Toolkit: Choosing a Stylebook   41

Chapter 4: Polishing Writing   43
From Writer-Centered to Audience-Centered   43
Using the Appropriate Writing Style   44
Offer a Unique Voice   45
Case Study: SmittenKitchen   **46**
Avoiding Verbosity and Achieving Clarity   46
Worry About This/Not About That: The Truth About Short and Long Sentences   **49**
Limiting Sentences to One Idea Each   50
- Wrapping Up   52
- Key Points   52
- Chapter Exercise   52
- Write Right: Avoiding Fragments and Comma Splices   53
- Editor's Toolkit: Blogs Editors Should Follow   54

Chapter 5: This One Weird Chapter Will Help You Grab Readers   57
Keep It Simple   57
Headline Style Rules   **58**
Make It Specific   59
Size It Right   60
When It's Time for a Subhead   61
How Print and Online Headlines Differ   62
SEO and Why It Matters   62
Trends in Online Headlines   63
Case Study: Crafting the Most Attractive Headlines   **64**
Worry About This/Not About That: Why Headline Writers Need Dirty Minds – and Shouldn't Hesitate to Ask Questions   **65**
Captions and Cutlines   66
Writing the Ultimate Cutline   **66**
- Wrapping Up   67
- Key Points   67
- Chapter Exercise   68
- Write Right: Avoiding Passive Voice   68
- Editor's Toolkit: Resources for Writing Better Heads   70

Chapter 6: Defamation   71
Defining Defamation   71
Case Study: Sending a Blogger to Jail to Keep Him From Publishing   **72**
What's the Difference Between Libel and Slander?   **72**
Case Study: When a Blogger Is Not a Journalist – and Then Is   **74**
Journalistic Privilege   75
   The Opinion and Fair Comment Privilege   75
Case Study: Truthful Blog Post Costs Subject a Job – Should Blogger Pay $60,000?   **76**
   The Fair Report Privilege   77
   The Neutral Report Privilege   77
Differences in Status   77
Case Study: Courtney Love's Costly Tweets   **78**
   Private Figures   78
   Public Figures and Public Officials   78
Worry About This/Not About That: The Risks of Relying on Allegedly and Inference, and the Safety of Publishing Online Comments   **80**
   Satire and Parody   81
Publishing Anonymously   82
SLAPP Suits   82

Case Study: Getting SLAPPed for Calling Someone a Dumb Ass **83**
The Importance of Corrections and Clarifications 83
- Wrapping Up 84
- Key Points 84
- Chapter Exercise 84
- Write Right: Using Commas Properly 86
- Editor's Toolkit: Resources for Free and Affordable Legal Help 87

Chapter 7: Privacy, Copyright, International Regulations and Other Legal Issues 89
Privacy Issues 89
Copyright Infringement 92
Case Study: When Using 99 Percent Is Fair Use **93**
Responsibility for Publishing the Statements and Content of Others 94
Publishing Product or Service Endorsements 94
Case Study: When Copyright Meets Privacy **95**
Laws Affecting Recordings 95
New Technologies 95
Employment Issues 96
Governmental Risks 97
Worry About This, Not About That: "Borrowing" Copyrighted Material Is Never OK, but Naming Minors Can Be **97**
Fending Off Foreign Legal Threats 98
- Wrapping Up 100
- Key Points 100
- Chapter Exercise 100
- Write Right: Using Apostrophes Properly 101
- Editor's Toolkit: Online Sites for Editing Practice and Learning 102

Chapter 8: Handling Matters of Ethics, Fairness, Taste and Sensitivity 103
Ethical Issues 104
　　Fabrication 104
　　Plagiarism 104
Case Study: Printing a False Story to Prevent Murders **105**
　　Image Manipulation 106
　　Getting Information via Deception 107
　　Funding Issues 108
　　Transparency 109
Case Study: Stopping the Presses **110**
　　Balance and Fairness 110
　　Conflicts of Interest 111
　　Anonymity and Confidentiality 112
　　Withholding Information That Could Lead to Harm 113
　　Taste and Sensitivity 114
Making the Right Decisions 116
Is It Time for New Ethics Codes? 117
Diversity as an Ethical Concern **117**
Worry About This, Not About That: Using Public Social Media Posts Is OK, but Private Ones Probably Are Off-Limits **118**
- Wrapping Up 120
- Key Points 120
- Chapter Exercise 120
- Write Right: Avoiding Dangling Modifiers 121
- Editor's Toolkit: Journalism Ethics Codes 123

Chapter 9: Managing Engagement 124
Internal Engagement 124
External Engagement 125
What If Readers Chose the News? **128**
Crafting and Using Social Media Guidelines 128
Case Study: When Tweets Break Bad **129**
Using Analytics to Learn More About Audience Usage and Preferences 129
- Wrapping Up 131
- Key Points 132
- Chapter Exercise 132
- Write Right: Untangling Words That Sound Like Each Other (Part 1) 132
- Editor's Toolkit: Organizations for Editors 136

Chapter 10: Curation, Aggregation and Creation 138
Curation and Aggregation 138
    Curation as Distribution or Relay 138
    Curation as Aggregation or Combination 139
A Mouse That Roars **141**
    Curation as Filter or Distillation 141
The Importance of Links **141**
Creation 142
    Listicles 142
    Photo Galleries and Slide Shows 143
Case Study: Creating Lists at BuzzFeed **144**
    Quizzes 145
    Timelines and Chronologies 145
    Maps 146
    Animated GIFs 146
    Other Possibilities 147
- Wrapping Up 147
- Key Points 148
- Chapter Exercise 148
- Write Right: Untangling Words That Sound Like Each Other (Part 2) 148
- Editor's Toolkit: Creating an Engaging Storify 153

Chapter 11: Editorial Triage 155
- Wrapping Up 157
- Key Points 157
- Chapter Exercise 157
- Write Right: Other Confusing Words 157
- Editor's Toolkit: Automated Editing Tools 161

Notes 162

Index 179

About the Author 187

PREFACE

On the surface, editing seems like a simple and relatively timeless process – and a natural one, too. As the comments section on any Web page proves daily, one of humankind's most basic instincts is to correct other people's grammatical mistakes and otherwise try to improve their writing. It probably wasn't long after the first words were chiseled in stone or inked on papyrus that someone looked at them and said, "You know what would make that read better?"

For a long time, that was pretty much the definition of editing. But as soon as the first graphics were added to words, the role of the editor began to expand, and that expansion continues through today, when editing has reached a point far from its origins. In fact, in this age of computerization, many of what were once the basic tasks of editing – checking spelling and correcting grammar – now can be handled largely by software. Further, many of the most important tasks editors perform today were barely imagined even 20 years ago. And perhaps most important: In the digital age, everyone has to act as an editor, if only on his or her own work.

As the author of two previous editing textbooks, I have seen many of these changes firsthand. My first book was published just as the World Wide Web was coming into existence, and the focus was on traditional print media and the skills needed to edit in that arena. The second edition of that text came at a time when the Web was well established as a publishing medium, but long before social media, mobile news and other new factors came into play.

With this book, I decided it was time to start with a blank slate. The guiding question for this entirely new text was "How is the job of editing practiced today, and how will it likely change in the near term?" That approach meant leaving behind some of the points that were central to my other texts and adding in many new aspects that I had not addressed before.

Along the way, I checked in daily with a wide range of practicing editors, through their online writings, personal correspondence, online chats and webinars, in-person conferences and a multitude of other means. I wanted to make sure that the editors of tomorrow would get the timeliest advice from some of the best editors today. I have to admit that I learned a lot in the process – always one of the nicest benefits of writing.

The result is a text that offers journalists and journalism students the most up-to-the-minute information on how to best do their jobs – even if their jobs are just to edit their own material.

In order to keep the text relevant and timely, I will be posting regular links to articles and other material that complement the text on my Twitter account: http://www.twitter.com/thomlieb. Readers will be able to find the most relevant links by searching for the hashtag I use for my own News Editing course, #mcom358. My hope is that this hashtag will become the center of an interactive forum for users of the book. Therefore, I invite you to tweet your own links with that same hashtag, as well as to ask questions of me and other users. I look forward to continuing the discussion.

Visit the companion website at **http://study.sagepub.com/lieb** for open-access student resources including chapter-by-chapter **web quizzes** for independent assessment of course material, and a list of **online web links** and **general resources**. The password-protected instructor resource site includes additional **Editing Practice Exercises** for each chapter designed to enforce chapter lessons and provides additional experience of hands-on editing.

Thom Lieb

ACKNOWLEDGMENTS

Even when a book like this bears a single author's name, it's no secret that it takes the help of a lot of people to make it a reality. Truer words were never spoken than "I could not have done it without your help."

Many of my helpers did not even know they were doing so: they were speakers at Online News Association, SPJ Excellence in Journalism, American Copy Editors Society and Journalism Interactive conferences, as well as bloggers and prolific tweeters who alerted me to new topics, methods and tools I never would have come across on my own. One of those people who deserves special mention is Steve Buttry, whose long and varied writings on digital journalism have been the equivalent of graduate study in that discipline.

Those who directly helped are many, but a few deserve particular accolades. As has been the case many times in our long friendship, Mark Sullivan deserves a special thanks for a wide range of contributions. From my earliest drafts of the proposal through questions about structure, examples and much more, Mark was there to offer vital feedback over and over again.

My good friend and colleague at Towson University, Beth Haller, was very helpful in offering feedback on the material in Chapter 6, an area in which she has developed great expertise over the years.

Ian Hill, executive producer of Digital & Social, News10, Sacramento, California, went way beyond the call of duty in helping me understand the full range of engagement efforts and tools.

Rebecca Huffman and Adam Marton of The Baltimore Sun – both people I am proud to say are former students of mine – helped immensely with suggestions and feedback, particularly on Chapter 10.

Another former student – and at this point, longtime friend – Maria Stuart offered feedback on chapters along the way and provided one more set of eagle eyes during the editing process. Marketing writer and consultant Angela Davids, another former student, went through the page proofs and found even more things that needed to be corrected.

Mary Hartney Nahorniak, social media editor at USA Today, provided great feedback on Chapter 9 and graciously agreed to let me quote some of her more insightful observations.

I would be remiss if I did not thank Cynthia Cooper, my chair in the Department of Mass Communication and Communication Studies at Towson University. Throughout the long process leading up to the completion of this book, she has provided support in a multitude of ways. I am grateful for all the help.

I would also like to thank the following reviewers of the book: Andrew Bechtel, University of North Carolina; JoAnne Broadwater, Towson University; Andrea W. Dilworth, Jackson State University; Nancy Heiz, SUNY–New Paltz; and Ray Murray, Oklahoma State University. And a special thanks to the staff at SAGE, especially acquisitions editor Matt Byrnie, editorial assistant Gabrielle Piccininni, and production editor Jane Haenel. Mark Bast, the copy editor selected to copy edit this book on copy editing, did a great job of finding missing words, misspelled names and other errors that would have been mightily embarrassing to have appearing in print.

Finally, I tip my hat to Vince Rinehart, multiplatform editor, The Washington Post. For more than 20 years, Vince has been a valued friend and professional colleague who – no matter how hectic his schedule or personal life – has been quick to offer assistance in any way I needed.

CQ Press, an imprint of SAGE, is the leading publisher of books, periodicals, and electronic products on American government and international affairs. CQ Press consistently ranks among the top commercial publishers in terms of quality, as evidenced by the numerous awards its products have won over the years. CQ Press owes its existence to Nelson Poynter, former publisher of the *St. Petersburg Times*, and his wife Henrietta, with whom he founded Congressional Quarterly in 1945. Poynter established CQ with the mission of promoting democracy through education and in 1975 founded the Modern Media Institute, renamed The Poynter Institute for Media Studies after his death. The Poynter Institute (www.poynter.org) is a nonprofit organization dedicated to training journalists and media leaders.

In 2008, CQ Press was acquired by SAGE, a leading international publisher of journals, books, and electronic media for academic, educational, and professional markets. Since 1965, SAGE has helped inform and educate a global community of scholars, practitioners, researchers, and students spanning a wide range of subject areas, including business, humanities, social sciences, and science, technology, and medicine. A privately owned corporation, SAGE has offices in Los Angeles, London, New Delhi, and Singapore, in addition to the Washington DC office of CQ Press.

Chapter 1 **You, the Editor**

It used to be easy to distinguish between writers and editors. The former undertook the necessary research and reporting to put stories together; the latter made sure those stories were accurate, fair, grammatically and stylistically correct, and free of legal problems. But today, that distinction essentially has vanished. While not every editor also has to be a writer, every writer now needs to be his or her own best editor.

That shift has come as the Internet transformed the publishing industry. The World Wide Web and later offshoots such as blogs opened the way for anyone with something to say to become a publisher. For the first time in history, there were no large staffs needed, no high costs – in many cases, no costs at all – and no long delays in getting a message out to a large audience.

People who had never thought of themselves as publishers jumped at the opportunity. And by mid-2014, barely 20 years after the birth of the World Wide Web, users had set up more than 1 billion websites on the Internet.[1] At the same time, more than 180 million blogs were being published around the world.[2] The Internet, it turned out, was as revolutionary a publishing tool as Gutenberg's printing press.

Other trends accelerated the momentum of average people taking up publishing. As mobile phones became miniature computers – and were joined by tablets and music players that were also computers – people who so far had sat out the online publishing revolution were able to jump in. And as the world turned toward mobile, new platforms like Twitter and Tumblr and even the hulking giant Facebook offered more opportunities for anyone to publish.

Clay Shirky, professor at the renowned Interactive Telecommunications Program at New York University, summed up the changes in an interview with Findings.com:

> Publishing is not evolving. Publishing is going away. Because the word "publishing" means a cadre of professionals who are taking on the incredible difficulty and complexity and expense of making something public. That's not a job anymore. That's a button. There's a button that says "publish," and when you press it, it's done.[3]

That huge transformation has brought with it unimaginable benefits. Now that anyone can be a publisher, it becomes harder for a few powerful voices to dominate any conversation. From the trivial – the countless movie and music fan blogs – to the critically important – dissident news sites that help rally citizens to take up the cause of freedom – there can be no doubt that the conversations of the times have become more democratized.

Meanwhile, in part as a direct result of the rise of these new forms of media, traditional publishers found their revenues steadily plummeting. Newspapers that could once count on financial support from classified advertising and retail display ads saw that revenue disappear in the wake of eBay, Craigslist and retailers' own websites and mailing lists. Magazines suffered a similar if not as great loss.

Because newspapers and magazines need writers (and photographers, artists and designers) to fill their pages, many of them found that an easy way to cut costs was to reduce the number of editors. A study conducted by the American Society of News Editors found that the number of copy editors in newsrooms decreased by almost 50 percent from 2002 to 2012 (for reference, the number of reporting and supervisory positions was cut by about 25 percent).[4]

And even when positions were not eliminated, highly paid experienced editors sometimes were let go in favor of younger editors. Those newcomers would work for less money, but they did not have the depth of knowledge of the publication or its content areas, so they were more likely to let mistakes slip through. As a result, writers even at established media now found they too needed to be their own editors. It's not surprising that Steve Buttry, former digital transformation editor for Digital First Media, has noted that "Journalists who have treated the copy desk as a safety net need to take more responsibility for the quality of their own work."[5]

Traditional Editors' Roles

Editors long served as the last line of defense in picking out errors large and small before they reached the audience. Editors check for holes in stories, verify facts, look for legal and ethical problems with material, and much more. Most of the time, the lack of editors shows up in ways that mainly serve to irritate cranky grammar fanatics: a misused word here, a missing comma there, a subject that doesn't agree with its verb. But too many of these little things inevitably cause readers to ask, "If they can't get the little things right, how can I trust that the big things will be correct?"

In truth, the loss of editors has resulted in a situation that's even worse than that. As longtime editor John McIntyre has written in regard to elimination of copy editors in newspaper newsrooms:

> What you can expect from the copy-editor-free newsroom is a first-draft text from a writer to which someone bearing the title of editor will have made a quick swipe before posting it online. You will notice the typos and lapses in grammar and usage, which stand out. What you may not be so quick to notice is that the reporting is often thin, superficial, uncritical, because no one was there to pose hard questions.[6]

Further, the warp speed at which online and mobile publishing operate often results in much more serious errors, even from people who know better but just did not have (or take) the time to double-check things. So errors like these show up:

- A news item about the death of the first man to walk on the moon that identified him as musician Neil Young, rather than astronaut Neil Armstrong.
- A map that reversed the location of North and South Dakota.
- The logo of United Nation Space Command from the videogame Halo used unintentionally in place of the logo of the United Nations.
- Breaking news reports that the Supreme Court had overturned the individual health care mandate in a landmark case – when in fact it had upheld it.
- A column about new DVD releases that misstated the name of the creatures that appeared in the "Gremlins" movies, calling them mowglis. They actually were mogwais; Mowgli was a character in Rudyard Kipling's "Jungle Book."

While those errors range from the silly to the serious, they have one thing in common: They were committed by large, well-established news organizations that should have known – and done – better. (In case you are wondering, the culprits were NBC News; The New York Times, in a repeat of an error The Washington Post had recently committed; the BBC; CNN and Fox News; and The New York Times.)[7] And all were published within a short time period, illustrating the fact that it's not hard to find such mistakes regularly being made by trained and well-staffed organizations, let alone by a multitasking individual.

New Challenges

The digital era also presents a number of other challenges that did not exist in the pre-Web era. For instance, when news was written to be delivered in a newspaper or magazine, it was a simple matter to indicate when it had happened – yesterday, last week – or when a follow-up would occur – tomorrow, next week. But when information is distributed all over the world instantaneously, it might already be tomorrow or still be yesterday where some people are reading. Further, unlike a newspaper that gets thrown away once it has been read, digital information tends to stick around. So a reader might come across those references months or even years after they were written. As a result, writers now have to make it clear what specific day or date is being referred to.

In addition to avoiding embarrassment and confusion, digital publishers also want to avoid legal problems. Wrongly connecting a person with a crime or using someone else's material without proper permission can lead to criminal charges. Conversely, shying away from potentially libelous material can lead to bland writing that overlooks important news, and being overcautious about getting permission can waste valuable time.

In some cases, the legal concerns go beyond those that govern publishing. For example, one blogger who offered free advice to help readers lose weight and become healthier – something newspapers and magazines have done for decades with no problems – was told by the state that he was breaking the law by "providing nutrition care services without a license."[8] Clearly then, digital publishers need to know how changes in the interpretations of publishing laws affect them.

That's where this book comes in. While no volume can turn someone into an editor overnight, this one serves as a guide to get readers up to speed as quickly as possible on all the critical elements of editing. Whether the reader intends to self-publish or write for an established organization, this book offers the tools to work effectively and to avoid looking stupid and inviting legal action.

The points just discussed are only some of the topics covered in this book. In addition, sections provide guidance on the following topics and many more:

- Refining the focus – finding and reaching the target audience
- Getting the facts straight
- Writing tight (and clearly)
- Creating headlines and titles that summarize and attract
- Navigating the shifting legal landscape
- Handling matters of fairness, ethics, taste and sensitivity
- Engaging an audience and acting as a curator
- Finding and creating multimedia
- Performing triage

Wrapping Up

In the immortal words of Spider-Man's Uncle Ben (and earlier, someone named Voltaire), "With great power comes great responsibility." Now that virtually everyone has the power to be a publisher, it's important that people also keep in mind the responsibilities to publish accurate, fair and error-free material. We begin learning how to accomplish that in the next chapter.

Key Points

- In the digital age, anyone can be a publisher.
- The increase in small publishing operations and cuts in traditional newsrooms have led to a lack of editing, lowering quality in many publications.
- At a minimum, lack of editing leads to lots of minor errors. But combined with the quick pace of online publishing, it also can lead to serious problems.
- New problems arise in the digital age, ranging from how to denote the time element when readers are spread around the world to how to handle emerging legal issues.

CHAPTER EXERCISE

In the following sentences, choose the correctly spelled word in each group.

1. ___ Her tooth needed to be pulled because of the underlying **a) abcess b) abscess c) absess**.

2. ___ Because he was close to graduation, he thought it would be a good idea to check in with his **a) adviser b) advisor**.

3. ___ While the plan was not their first choice, they said they were **a) alright b) all right with it**.

4. ___ The question was how well the hotel could **a) acommodate b) accommodate** such a large group.

5. ___ Summer is the perfect time for **a) backyard b) backyard** grilling.

6. ___ While the show was a critical success, poor viewership led it to be **a) canceled b) cancelled** after just a few episodes.

7. ___ Walking through a **a) cemetary b) cemetery** always made him nervous.

8. ___ There was no clear **a) concensus b) consensus** on how the noise problem could be resolved.

9. ___ They decided to splurge and hire a **a) chauffer b) chaufer c) chauffeur** for the evening.

10. ___ No one on the jury seemed to find the **a) defendant b) defendent** credible.

11. ___ It might not have been the most **a) disasterous b) disastrous** first date in history, but it ranked in the top 10.

12. ___ Getting the job of her dreams right out of college put her in a state of **a) ecstacy b) ecstasy**.

13. ___ Young people spend less time with **a) e-mail b) email** than virtually any other form of communication.

14. ___ He realized that if anyone came across the photos he had posted, it would **a) embarras b) embarrass** his family.

15. ___ Spending the day working under **a) flourescent b) fluorescent** lighting gives many people a headache.

16. ___ Her loss of vision was caused by a **a) hemorage b) hemorrhage** in one eye.

17. ___ The group needed someone to act as a **a) liason b) liaison** with the local police.

18. ___ She made no effort to be **a) likable b) likeable**, but most of her colleagues enjoyed working with her anyway.

19. ___ The **a) limosine b) limousine** sped away before the onlookers could catch a glimpse of who was inside.

20. ___ World events indicated that it was probably time to **a) liquefy b) liquify** some of their assets.

21. ___ A good editor is careful to never **a) mispell b) misspell** a word that a writer had used correctly.

22. ___ While pancakes were tempting, she decided to have an **a) omelet b) omlette**.

23. ___ No one realized at the time of his signing what a **a) phenomenon b) phenomenom** he was.

24. ___ Everyone at the university realized what a **a) priveledge b) privilege** it was to be a student there.

25. ___ To help measure satisfaction, customers were asked to fill out a **a) questionaire b) questionnaire**.

26. ___ It was becoming more common for law enforcement officials to **a) seize b) sieze** the assets of people arrested for drug sales.

27. ___ They did not know what to do when they were told they could not obtain **a) separate b) seperate** rooms.

28. ___ Her family was proud that she had made the rank of **a) sargent b) sergeant**.

29. ___ The correct term for those who tend flocks of sheep is not cowboy but **a) shepard b) shepherd**.

30. ___ It's **a) weird b) wierd** how even words spelled correctly can appear incorrect after staring at them long enough.

 ## WRITE RIGHT

Choosing the Correct Word

With estimates of the number of words in the English language ranging as high as 750,000, it's hard to keep track of them all. (See "How Many Words Are There in the English Language?" Oxford Dictionaries, http://oxforddictionaries.com/words/how-many-words-are-there-in-the-english-language.) But a small number of those words are particularly troublesome to most people, and understanding how they are properly used goes a long way to creating a professional publication. This list might be considered the Top 10 Common Word Errors. The Write Right sections in Chapters 10 and 11 highlight other word errors.

Affect, effect: The distinction between these two is simple and clear – but with a small catch. *Affect* is a verb; *effect* is a noun. An easy way to keep them straight is to keep in mind the word *RAVEN*: Remember Affect (is) Verb (and) Effect (is) Noun.

For example:
The voters were worried how the changes in the tax code might affect them.
A year after the hurricane, residents were still dealing with its effects.

But now the catch: Both words can also be used as a different part of speech, *affect* as a noun and *effect* as a verb. In such uses, their meanings change completely, with *affect* meaning the observable manifestation of an emotional state, and *effect* meaning to bring about:

Despite the horrible crimes he had confessed to, the young man displayed a positive affect.
The student group hoped to effect changes in the levels of fees used for athletic spending.

Anxious, eager: Unlike the previous pair, these two are commonly misused in speech as well as publication. Again, a simple distinction determines which of these two to use, and there is not even a catch this time. The trick is just remembering that the root of *anxious* is the word *anxiety* – something that comes with dentist visits, exams for which one has not studied, and other uncomfortable situations. Most people are not filled with anxiety when they have the chance to hear their favorite band play, visit a new city or eat at a great new restaurant. So these would be fine:

Knowing that breast cancer runs in her family, she was anxious about getting the mammogram.

(Continued)

(Continued)

Based on the glowing coverage of the movie, he was eager to see it as soon as possible.

Notice that one is anxious about something and eager to do something.

Could of, should of, would of: These three versions of the same mistake are all too commonly spoken and written. This is one that just takes a moment of reflection: What in the world could those constructions mean? The answer: nothing. The proper usages are could have, should have and would have, as in these examples:

She could have been a dancer had it not been for the bus accident.
They should have gotten permission before entering the building.
He would have gotten the last lobster roll if he had been just five minutes earlier.

Fewer, less: If there's anything word geeks like less than waiting in line, it's waiting in line under a sign that says "10 items or less." That's because *fewer* should be used when referring to individual items that can be counted; *less* to quantities that cannot be broken down into individual units. For example:

Fewer students were admitted to the college last year, which led to less congestion on the local roads.

Its, it's: Remembering that an apostrophe indicates that something has been omitted (e.g., the '90s means the 1990s) makes this pair easy to keep straight. The one with the apostrophe omits the second *i* from *it is*:

It's widely known that spending too much time sitting at a desk can lead to health problems.

The other word should be saved for possessive usages:

The dog took months to adapt to its new surroundings.

Lay, lie: At least when using present tense, there's nothing all that tricky about this pair that would explain why so many people confuse them. *Lay* means to place; *lie* to recline. One easy memory aid is to think of the vowel sounds in those words and match them with *lie* and *lay*: lay = place (long *a* sound); lie = recline (long *i* sound).

The students were instructed to lay their books on the desk in the corner before the exam began.
I was so tired after the race that all I could do for the rest of the afternoon was lie on the sofa.

It's that easy. At least until the past tense is needed. That's because while the past tense of *lay* is relatively straightforward – *laid* – the past tense of *lie* is *lay*. So as strange as this might sound, it is correct:

He lay around the house yesterday instead of doing the yard work he promised to do.

Than, then: The easy way to keep these straight is to remember that *then* refers to time. In contrast, *than* is used to compare things or people.

She is in better shape now than she was when she was younger.
He plans to drive to the market and then to the library.

Their, there, they're: Remember the lesson from *its* and *it's*? That apostrophe means something has been removed. In this case, it's the letter *a* from *they are* that is missing from *they're*. *There* is easy to remember, since it indicates a direction. So the only remaining source of confusion is *their*, which is the possessive form of *they*.

Their jobs are too demanding for them to take on any additional work right now.
I liked the desk better when it was over there.
They're happier in their new apartment than they were in the old one.

Who, whom: The simple rule for these two is that *who* acts as a subject, directing some action; *whom* is an object that is acted on. (*Whoever* and *whomever* follow the same rules.) In the simplest sentences, the distinction is obvious:

Who invited him to the party?
It took her a long time to figure out for whom she was working.

Things can get trickier, though, as this sentence illustrates:

Just give the package to whoever answers the door.

While it might initially seem that *whomever* is more appropriate, since it is the object of a preposition, *whoever* is the correct choice since it is performing the action of opening the door.

Your, you're: *You're* is just like *they're*: the letter *a* from *you are* is missing from *you're*. *Your*, like *its*, is the possessive form of *you*:

Your plans will come to nothing if you don't start working to make them happen.
If you hope to get a good job with little education, you're dreaming.

Exercise

Choose the correct word in each sentence.

1. ___ I knew the type of car she owned, but I wasn't sure about **a) its b) it's** year or color.

2. ___ From all indications, **a) its b) it's** going to be a great season for our team.

3. ___ I have no idea where **a) their b) there c) they're** going when they leave here.

4. ___ It's **a) their b) there c) they're** choice, but I can't help feeling I should offer my advice.

5. ___ Whenever **a) their b) there c) they're** is the slightest chance of snow, local schools close.

6. ___ If **a) you're b) your** too tired to go to class, I can take notes for you.

7. ___ **a) Your b) You're** lack of sleep will surely

8. ___ **c) affect d) effect** your performance on the quiz.

9. ___ They are going to the mall and **a) than b) then** to a movie.

10. ___ With his analytical mind, he **a) could of b) could have** been a scientist.

11. ___ With the team's recent wins, the fans were all **a) anxious about b) eager for** the upcoming playoff game.

12. ___ Many supermarkets have increased the capacity of express checkouts to 15 items or **a) less b) fewer**.

13. ___ She had no energy yesterday and just wanted to **a) lay b) lie** around all day.

14. ___ Sara would much rather read a book for enjoyment **a) than b) then** study for the exam.

15. ___ No one was sure what side **a) affects b) effects** the new medicine might have.

EDITOR'S TOOLKIT

Choosing a Dictionary

The most important book for any writer or editor is one he or she probably already owns: a dictionary. But which dictionary is the best? It depends.

That might be a surprising answer, because it would seem only reasonable that words mean the same thing and are spelled the same way no matter what dictionary they appear in. But that's not the case. No dictionary includes all the words in usage at a given time. For one thing, many words are used only in specialized settings like law and medicine. So for people working in a field such as law, the best dictionary is probably Barron's Law Dictionary or an online equivalent such as Dictionary.law.com.

But such dictionaries contain only a small subset of words used in one specialized field. For general use, something more comprehensive is in order. Some purists swear by the Oxford English Dictionary, which surveys the use of 600,000 words over the last 1,000 years. But what makes OED so fascinating to word buffs is also its downfall for writers and editors in a hurry: Its focus on the origins of words means it is not always the best place to get a quick decision on how a word should be used. In addition, its heft (the print edition's more than 21,000 pages fill 20 volumes), its price (more than $1,000) and its lack of recent entries mean that for many the OED is not a practical choice. (Access to OED.com, an online version updated quarterly, costs nearly $300 a year.)

A far better choice for most writers and editors who want a comprehensive dictionary is Webster's Third New International Dictionary. At a little more than one-tenth the bulk of the OED, the Third International includes nearly 500,000 words, is available in print and online (free with purchase of the print edition) and costs far less. On the other hand, a decade or more can pass between new editions, and a weight of nearly 13 pounds makes this a volume that few users would want to carry around.

Fortunately, other options abound. A search for "English dictionary" on Amazon.com turns up nearly 200,000 results. Of those, three are generally regarded as the cream of the crop: The American Heritage Dictionary, Webster's New World Dictionary and Merriam-Webster's Collegiate Dictionary. Of those, the New World is the one most often used by journalists, and it is the standard cited by The Associated Press Stylebook.

But why even bother with a printed dictionary when so many online sites and dictionaries are built into word processing programs? The answer to that lies in the Amazon.com search results noted in the previous paragraph. The wide range of dictionaries on the market indicates that not every dictionary is the same. Similarly, while some of the electronic options might do the job just fine, there's no guarantee that they will perform at the same level as the recognized standards.

The bottom line, however, is that any dictionary is better than no dictionary. A key reason to choose and use one dictionary is to have a consistent style. For writers and editors not bound by an organization's choice of dictionaries, it's hard to go wrong – unless the dictionary sits unused.

Student Study Site

Visit the Student Resource Site at **http://study.sagepub.com/lieb** to access:

- Chapter-by-chapter **web quizzes** for independent assessment of course material
- List of online web links and general resources

Chapter 2   Choosing Content That Clicks

Publishing for Your Audience

General-interest newspapers and magazines were once at the top of the media pyramid. Life and Look magazines and big-city papers aspired to offer something to everyone. But there's a reason those publications are dead or dying: In today's media landscape, attempting to appeal to everybody ensures that a publication will appeal to *nobody*. Instead, every newspaper, magazine, blog and website needs to have a specific focus and target a specific audience.

That change marks a major departure from the not-too-distant past, when media producers functioned in a realm of information scarcity. In most geographical areas, a newspaper or two peacefully coexisted with a couple of television stations and a somewhat larger number of radio stations. But since the late 20th century, things have been markedly different as cable TV and the Internet ushered in an explosion of competing options.

That change has been particularly hard on daily newspapers. When a daily newspaper served as a primary source of news for its readership, it was important that it cover a wide range of topics from around the globe. Of course, few newspapers had the resources to do even part of that job well, so they heavily relied on stories provided by wire services such as The Associated Press and Reuters.

When newspapers moved online, however, it quickly became clear how little original content most of them offered. And many readers found themselves asking why they should continue reading wire service copy offered by the local paper when they could get the same coverage – or even higher-quality original coverage – from many other sources. As a result, newspapers that had not made a commitment to in-depth coverage of their local communities found their readers jumping ship, and many of those papers did not survive long.

What New Publishers Can Learn From Old Media

Not all general-interest news publications have folded. At any given moment, the list of the most popular news websites is guaranteed to include familiar names such as The New York Times and The Washington Post.[1] But even though they cover a wide range of topics, each has its own area of expertise or its own slant that attracts a specific audience. In other words, even these general-interest news websites serve a somewhat specialized audience.

That has become increasingly important as news organizations and other online publishers have struggled to find funding. Classified and display advertising, once the lifeblood of newspapers and magazines, has largely dried up thanks to Craigslist, eBay and merchants' own online presence. As Hamilton Nolan of gossip and media news blog Gawker.com notes, people will not pay for the vast majority of online content. "The fact that readers like you is not enough to support an online paywall," Nolan adds. "Readers must need you." Nolan notes examples that illustrate such needs:

> High quality national newspapers (NYT, WSJ, probably the WaPo, and … ?); sites that offer quality financial news to an audience for whom a paywall's cost is negligible (WSJ, FT, Bloomberg); sites that cater to very specific niche audiences with highly specific news that can't be easily found elsewhere (Politico, trade publications of all types, small local newspapers); [and] sites offering very high quality proprietary longform journalism published on a frequent basis.[2]

Gawker Media itself offers a good example of the importance of niches, with its stable of blogs, including seven titles in addition to the one bearing the corporate name:

- Deadspin, covering sports;
- Lifehacker, offering "tips and downloads for getting things done";
- Gizmodo, covering technology and design;
- io9, devoted to science fiction, fantasy, futurism, science and technology;
- Kotaku, billing itself as "the gamer's guide";
- Jalopnik, covering the auto industry and car culture; and
- Jezebel, focusing on women's issues from a feminist perspective.

Finding a Niche

In the early days of the digital revolution, carving out a niche was fairly easy. The Web was a new frontier where anyone with an idea and a little technical skill could set up shop. But at a time when millions of blogs and websites – not to mention hundreds of television networks and magazines as well as the constant pull of social media – compete for an audience's limited time and attention, standing out from the crowd takes much more work.

Whether launching a new publication or rethinking an existing one, it is essential to give it a unique slant sure to draw a crowd. Taking a few simple steps can help make that a possibility.

1. *Start with something that interests you:* It's no secret that people want to watch, read and interact with news on topics of interest to them. Thus they gravitate to blogs, magazines and websites that share their passions. (It's hardly surprising that Gawker's blogs on sports, women's issues and technology are typically among the 20 most visited blogs.) Therefore, anyone thinking about a new publishing venture, or rethinking an existing one, should start by examining the passions of the people behind the site. It's almost impossible to fake sincerity, and the audience can see quickly who shares their interests and who is just milking those interests for profit.

2. *Find some new interests:* Unfortunately, many of the most common interests are already overrepresented in the media universe. Sports, fashion, food, celebrity news and a few other topics long ago reached their saturation points. So unless a publisher can bring a truly fresh and unique perspective to the topic, there is little chance of breaking through the clutter. Let's face it: What can the average sports fan bring to the table that ESPN cannot? It is best to think outside the box and try to come up with a unique angle or an overlooked and underplayed idea. For instance, a blog about baseball generally is not a great idea, but one that provides inside information for fans – how to get the best deals on tickets, where

to eat near the stadiums, how to increase the odds of getting autographs – could attract an audience. Similarly, a website or blog about a niche sport such as independent professional wrestling might fill an important gap.

3. *Try to mix and match topics for ideas:* Sometimes the best way to find fresh ideas is by taking two seemingly disconnected topics and trying to find common ground. A person who likes skiing and smartphones might come up with a blog that looks at the best smartphones and apps for skiers.

4. *Go narrow but deep:* The focus always should be kept tight, but with as much information on that narrow topic as time and resources allow. In the previous example, broadening it to "technology for active people" waters things down too much to be of interest to almost anyone. At the same time, reining things in too tightly will limit the audience. A blog that is limited to iPhone apps for heli-skiers is likely to produce few ideas for posts – and draw even fewer readers.

5. *Make sure the topic has continued appeal:* While attracting an audience is tough, keeping an audience is even tougher. For instance, many magazines lose up to half their readership every two years and have an almost completely different audience after five years. So a good topic has to be more than a primer on how to do one basic thing, or it needs to offer information that will continually appeal to a new audience. For instance, the leading bridal magazines remain hugely popular with women, but their readers don't stick around long. On the other hand, a magazine like Bicycling can keep readers coming back for years by regularly running features on new places to ride, new bikes to lust after, and so on.

6. *When all else fails, look for the local angle:* Sometime the best way to find a fresh way to approach a topic is simply by looking at it from a local perspective. For instance, bartering recently has become a big topic. Millions of hits on a Google search attest to that. So no one needs another generic website or blog about bartering. However, a site or blog that focuses on how bartering works in a specific area could be a valuable resource. The trick is finding the right geographical focus that makes coverage useful but not too limited. A medium-sized town, a large university campus, or a small city would probably work. Bigger than that, and the focus is lost; smaller, and it will have trouble finding an audience.

Defining the Target Audience

It might seem that defining a topic automatically defines the target audience. And in many cases, that is true. For instance, a publication that focuses on bargain weddings would obviously draw most of its audience from young people who are planning to get married.

However, in other cases the target audience might not be who it first seems to be. As one example, the target audience for a publication that focuses on finding financial resources to pay for college is probably less likely to be college students and more likely to be their parents.

Learning as much as possible about an audience is essential to helping focus the content of a publication. Two key aspects of any audience are its *demographic* and *psychographic* traits.[3] Demographic factors include a person's

- age,
- race/ethnic background,
- gender,
- geographic location,
- income, and
- marital/parental status.

Psychographic factors include a person's

- psychology,
- interests,
- hobbies,
- values,
- attitudes, and
- behaviors and lifestyle.

The more an editor or publisher knows about these traits, the better the content will be tailored to that audience. In addition, such information is crucial in attracting advertisers, who want to make sure they are reaching their own target audiences.

When launching a new publication, gathering that information can be challenging. The most useful method of obtaining it is by turning up at places and events where a potential audience is likely to gather. Someone who is thinking about creating a new music blog would do well to spend time at clubs where the genre she is interested in is played; a person interested in starting a new publication on environmental issues should attend conferences and meetings on that topic. In all cases, the point is to pay careful attention to the topics and perspectives that are discussed and to make careful note of as many traits of the potential audience as possible.

For existing publications, several tools can help gather demographic and psychographic information. First is the **reader survey**. Free and inexpensive online tools such as SurveyMonkey and Zoomerang make it easy to collect information from readers. Offering a chance to win a small gift by taking the survey can increase the percentage of readers who participate and in the process collect email addresses for future contacts (with users' permission, of course).

A second option is the **focus group**. This is just what it sounds like: getting a bunch of readers (or prospective readers) together to discuss what they like and don't like about content, design and other aspects of a publication. Whether done in person with some free food thrown in as an enticement, or online using Skype, the focus group is a powerful tool.

Finally, it's important not to overlook information that has already been collected. Any existing publication with an advertising department is likely to house a gold mine of information there. An editor can learn a great deal about an audience by spending time with that information.

Creating Useful Surveys and Focus Groups

Technology has made it easier than ever to create surveys and focus groups. Unfortunately, it is just as easy to create bad surveys and focus groups as it is to create useful ones. If you have never been involved in setting up one before, these tips should help.

Surveys

Kiersten Frase of Oh My Veggies (http://ohmyveggies.com) is one of the many bloggers who advocate occasional audience surveys. She notes several reasons for doing so:

- To learn about reader demographics
- To find out how readers discovered the blog
- To see what readers like about the blog
- To see what readers think about proposed new features
- To test reader reactions to anticipated design changes
- To determine why traffic has dropped
- To check that the blog is on the right track

Frase said that she was reluctant to undertake her first survey, as she did not want to deal with criticism. But, she notes: "While I spent so much time dreading the criticism part, I completely overlooked the fact that people would say nice things about my blog too. It can be good to hear that!"[4]

Blogger and consultant Ramsay Taplin strongly agrees that bloggers should occasionally survey their readers. He offers several guidelines for creating effective surveys. Among them:

- Define your goals: As the previous list suggests, there are several reasons for conducting a survey. No single survey can tackle all of them, so choose the most important goals for the moment and focus on them.
- Keep it short: Taplin suggests that surveys should take no more than a minute to complete or else people will ignore them or quit in boredom. While that figure is pretty restrictive, it's far better to err on the side of shortness than to have a low response rate.
- Use simple language with minimal jargon: To minimize the time required to complete surveys, they should be as simple to understand as possible.
- Limit response options: In most cases, providing a small number of possible responses is better than asking open-ended questions.
- Take care in creating the email and subject line: The best survey is no good if no one bothers to read the email asking them to take it. So Taplin stresses it is important to carefully craft the subject line and body of such emails.[5]

Focus Groups

Sometimes focus groups offer the better alternative for collecting information a publisher is interested in. To make a focus group worth the time and effort, however, it's important to understand some ground rules. Businessweek.com offers several suggestions:[6]

- Define your goals: As with surveys, it is crucial that the purpose of the focus group is clear. That information should be used to create a list of questions and conversation starters, "but questions should be broad enough to encourage discussion."
- Choose participants: Think about who is best able to help you find the information you want. Is it your current audience, prospective readers, the audience of a competitor, or another group? Around a dozen participants are required for a typical group.
- Choose a site: Traditionally, a focus group is held in a neutral location that has plenty of room, video recording equipment and, often, one-way mirrors for observation. More recently, however, online focus groups have grown in popularity. Such focus groups can be conducted via webcams in real time or bulletin board asynchronously, "with researchers benefitting from the convenience, time and cost savings, and more in-depth insights," notes 2020Research.com.[7]
- Pick a moderator: The ideal moderator has no investment in the results, so he or she will not take feedback personally. In addition, a good moderator has the communication skills to ensure that all participants get the chance to join the discussion.
- Discuss results: Afterward, look for themes and ideas that emerged from the discussion. "And be prepared for any negative feedback about your company or industry," Businessweek.com advises. "After all, you wanted people to be honest."

Creating a Mission Statement

Armed with clear focus and a clear understanding of the audience, it becomes easier to choose the right material for publication. For instance, someone with a vague notion of publishing a magazine about business would be overwhelmed with information. But the top business magazines have specific roles and niches that help their editors choose the best content. For just a few examples:

- Fast Company magazine is known for keeping managers abreast of emerging business trends and ideas.
- Inc. magazine focuses on the tools and information needed to grow small to midsize companies.
- Barron's magazine features in-depth analysis and commentary on topics from Wall Street and abroad.
- Harvard Business Review focuses on ways to achieve managerial excellence, advice on strategic decision-making and profiles of industry leaders and trendsetters.

One of the most useful tools in achieving such clarity is a **mission statement** – in many people's opinion, a critical item:

> Would you ever drive your car with a bag over your head? If you did, it sure would be a challenging ride. You would get lost. You may veer off of the road or cross the yellow lines into someone else's territory. We all know this would be a very bad idea. This dangerous driving scenario comes to mind as we deal with an ongoing problem seen [over] and over again working in the publishing industry: Why are so many magazines being published "in the dark" without a mission statement?[8]

In a few sentences, a mission statement should define the publication's focus and approach, explain how it differs from its competition, describe its readers, and show how the audience benefits from reading it. The more detailed each of those are, the better the chance of success. For instance, this before and after study shows how a vague mission statement can be transformed into a true resource for an editorial team:

> *Original:* "Piano & Keyboard is the magazine for all who love to make music and choose to do so on a keyboard instrument. It is the one magazine that covers all keyboard instruments and all kinds of music made on them. P&K encourages its readers' greater involvement in keyboard playing, fuels their enthusiasm for and interest in the instruments themselves, and helps them be informed members of the global community of keyboard players."

> *Revised:* "Piano & Keyboard is a magazine for players. Through news and reviews, career guidance, insights from name players, sheet music, and articles on skills, technique, and instrument care, P&K inspires, informs, offers connections among, and solves problems for players of acoustic pianos. Musically, the main territory is classical and new music, though there are pockets of jazz and pop. Skill levels range from long-time dabbler to serious professional. Whether teachers, performers, students, or hobbyists, the readers all think of themselves as players – and that's how P&K serves them."[9]

Unlike the original, the revised version clearly states what type of keyboards, music and readers the magazine is going after, as well as what the magazine offers those readers.

Deciding What to Publish

No matter the focus or audience, there's rarely a better place to start when thinking about selecting content than the traditional list of news values:

- Impact
- Unusualness
- Prominence
- Timeliness

CASE STUDY

The Scientist Gets a Makeover

Just how much difference can tweaking the focus of a publication make? One case study drives home the point that the difference can be huge. The owners of The Scientist, a magazine for professionals in the life sciences (biology, genetics, pharmacology and many other fields), decided to request an outside editorial audit in 2004. As a result of that audit, consulting firm DrivingWheel noted that the magazine needed a tighter focus on its audience; needed better writers; and needed a more professional tone and design. With some reluctance, the publication's owners and top editors agreed to changes that would accomplish those goals – and substantially alter the magazine.

Over an 18-month period, the consulting firm worked with the magazine's staff to make the changes, as well as to develop a companion website that would focus "on rapidly changing news in the life sciences, while the magazine concentrated on deeper, more analytical articles."

After the magazine was relaunched, a survey showed it to be a great hit with its new target audience: "Opinion leaders (including lab chiefs, biotech executives and policy-makers) are spending much more time with the new publication than they did with the old one, and take its views much more seriously." In addition, the magazine won several prestigious awards over the next few years.

So yes, having a clear focus does make a clear difference – some would say all the difference.[10]

- Proximity
- Human interest
- Conflict
- Currency
- Visual impact

While those factors differ in relative importance depending on the publication and audience, they offer good basic guidelines to help generate article ideas and choose among many competing offerings.

Most writers and editors would agree that the top three news values are **impact, unusualness** and **prominence**. If none of those are present, there's probably really nothing worth publishing. Let's look at each of them.

Impact answers a reader's most important question: Why should I care about this? Most journalists would argue that information that has a direct impact on a reader's life is without question the most valuable type of information to publish. A few headlines illustrate this type of story:

Student loan rates double after Congress fails on fix

China smog cuts 5.5 years from average life expectancy, study finds

Tropical Storm Chantal races toward Caribbean

The first article would have a direct impact on every student in the United States (as well as many spouses and parents) in the process of paying off a college loan or considering applying for one. In the other two examples, the news in these articles would have a direct impact on people in the specific areas mentioned: northern China and the Caribbean. But the

Two of the best-known newspapers in the United States often offer a study in contrasts in what stories are deemed most worthy for their readers. The New York Times typically focuses on national and international stories that are high on impact or potential impact, as seen here in the selection of stories focusing on Middle East violence, the Ukrainian conflict and efforts to rebuild Detroit. The front page of The New York Times, on the other hand, on the same day features two sports stories – one of them local – and one local minor crime story, complete with tasteless pun headline. So the emphasis is much more on proximity and unusualness.

second and third articles might also have an indirect impact on people in the United States and elsewhere. The most obvious example of such an effect would be that felt by readers who have friends and relatives in the affected countries.

Many other stories have different types of indirect effects. For example, the deaths of more than 1,100 workers in the collapse of a clothing factory in Bangladesh in 2013 led to a consortium of 70 retailers and apparel brands agreeing to inspect all Bangladeshi garment factories that supply the companies.[11] That action could lower the supply of low-cost clothing or raise prices, either of which would ultimately affect many consumers around the world.

The news value of **unusualness** indicates that something out of the ordinary has happened that is not so much important to the reader as potentially interesting. While many journalists look with disdain on publications that feature mostly articles of this type, virtually every publisher uses them, if only to offer relief from the serious news of the day. Some examples:

In twist, prosecutors seek mercy for condemned man

Boy in Batman costume robs Colorado State Fair

Beaver bites through man's artery as he takes its picture

Woman rescues boy during engagement photo shoot

All of these are from general-interest news sites. There is nothing particularly compelling for a specific readership about any of these; rather, the hope is that they are strange enough to attract the attention of a wide variety of readers. Choosing such articles requires careful thought, lest readers end up asking, "Why am I seeing all this weird crap?" Some online news sites segregate such content so readers can skip it – or click right to it. For instance, The Huffington Post has a "Weird News" section; ABC News offers a similar "Watercooler" section.

The news value of **prominence** is based on the idea that "names make news." When routine things happen to famous people – or at least things that are routine for well-known people – those stories are deemed far more newsworthy than the same or similar things happening to everyday people. For example:

Prince William and Kate's royal baby to be Prince or Princess of Cambridge

Aaron Hernandez arrested, taken into police custody

Randy Travis in critical condition

In each of these cases, the story is a routine one: a pregnancy, a run-in with the law, and a health problem. When such things happen to ordinary people, no one (except perhaps the person and his or her close family) would argue that they are newsworthy. But because of widespread interest in royalty, celebrities, artists and sports figures, these stories can attract the attention of many, provided they are directed at responsive audiences.

Beyond the top three news values is another supplemental group. By themselves, they are unlikely to elevate an article to "must publish" status. However, they add to an article's appeal.

Timeliness is the first of these. Essentially, what it means is that the more recently something happened, the more newsworthy it is. In the days of traditional publishing, it was used to filter out stories when there were too many for the space or time available. For instance, if two car crashes occurred over a weekend but there was only room to report on one in the Monday newspaper, timeliness dictated that it would be the more recent of the two, presuming all else was equal. Timeliness takes on an even more crucial role in the digital age with its deadline-every-second pace: The audience is always looking for the next big thing. But it's important not to let those desires lead to posting information that has not been checked, something discussed in more detail in Chapter 3.

Proximity played a similar role in the days when newspapers and broadcast TV ruled the world. As with timeliness, the idea is that of two comparable events, the one occurring closest to the audience's location would be the most newsworthy, and if there was only room or time to cover one, it would be that one. And also as with timeliness, proximity has become more important today. That's because many news publications and sites have a specific geographical focus to them, in some cases being conceived as "hyperlocal" projects – that is, focusing on everything from PTA meetings to Little League games to community gardening projects. Such a focus can make a publication or site stand out from its competition, but in order to succeed every piece of content must exhibit proximity.

A second form of proximity also plays a role in story selection. This one is more of a kinship for others who share a heritage, religion or ethnic background. So for example, a largely Catholic audience would be interested in news concerning the pope; an audience of Russian background would feel connected with news from its homeland.

The news value of **human interest** is an important one that is sometimes hard to define. Essentially, it means something that affects the emotions. Anyone who has ever wondered why the Internet is full of pictures of cute kittens and other animals need only think about the "Aw" factor such pictures have. Sometimes a human interest story makes people feel good like that; other times, it makes them feel sad; still others, it offers inspiration and motivation. Some of the most popular websites focus primarily on unusualness and human interest in choosing their offerings. One example: Buzzfeed's article headlined *The Amazing Story Of The Soldier Who Was Reunited With The Dog He Left Behind In Afghanistan*.

Worry About This/Don't Worry About That

Long-Term Planning vs. Gradual Evolution

While it is vitally important to have a clear audience and focus, it is less important to try to develop a long-range plan for creating and delivering content to that audience. Instead, it's far more important to regard any publication as a living organism subject to changes in audience interests, tastes and demographics – and even changes in how they read.

One perfect example of an evolving publication is Wired magazine. At the time of the magazine's launch in January 1993, the World Wide Web was not even a year old, and the first graphical browser had not yet been released. So the debut issue was not very "wired" in the sense that most people would think of today. Articles covered videogames, phone hacking, digital special effects, Japanese otaku and a range of other topics. But just a few issues later, Wired was acknowledging the growing importance of online communication and added a "Net Surf" column to help readers find interesting online resources. The following year, the magazine started a companion website, Hotwired.com, one of the first commercial Web magazines, which in turn led to dozens of spinoff sites. (Hotwired.com is now dead for all intents and purposes. Wired's Web presence is now simply Wired.com. But some past issues of Hotwired.com can be browsed at http://web.archive.org/web/*/http://www.hotwired.com.)[12]

But as the print and online versions of the magazine evolved over the years, they did not shift to focusing only on the Internet. Far from it, the magazine's editors noticed how technology was creeping into every aspect of human existence and communication, and readers were continually treated to interesting articles they could hardly have imagined.

In addition to evolving content, the magazine also evolved technologically. Barely a month after Apple introduced its first iPad, Wired released its Tablet edition.

So Wired clearly had done its homework before its first issue was published. But it's the fact that it has continued to keep tabs on its readers and their interests and preferences that has continued to keep it relevant and vital more than 20 years later. That's an example every editor should follow.

A large percentage of news stories contain some element of another value, **conflict**. The value is found not just in stories about political contests, sporting events and military actions, but also in more mundane news such as court actions, stories about people facing adversity and news about unemployment. While the element of conflict can make a story more interesting, writers and editors should be careful not to create conflict in situations where it does not already exist.

The news value of **currency** may sound similar to timeliness, but it actually is quite different. Currency means that the presence of a topic in the news adds weight to similar stories on the same topic. So for instance, after a mass shooting or an airplane crash, stories about gun violence and airline safety are presumed to be of more interest to the audience than they were before that event happened. Eventually, things level off again and then something else happens and stories similar to the new one gain currency.

The final news value is **visual impact**, which is just what it sounds like: something that makes a person say, "You've got to see this!" No matter the medium, something that catches a viewer's eye will definitely improve the chances he or she will linger on it and read the accompanying story.

A photo that almost defines visual impact: The parents and grandmother of a young girl killed in the Sandy Hook shootings grieve at the launch of the Sandy Hook Promise, an initiative to encourage and support sensible solutions to prevent gun violence.

© GARYHE/Reuters/Corbis

Letting the Audience Lead You to Ideas

While brainstorming ideas based on the news values is a good starting point, the best way to make sure that content connects with an audience is to actually look at what the audience is already reading and talking about.

Ian Hill, the executive producer for digital and social media for News10 in Sacramento, California, notes that doing that sort of "in the trenches" research is crucial:

> Your community doesn't need you. They already have what seems like an infinite number of sources for news they find interesting. You're just another voice in that cacophony. If you want to be relevant, you need to pay attention to what your audience is talking about online and be part of their conversations. Hang out where they hang out, ask them what they're interested in and learn how to recognize patterns in their news consumption. Does your community have a huge subreddit where users are regularly upvoting items about housing? Try providing more housing coverage. Are there no comments on your competitor's education blog? Spend less time reporting on education.[13]

Hill's advice is echoed in that of James Mathewson, search strategy and expertise lead for IBM and coauthor of "Audience, Relevance, and Search." Mathewson works to make sure IBM's publications connect with their audiences, and much of that work is monitoring what members of the target audience are discussing. Mathewson is particularly interested in the words audiences use in searching and social media interactions. But that doesn't mean just peppering material with keywords. Instead, he is talking about using research to determine which topics are most likely to connect with the audience:

> I think that we get caught up – and this is a typical thing across all information development – we get caught up wanting to tell our story and wanting to write our interesting things. And that's great. But if nobody finds it and nobody uses it, then it's basically a waste of time and effort.
>
> So if you do the research up front and you figure out what people want and you try to cater to those market forces in your writing, you'll have a much better chance of not

only connecting with that audience but creating things that are well used and passed along and ultimately have the desired effect.[14]

The process Mathewson describes is similar to what has become known as **content marketing**, also known as **brand journalism** or **custom content**. The Content Marketing Institute defines those terms as "a marketing technique of creating and distributing relevant and valuable content to attract, acquire, and engage a clearly defined and understood target audience – with the objective of driving profitable customer action."[15] Rather than buying ads in traditional media, companies create their own online and print publications that they control and distribute, write the stories themselves and own all the ads. "This is what makes people actually want to consume a brand's content; it looks like something they'd read anyway," notes Poynter.org. While journalists might take offense at having their work lumped in with corporate branding efforts, understanding the concept of content marketing is essential in appreciating how things work in the digital age.[16]

Objectivity in the 21st Century

For decades, the ideal of journalistic objectivity underpinned journalism. That ideal held that journalists should not bring their opinions or analysis to their writing, instead offering readers "just the facts."

But that notion has undergone serious reexamination in recent years, and some people believe that it often has led to poor journalism. Media critic and New York University professor Jay Rosen has coined the phrase "the view from nowhere" to describe the problem. As GigaOm notes, it

> developed over time as the newspaper business stopped being about independent voices and became more of a professional phenomenon – in other words, an industry made up of a few large chains owned by corporate conglomerates. Among other things, the practice of objectivity was designed to make these businesses appear less politically controversial and therefore more appealing to advertisers, who were trying to reach a mass market. But just as advertisers seem to be deserting that model, readers are also gravitating towards outlets with strong voices, regardless of whether they happen to be traditional or mainstream sources.[17]

It's that last sentence that is most important for today's publishers: The audience wants a point of view.

But at the same time, it's important for journalists to be fair. Contrary to what passes as journalism on cable television, just shouting one-sided opinions does not make for the most convincing or compelling content. Instead, it's best to acknowledge all sides of an issue and use evidence to support one point of view – and dismiss the rest. As Rosen notes, "In journalism, real authority starts with reporting. Knowing your stuff, mastering your beat, being right on the facts, digging under the surface of things, calling around to find out what happened, verifying what you heard."[18]

Wrapping Up

In a highly competitive environment, attracting and keeping an audience requires constant work. The key initial steps are finding a unique niche, defining a target audience and creating a focused mission statement. Once the foundation for success has been laid through those actions, an editor needs to call upon the news values to select the most appropriate content for the audience and monitor what the audience members are discussing and searching for. All that put together will greatly increase the odds that the audience will become a loyal one, ensuring the success of the publication.

Key Points

- Every publication must have a clearly defined audience. Attempting to appeal to everyone means the content will appeal to no one.
- Similarly, every publication must have a specific niche. Evaluating one's interests is a good starting point, but that in itself is usually not enough.
- The target audience is not always who it might seem to be. Editors need to be clear who the target is, then gather as much demographic and psychographic information as possible.
- A clear, short mission statement provides great help in steering a publication in the correct direction.
- One of the most important things an editor does is select what material should be published. The traditional news values offer guidance here, particularly those of impact, unusualness and prominence.
- Monitoring the audience on a continuing basis is critical if a publication is to stay a step ahead of it in offering just what readers are looking for – before they know it.

CHAPTER EXERCISE

Pick a category of magazines or websites and compare at least three of the top titles. Try to write out their mission statements in 10 words or fewer, and try to determine as much as you can about their readers. (Hint: The ads are a great help on the second part. The likely target market for products advertised in the magazine is probably the same target market that the magazine is aiming to reach.)

WRITE RIGHT

Making Sure Subjects and Verbs Agree

Almost as soon as children begin putting sentences together, they come to understand the importance of subject-verb agreement. That is, a singular subject needs a singular verb, and a plural subject needs a plural verb. That's a straightforward rule, and it is rare to encounter errors in simple sentences. Everyone knows *He run to the store* is not correct (even though Microsoft Word does not flag it as an error!).

However, errors do pop up regularly when sentences become more complicated. The following are the main problem areas:

- Compound subjects: When two or more words serve as the subject of a sentence, they require a plural verb: *Amy and Brenda run faster than we do.* That's relatively simple to remember. Where things become more difficult is when *or* or *nor* is used in place of *and*. In such cases, the verb must agree with the noun closest to it: *Neither his grandparents nor his father agrees with his investment plan. Neither his father nor his grandparents agree with his investment plan.*
- Group (collective) nouns: Some nouns can be used to denote either a collection of people or the individual members of that group (for example, *club, company, group, committee, board*, and so on). When one of those nouns is used as the subject of a sentence, it's important to understand the writer's intentions in order to make sure the verb agrees. In the first example that follows, the word *couple* refers to the collection of people and therefore takes a singular verb; in the second, it refers to the individual members and therefore takes a plural verb: *The couple has always been a model of compatibility.* But *The couple have decided to separate.* Note that any time the plural of a group noun serves as the subject of a sentence, the plural verb is required: *The committees repeatedly disagree over which set of bylaws should be followed.*

(Continued)

(Continued)

- Plural form/singular-meaning nouns: Some nouns sound like they are plural, but they actually function as singular words. Examples include *aerobics*, *blues* (music), *economics*, *gymnastics*, *headquarters*, *mathematics*, *measles*, *mumps*, *news* and *politics*. All of these take a singular verb (e.g., *Aerobics is a great form of exercise*), but other similar words require a plural verb (e.g., *Those eyeglasses look great on her*). And just to make matters more complicated, some words in this category can go both ways (*Statistics is not a popular course; The statistics show that more women than men are choosing to major in communication.*)

- Indefinite pronouns: These are words like *somebody*, *everything* and *each*. Most of them always take singular verbs. This group includes *anybody*, *anyone*, *anything*, *each*, *either*, *everybody*, *everyone*, *everything*, *neither*, *nobody*, *no one*, *nothing*, *somebody*, *someone* and *something*. A few (*both*, *few*, *many*, *several* and *others*) always take plural verbs. And a small group (*some*, *any*, *none*, *all* and *most*) can take either one, depending on how the word is used. For example, *Some of the cost of an electric car can be recouped in tax credits.* But *Some of the costs of attending college are likely to surprise new students.*

- Prepositional phrases: When a prepositional phrase sits between a subject and its verb, it can make it harder to ensure that the subject and the verb agree. That's because in addition to containing a preposition such as *to*, *in*, *from* or *over*, a prepositional phrase contains a noun, and a casual writer or editor might make the verb agree with that word. For example, *The employees of the store are donating some of their sick days to help their coworker who has cancer.* The verb *are donating* agrees with the subject *the employees* – as it should – not with *the store*, the object of the preposition.

- Sentences beginning with *there is/are* or *here is/are*: The problem in these cases – aside from the fact that they are a poor way to begin a sentence – is that the verb comes before the subject instead of after it. For example, *There are many ways to approach that problem.* The correct verb is *are*, as it must agree with the subject *ways*.

- Clauses placed between the subject and verb and beginning with *who*, *that*, or *which*: These are similar to the previous problem, the main difference being that clauses include a verb as well as a noun. The net result is the same: Agreement can easily suffer when a writer or editor tries to make the following verb agree with the noun that is closest to it, which is not the subject. For example, *A cat that is allowed to eat wild birds poses a threat to the ecosystem.* The correct verb is *poses*, since it needs to agree with *cat*.

Exercise

Correct errors in subject-verb agreement in the following sentences.

1. Is Ray Lewis and his two codefendants guilty?

2. There was 70 students hoping to get overrides on the first day of the class.

3. It is the details that makes a wardrobe complete.

4. The group plan to announce a decision Tuesday.

5. The group plan to go their own ways after the next recording is finished.

6. The reason for collecting all the pop-top tabs were to show the students how many a million is.

7. A year earlier she had discovered the delights of Cordele, Georgia, the town that bill itself as the "watermelon capital of the world."

8. The defense is preparing its own sentencing arguments and are set to call two psychiatrists to testify for Price.

9. One of the victims said she noticed that her silver tea services and flatware was missing upon returning home at 4:30 p.m.

10. The use of visuals to help explain complex issues are a good feature of the book.

11. Romantic dinners at home are less expensive than dining out and displays much more love than just ordering items off a menu.

12. An example of the craftsmanship were lovely crystal cherubs.

13. In the misty air was the shadows of hundreds of students.

14. The scamper of squirrels were the footsteps of someone running after me.

15. Sitting perfectly still were more than 100 geese.

EDITOR'S TOOLKIT

Using an Editorial Calendar

In traditional media, scheduling was something pretty much taken for granted. A daily newspaper had one or more deadlines each day it was published; a magazine had a more complex set of deadlines every week or month.

But in the digital world, the deadline is all the time – but at no specific time. Yet one of the most important things an online publication can have is a regular schedule of ongoing content built around a consistent editorial mix. Otherwise, readers will grow impatient after making multiple trips to a website or blog and seeing the same material they saw on their last visit. That state of affairs sends a clear message: "There's nothing (new) to see here – move along."

One of the best resources to help avoid that problem is an editorial calendar. At a minimum, an editorial calendar is no more than a simple publishing schedule: "Blog post due every Tuesday at noon." But it can be much more than that.

Bloggers in particular can benefit from an editorial calendar, as many are one-person operations who often find themselves struggling for inspiration. As one overview of editorial calendars notes:

> If you have an editorial schedule, you won't be left staring at a blank screen, thinking … "What am I supposed to blog about?" An editorial schedule helps you plan not only what you are going to say but also when and how often you're going to say it.
>
> Now that you know who you're creating content for and why, you can create an editorial calendar with publishing dates, blog categories, keywords, blog titles, and even columns for social media posts promoting your content.

Identify 3-5 content buckets or categories that will help you organize and streamline your topics for consistency. Those categories should repeat throughout your editorial calendar to help guide your content, keep your blog on track, and meet goals.[19]

The key to creating a useful editorial calendar is backing it up with research. One expert's list of research requirements includes finding out what trade publications are writing about; determining "what industry news/posts are shared and retweeted the most"; finding out what competitive publications are covering; and looking for trends concerning the topic.[20]

Bloggers and editors of smaller publications may be able to meet their calendar needs with simple bullet lists or an Excel spreadsheet. For larger publications, a number of free and paid services are constantly being introduced, with some offering online collaboration between team members and cloud storage of article ideas, drafts, and so on. These offerings can be found by searching online for "editorial calendar."

Plenty of additional useful information on this topic can be found in Georgy Cohen's "Guidelines for Effective Editorial Calendars" (http://meetcontent.com/blog/guidelines-for-effective-editorial-calendars) and Matt Lee's "Content Marketing 101: Developing an Editorial Calendar" (http://www.adherecreative.com/blog/bid/144931/Content-Marketing-101-Developing-an-Editorial-Calendar).

Student Study Site

Visit the Student Resource Site at **http://study.sagepub.com/lieb** to access:

- Chapter-by-chapter **web quizzes** for independent assessment of course material
- List of online web links and general resources

Chapter 3 **Getting the Facts Straight**

The story was amazing. Jay Forman submitted an article to Slate.com that detailed a trip on which he claimed to have gone "monkeyfishing" on an island off Florida where "A pharmaceutical company had released a bunch of rhesus monkeys ... and left them to breed, thereby supplying research labs around the country with a fresh supply of experimental test subjects."

In his 2001 article, Forman recounted a tale of "catch-and-release" fishing for the monkeys, which was apparently done just for the sport of it (the article was one of three he wrote on the subject of human vice):

> Fruits were the bait of choice. ... Once the bait was on the hook, I watched as the monkeyfisherman cast it onto the island, then waited. Not for long. The monkeys swarmed round the treat, and when the fisherman felt a strong tug he jerked the pole. I knew he had hooked one by the shriek it made – a primal yowl that set my hair on end. The monkey came flying from the trees, a juicy apple stapled to its palm.[1]

The story was too good to be true – literally. The New York Times and The Wall Street Journal quickly set about tearing into it.[2] Slate acknowledged that it had "published falsehoods," but still noted that "Despite suggestions by others that the entire episode was fiction, this excursion did take place."[3]

And there the matter sat for nearly six years, until student journalists writing about the incident contacted the author, leading him to admit that he had made the entire thing up. Another apology followed from Slate.com, bringing a great deal of embarrassment to the publication.[4]

In the intervening years, the hoaxes have not let up. In early 2013, for example, The Associated Press was forced to run this retraction:

> In a Sept. 15, 2012, story about Notre Dame's college football victory over Michigan State that highlighted linebacker Manti Te'o's performance, The Associated Press erroneously reported that he played in the game a few days after the death of his girlfriend, who had a long battle with leukemia. Other AP stories through Jan. 3, 2013, also contained references to the girlfriend's death, including some directly quoting Te'o and his father, Brian Te'o, about how he played through personal grief. On Jan. 16, Notre Dame officials and Manti Te'o said there was never a girlfriend or a death, and that Te'o was victimized in a hoax. Others have since come forward to say Te'o was duped in a series of phone calls and online messages purporting to be from a girl he never met in person.[5]

The Associated Press was hardly the only news organization to fall prey to the "imaginary dead girlfriend" story – Sports Illustrated and ESPN were among others that bit. In fact, it took an unconventional sports website, Deadspin, to research the story and call it a hoax.[6]

The story left many inside and outside of the news business wondering how such a thing could happen. Unfortunately, it was hardly an isolated incident. During the same year the Manti Te'o story broke, news organizations also got duped on a number of other stories, including one that claimed Abraham Lincoln invented the Facebook of his day.[7]

So how did these stories spread unchallenged? While it might seem that factual errors would have nearly disappeared now that access to a vast majority of the world's knowledge is only a few keystrokes away, the reality is that the deadline-every-second environment of that same online environment has increased the chances of factual errors occurring. As Nate St. Pierre, the author of the Lincoln Facebook hoax story, recounted in a fascinating postmortem:

> From all the clues I put in there, I thought it would take maybe an hour or so for enough comments to be piled on the site calling it a hoax, and of course those would be voted up by people who actually read the article, and then any legitimate news source that read it would A) figure it out on their own just from reading B) see those comments there or C) do the 30 seconds of fact-checking it would take to debunk the story.
>
> I figured I'd have a blast of a few hundred shares in the first hour or two, maybe a couple of bigger orgs would promote it for a hot minute, and then a few sources would report on the hoax, and the whole thing would rise and fall by afternoon, leaving me with a few thousand pageviews, some kudos from around the web, and [a] nice little day.
>
> Pretty much the whole internet picked this thing up and ran with it. ... In addition to social media and bloggers, it ran as fact on a lot of big-name sites and news aggregators. That's the thing that surprised me the most. I knew it would happen, but I thought only one or two would run it without fact checking, and the rest would shout it down. But only one or two actually caught the joke, and the rest just kept promoting it! It was crazytown for a good long while.
>
> I can tell you that virtually nobody checked with me to ask if it was true. I think I got a few tweets and one email the whole day asking about the veracity of the article.[8]

In other words, many of those who passed along the story – and similar ones – probably thought it was too good to be true, but also found it too good to pass up. As St. Pierre noted, debunking the story would have taken virtually no time, as long as someone was motivated to do so.

Why wasn't that motivation present? That's a great question. There are few worse things a news source can do than to pass along faulty information. As one journalist told researchers looking into how news writers verify information, "There's no point in being a journalist if you're not going to relay accurate, correct factual information to the public."[9] And yet even the most respected news organizations can find themselves doing just that, as The New York Times did in the aftermath of the Newtown, Connecticut, school shootings. As a look at accuracy in The Times noted, the publication "briefly named the wrong person as the gunman online, and, even the next day in print, it made serious errors about how Adam Lanza entered Sandy Hook Elementary School, about his weapons, and about his mother's role at the school."[10]

In this chapter, we look at two common problems affecting accuracy. The first is **factual errors** – all those cases in which incorrect information is passed along to the audience. The second is **holes** – those cases in which the audience gets incomplete or misleading news because of missing information.

Common Factual Errors

While factual errors span the gamut from trivial (getting a score wrong in a sporting event) to the monumental (misreporting a key Supreme Court decision, one of the examples cited in Chapter 1), each mistake diminishes the credibility of the media outlets responsible for them.

Unfortunately, even under the best of circumstances, it is impossible to double-check every factual assertion, especially since a single sentence might contain five or six of them. This lead sentence from a Reuters news article is a good example: "British regulators investigating the fire on a Boeing 787 Dreamliner identified the plane's emergency locator beacon as a likely source of the blaze and said on Thursday it should be switched off, spurring a rally in shares from relieved investors."[11] The facts in just that one sentence include:

- British regulators are investigating the recent fire on a Boeing 787 Dreamliner;
- The regulators suspect the plane's emergency locator beacon caused the fire;
- The regulators said the beacon should be switched off to prevent similar fires; and
- Boeing's stock price rose as investors were relieved to have a potential cause identified.

While there is nothing to suggest that any of these assertions is incorrect, one or more *could* be. The trick for time-pressed writers and editors is knowing which types of things should get the most scrutiny. The following sections cover the most important areas to check.

Names and Titles

Two of the basic items that demand verification are names and titles. Even common-sounding names come in a variety of spellings: John and Jon, Chris and Kris, Amy and Aimee, and so on. Unusual and foreign names increase the challenge of getting things right. So names should always be double-checked.

Verifying names becomes especially important when the person being discussed is involved in any kind of legal trouble. Getting a name wrong in such a situation could lead to libeling another person, a serious matter for that person and for the publication that made the mistake. (See Chapter 6 for more on libel.)

While incorrect titles rarely present such serious potential problems, it is also crucial that they be double-checked, either with the person or employer. Many titles sound similar, but often two titles that sound close to each other are miles apart in terms of responsibilities and prestige. For example, these titles can easily be confused, but the jobs are different:

- psychiatrist/psychologist
- genealogist/geologist/gynecologist
- aesthetician/anesthetist
- copywriter/copyright lawyer.[12]

Far worse than simple confusion among similar-sounding titles is giving someone a title that has nothing to do with his or her job. For instance, Vogue magazine had to run a particularly embarrassing correction in 2012:

In the September profile of Chelsea Clinton, "Waiting in the Wings" by Jonathan Van Meter, Dan Baer was mistakenly identified as an interior designer. He is a deputy assistant secretary for the Bureau of Democracy, Human Rights and Labor at the U.S. Department of State.

With both names and titles, the best source is always the person they apply to. Having the person literally spell them out is the best bet for ensuring accuracy.

Place Names

Once again, it might seem that ready access to a great deal of the world's information would solve this problem. But once again, it does not. One study found the following were the most commonly misspelled places in the United States:

1. Pittsburgh, Pennsylvania

2. Tucson, Arizona

3. Cincinnati, Ohio

4. Albuquerque, New Mexico

5. Culpeper, Virginia

6. Asheville, North Carolina

7. Worcester, Massachusetts

8. Manhattan, New York

9. Phoenix, Arizona

10. Niagara Falls, New York

11. Fredericksburg, Virginia

12. Philadelphia, Pennsylvania

13. Detroit, Michigan

14. Chattanooga, Tennesee

15. Gloucester, Massachusetts[13]

Granted, some of those are tricky because of silent or repeated letters (curse you, Cincinnati) or unusual pronunciations (Gloucester is pronounced "gloss-tah"). But others just should not be so problematic. Even more troubling is that a smartphone app released by presidential candidate Mitt Romney in 2012 misspelled America itself ("A Better Amercia," it promised, undoubtedly costing Romney the vote of spelling bee winners).[14]

Another common problem is failing to clarify which place is being referred to when there is more than one possibility, such as Berlin, Md., or Paris, Texas.

And of course, moving out of North America only makes matters worse. Among the most common foreign place names that trip up writers are Bosnia and Herzegovina, Kazakhstan, Kyrgyzstan, Liechtenstein, Luxembourg, Mauritania, Nicaragua, Philippines, Uruguay and Yugoslavia.

Numbers

Many people who work with words for a living have chosen to do so in part because they fear numbers. Yet just like the fear of water increases the likelihood of a non-swimmer drowning in a pool, so does the fear of numbers increase the chances of numerical mistakes.

Therefore, it's best to confront numbers head-on to make sure they add up. Otherwise the result is mistakes like this one The Associated Press was forced to correct: "In a story June 23 about expansion of the St. Louis Art Museum, The Associated Press reported erroneously that the museum is debuting a 210-square-foot expansion. The expansion is actually 210,000 square feet."[15]

Ages should be checked against other material in the article or post to make sure things match. For instance, a writer noted that a 22-year-old woman had three children. That is not common, but it is definitely possible. But then the writer noted that the oldest of her children

The Mitt Romney campaign iPhone app.

© BRENDAN MCDERMID/Reuters/Corbis

was 11. That would have meant the mother became pregnant at 10 or 11. That is not outside the realm of possibility, but it is rare enough that it should have raised a red flag. As it turned out, the writer had the mother's age wrong: She was 32, and therefore had her first child at 21.

Similarly, **dates and chronology** call for careful inspection. Sometimes such errors are so obvious it seems impossible that they could be missed. For example, a cutline accompanying a photo of the Titanic on the 100th anniversary of its ill-fated voyage noted that "The ship sank on April 15, 2012, after striking an iceberg off the coast of Newfoundland."[16] And The New York Times mistakenly reported that E.B. White wrote for The New Yorker magazine for five centuries, apparently forgetting the difference between decades and centuries. Dates and chronologies are especially important to double-check when an age is also cited: Often, the numbers do not add up.

Percentages present a number of challenges. First is that many writers do not understand the difference between a percentage and a percentage point. Percentage points actually are easy to compute: Doing so requires only simple subtraction. For example, if 25 percent of the students at a university had in previous years received financial aid but now only 20 percent do so, that is a change of 5 percentage points ($25 - 20 = 5$). To determine the percentage change, however, requires a little more math. Once the previous calculation has been made, the smaller number is divided by the larger number (5/25), in this case yielding 0.20. Finally, the decimal point moves two places to the right, so the percentage change is 20 percent. (Of course, the truly math-adverse could get the same results simply by plugging the numbers into an online percentage change calculator, such as the one at http://www.csgnetwork .com/percentchangecalc.html.)

Conversions (metric, monetary) also require careful attention. In the real world, such errors can have costly and even fatal consequences. For example:

- The $125 million Mars Climate Orbiter became lost in space after NASA engineers failed to convert from English to metric measurements when exchanging data before its launch.[17]
- An Air Canada jet ran out of fuel in midflight after mistakes were made in figuring the fuel supply of the airline's first aircraft to use metric measurements.[18]
- An axle, mistakenly sized because of an error in metric conversion, broke on a roller coaster train at Tokyo Disneyland's Space Mountain, causing it to derail.[19]

While things generally don't turn out as bad when such errors appear in consumer publications, they can be embarrassing. But with online resources such as the convertors at http://www.metric-conversions.org, such mistakes should not appear at all. Similarly, any cross comparisons of currency should be checked with the latest rates at http://www.xe .com. And references to sales and transactions in foreign countries should be double-checked as to whether those references refer to the local currency or have already been converted to U.S. dollars.

Myths, Hoaxes and Urban Legends

Beyond the basics of fact-checking, a few other areas also demand special attention. The first is a conglomeration of myths, hoaxes and urban legends. These take many forms and tend to shape-shift over time. As Herb Weisbaum of MSNBC.com has written:

> Thanks to the Internet, every day is April Fools' Day. There are literally thousands of myths like these circulating in cyberspace. Unlike the malicious messages sent by cyber-thieves – designed to steal your personal information – these hoax e-mails simply spread rumors and false information.[20]

In most cases, these are little more than nuisances, cluttering people's email inboxes and wasting their time. But in some cases, they actually can disseminate dangerous information. For example, a commonly circulated myth is that if a person is held up and forced to withdraw cash from an ATM, entering the account PIN in reverse will alert the police. This is a total fabrication, and it could lead to the victim being harmed for delaying the withdrawal.

What makes myths, hoaxes and urban legends so problematic is that they tend to be persistent and often sound plausible. The lack of source details ("My cousin Bob heard this from his mechanic ...") adds a third problem: They often are hard to pin down. Fortunately, several websites routinely debunk these types of bad information. The best known is Snopes.com, which maintains a constantly updated list of the "25 Hottest Urban Legends" (http://www.snopes.com/info/top25uls.asp). Snopes has been cited by major news organizations, including CNN, Fox News and MSNBC. Other good sites to check out such information include Scambusters.org and Hoaxbuster.org. Plenty of other resources are available at the Society of Professional Journalists' website (http://www.journaliststoolbox.org/archive/urban-legends-hoaxes-and-scams) as well as at http://www.sree.net/tips/hoax.html.

It's important to be aware that scammers know about these sites, and in many cases attach notes to their hoaxes and urban legends that claim that the information is "Snopes approved." Just because that phrase appears on a bit of info does not absolve the journalist from checking it out.

And even though as Herb Weisbaum of MSNBC.com has noted, every day is April Fools' Day on the Internet, stories published on or around that actual date should be scrutinized especially carefully. Both journalists and the public have been fooled countless times by April Fools' prank stories that upon reflection were obviously untrue.[21]

Similarly, many traditional media (and, for some reason, politicians) have fallen victim to passing along stories from the satirical publication The Onion as real. In one example, Deborah Norville of MSNBC cited a new study (the results of which were published only in The Onion) that claimed that 58 percent of all exercise done in America was done on broadcast television. "For instance, of the 3.5 billion sit-ups done during 2003, two million [*sic*], 30,000 of them were on exercise shows on Lifetime or one of the ESPN channels," she said. And in an article about Tiger Beat magazine, The New York Times mistakenly included a magazine cover that featured a Photoshopped image of President Barack Obama that accompanied a fake story in The Onion.[22]

Manipulation of Images and Videos

It's not just words that can contain lies: Photographs can and do often lie (something true not just in the age of Photoshop but since the earliest days of photography).[23] In some cases, employees of media outlets have created the doctored images themselves. Such cases are considered serious matters – usually grounds for termination – and are discussed further in Chapter 8.

In many other cases, however, media outlets have been duped by outsiders. One such infamous image was of the "tourist guy." The photo, circulated a few weeks after the September 11 attacks, purportedly shows a tourist standing atop the World Trade Center in New York City as a plane approaches from behind him.

Supposedly the photo, bearing a digital time stamp of the day of the attacks, was found on a camera retrieved from the rubble of the towers after the attacks." The image seemingly captured the last fraction of a second of a man's life, and also of the final moment of normalcy before the universe changed for

The 9/11 "tourist guy" photo was proven to be a fake.

http://graphicleftovers.com/blog/marketing-viral-images/

CASE STUDY

Fox News Channel Finds Itself Outfoxed

It's not just The Onion that confuses people as to what is real news and what is satire. Ray Richmond, cofounder of the satirical Internet webzine HollywoodPulse.com, found himself mystified when asked to appear on a Fox News Channel program to discuss a (real) story about whether comedian Paula Poundstone had received preferential treatment in a case involving suspected child abuse.

True, HollywoodPulse.com had written about Poundstone. It's just that what the zine had published were articles like "Poundstone: 'I'm a Drunk Driver, Not a Child Molester!'" and "Poundstone Granted 'Supervised' Child Abuse." As Richmond noted, the coverage was "hardly the kind of credible journalism one might associate with expert opinion."

As a result, Richmond said he was astonished when he arrived at Fox's studio and was not turned back because someone had discovered the truth about his site. Instead, he was ushered inside and appeared on a nationally aired program. And even though the program did not air for a full week, still no one at Fox caught on. He speculated as to how the sequence of events occurred:

> A researcher probably entered the words "Poundstone" and "court" into the Yahoo! search engine. Positioned at No. 17 on the resultant list is a HollywoodPulse.com story from Nov. 17, 2001, headlined, "Paula Poundstone Plays Dumb After Violation." The utterly fabricated piece found the comedian expressing purported shock and outrage that a recent liquor-drinking, pot-smoking, coke-snorting binge represented a true violation of her probation. ... Someone probably scanned a headline, scribbled down the Web address – which sounds legitimate enough on its face – and it was off to the races.
>
> It would be one thing if I had set out to dupe Fox News and somehow succeeded. The truth is scarier. The network duped itself, through either sheer laziness or cluelessness.[24]

all of us. . . . Whether or not the picture was real, the emotions it stirred up certainly were. It was because of those emotions that the photograph began to speed from inbox to inbox at the end of September 2001."[25]

However, even a casual glance at the photo should have made any viewer skeptical of its authenticity. Shadows and lighting are not consistent, and the "tourist" was wearing a much heavier coat and hat than the weather would have called for. As Snopes.com points out, more careful research would have shown the photo to be even less believable:

- The plane is shown approaching from the north and so would have had to hit the north tower. However, that tower did not have an outdoor observation deck;
- The outdoor deck of the south tower opened only at 9:30 a.m., nearly an hour after the first plane hit the towers; and
- The plane in the photo is a standard-body American Airlines 757 jet, but the AA jet that hit the towers was a wide-body 767.[26]

A little more than a decade later, when Hurricane Sandy struck the East Coast of the United States, the image manipulators were out in force. During the storm, journalist Andrew Katz tweeted that "Half of Twitter is debunking #sandy photos posted by the other half. Second half should vet images so everyone can focus on news." Photos showed sharks swimming through the streets of New Jersey, a storm-battered Statue of Liberty, a soldier guarding the Tomb of the Unknown Soldier, a flooded McDonald's restaurant, and more.[27] And the fake images arrived with the force of the storm itself.

So what should a careful publisher do amid such an onslaught? As Craig Silverman wrote at the time for Poynter.org: "Step one is to not retweet or repost any image you see circulating online. Verify it, or don't spread it. Those are your choices."[28]

Silverman offers three tips for helping to detect fake images:

1. *Check the file and metadata.* Digital photos contain metadata, including the type of camera and editing software used. This is often contained as EXIF data, which can be viewed with an EXIF viewer such as the one found at http://www.exifviewer.org.

2. *Look for telltale tool marks.* Many fake photos show evidence of using the Photoshop clone tool, for example, the same faces or clouds repeated many times. And using image enhancements may create halos around parts of the image.

3. *Search shadows and reflections.* Discontinuities in shadows, reflections and perspective lines are often tipoffs to altered images. But these kinds of red flags are often easy to overlook.[29]

One tool that can be used to verify eyewitness tweets also can be used to help authenticate photos. Jennifer Preston, who was the first social media editor for The New York Times, suggests using Twitter's advanced search to find eyewitnesses. Typing in a keyword and a location in the field that says "near this place" will compile tweets from people who include that location in their profiles. Using *pic.twitter.com* for a keyword can help locate photos they have taken and posted.[30]

Videos, too, can be altered, usually through staging or careful editing that can be harder to detect than a doctored photo. But sometimes the trickery occurs in the actual scene being recorded. As Kelly McBride, the senior faculty for ethics, reporting and writing at the Poynter Institute, has noted, it is the "obligation of journalists [to] vet information, because the journalists have made a promise to their audience that they will tell the truth. ... When there's so many nuggets of raw, unfiltered information out there, our job increasingly becomes to find the most meaningful ones and tell the story behind it."[31]

In one widespread example of journalists failing to do their job of checking out a story, a number of major news organizations were utterly taken in by what turned out to be a staged YouTube video of a pig rescuing a baby goat that had become stuck in the pond of a petting zoo. As The New York Times noted:

> Within hours the video had been posted around the Web; it had been shared with the Twitter followers of Time magazine and Ellen DeGeneres; and it had been broadcast on NBC's "Today" show and its "Nightly News" program, ABC's "Good Morning America" and Fox News, where the "Fox & Friends" co-host Brian Kilmeade said of it, "You couldn't do this at Warner Brothers as a cartoon and make it seem more realistic."[32]

But the video had been staged for an episode of an upcoming Comedy Central series, "Nathan for You," a documentary-style show in which host Nathan Fielder helped small businesses gain exposure.

And the exposure came much more widely and quickly than expected. Fielder was surprised that even major news media did not ask how the video was made. And when one of the presenters on "Good Morning America" asked her fellow presenters how the pig had freed the goat, they merely laughed at her. The Times noted, "That a faked video had been so rapidly disseminated by unskeptical news outlets was both surprising and dispiritingly familiar to professional experts on the news media."[33]

Filling Holes

Even trickier than checking facts is noticing when useful facts might have been omitted from a piece of writing. But it's always important to look for such problems and correct if possible.

CASE STUDY

The Manipulated Image That Wasn't

It began with a Facebook post. In March 2013, the Facebook group Women's Rights News posted a photograph of a plus-size mannequin. The accompanying caption read: "Store mannequins in Sweden. They look like real women. The U.S. should invest in some of these." Despite the fact that there was no indication of who shot the photo or when or where it was taken, many major media outlets, from Yahoo to Huffington Post to iVillage to the San Francisco Chronicle, reposted the photo, "prompting it to rapidly go viral, with hundreds of thousands of bloggers, Facebookers and tweeters distributing it far and wide across the social media landscape," Jeff Yang wrote for the online publication Quartz.[34]

As the image made the rounds, some of the reposters retroactively attributed it to H&M, even though there was no evidence the store had anything to do with it. But after nearly a week in circulation, The Washington Post contacted H&M, which denied it had ever used such mannequins. Rather than continue digging, the Post reporter concluded that the photo must be an altered hoax.[35]

As it turned out, the image was real – and nearly three years old. It had been picked up from a Swedish blogger's post, in which she identified the location as H&M's competitor Åhléns. The blogger, Rebecka Silvekroon, wrote: "I don't know who originally found and took the photo from Becka.nu, but my guess is that they didn't know Swedish and saw that I had written 'H&M' in the text, which caused the misattribution."[36]

Dealing with holes is difficult for several reasons. First is that the editor is looking for a problem that by its very nature is not obvious – something is missing. Second is that virtually *no* piece of writing ever includes every bit of information that might interest a reader.

A few tips are helpful in looking for holes. First, unless a piece of writing is directed only at a specialized audience, the assumption that "everybody knows that" is a bad one. For instance, a Page One story in a suburban newspaper reported that the recent graduation of 12 students from a local prep school signaled it had come back from financial problems. But the article never explained what had caused or solved the problems, how big graduating classes were before the financial problems, or whether the fact that all the graduates were female indicated it was a single-sex school. The editors' reasoning for omitting all this information (and more): "Everybody knows that." In a transient society, that justification just does not fly.

Second, writers and editors need to distinguish between information that would be "nice to know" for readers and that which they "need to know." As Vince Rinehart, a multiplatform editor at The Washington Post, notes:

> "Need to know" means basic things essential to understanding the news being presented – the what, when, where, why, how. "Nice to know" encompasses the deeper, more detailed aspects of story – the history of an age-old conflict, a full explanation of what a piece of legislation would do, etc. Vox and other sites – including The Post, with all the "verticals" and explanatory sites we have created – are predicating themselves on the "nice for them to know" market.[37]

If the "nice to know" information is available and fits time and space constraints, it should be included. But the "need to know" information *must* be included, even if it means delaying publication.

Holes are generally the result of one of the following problems:

- Buried leads
- Lack of information

- Source credibility problems
- Misunderstood reports
- Overzealous editing

Buried leads (also spelled **ledes**) occur when a writer has overlooked the most interesting or important aspect of a story and "buried" it deep in an article. Beginning writers are notorious for doing this, often writing leads that focus on the mere fact that someone spoke rather than on the content of what he or she said. For example, here's the lead on a college sports story, as posted to The George Washington University sports website in 2011:

> The George Washington baseball team held No. 1 Virginia to just two runs on Tuesday evening at Davenport Field but were unable to compliment [*sic*] the strong pitching performance at the plate, falling 2–0.

While it is customary to focus on one's own team in reporting on a sporting event, in this case readers would have been better served by an article that started with this tidbit about the opposing team, buried in the seventh paragraph:

> The two runs were all the Cavaliers would need as starting pitcher Will Roberts was perfect on the mound, striking out 10 batters en route to the eighth nine-inning perfect game in NCAA Division I (since 1957) history and the first since 2002.

So for the first time in nearly a decade, and only the eighth time ever, the opposing pitcher threw a perfect nine-inning game, and that's somehow not the lead?[38]

In another example, the writer summarized the remarks made by a researcher in a speech about the dangers of drinking while pregnant, but then he waited until the 15th paragraph to drop this bombshell: "In [his] research, he hasn't been able to detect any harmful effects of minimal drinking during pregnancy." So the entire point of the speech was seriously undermined by the fact that the speaker had *no* evidence on which to base his recommendation.[39]

Sometimes what appears to be a buried lead actually indicates a deeper problem with the story structure. Longtime journalist Curt Hazlett recalls a story in which this was the case:

> A while back I read a pretty routine story about unsolved homicides in a southern county. The lede was about a family still mourning the loss of a son, and the story went on to talk about other victims and about progress in a few of the cases. But [it] wasn't until the jump, deep in the story, that readers learned the sheriff couldn't even find a lot of the murder-case files, and that evidence was missing, too. It could have been a great story if the reporter had stopped and asked: What exactly is this about? That's a question more copy editors also need to ask.[40]

Lack of information is another typical cause of holes. Sometimes the writer knows the information but doesn't think to include it, but in other cases the writer didn't even think to ask the right question. For instance, a story from ABC News begins this way:

> New York cops are trying to determine whether to file charges against a retired police captain who mistook his son for an intruder and shot him at an Adirondacks motel.

The father and son were on a weekend motorcycle club outing, and both had reportedly been drinking. The article notes that after the shooting, the father "called 911 to report that he had shot his son, Matthew Leach … thinking he was an intruder." But the article does not clarify whether the two were sharing a room or had separate rooms, a detail that could make the shooting more or less defensible. (And just to make matters worse, the writer managed to wait until the ninth paragraph to mention that, oh by the way, the shooting proved fatal.)[41]

In another example, an article about cable TV providers joining in efforts to allow customers to buy channels "a la carte" rather than in expensive packages noted that one of the providers, Cablevision, was suing Viacom for requiring Cablevision to buy and distribute 14 channels that had little viewership. Then came this sentence: "The penalty for not carrying those channels is more than $1 billion." The writer moved on without any attempt to explain how that figure was calculated, who would enforce the penalty, how long a period that $1 billion cost would be based on, and so on.[42] (An even bigger hole in the article was that it took at face value cable providers' assertions that a la carte services would cut the cost of service for most customers; doing so actually could cost the same as or more than bundled packages.)[43]

Sometimes holes occur because of **source credibility problems**. That is, a writer relies on a single source (never a good idea) or even multiple sources who have a reason to present only one side of a story. Often, such articles leave the reader with the impression that he or she is getting the full story, but in other cases the writer belatedly slips in the fact that this perspective could be biased.

For example, an article in The Atlantic begins:

> It's not often that a government eagerly announces a military facility in its capital city has been destroyed in a stunning and audacious sneak attack, even in light of plausible evidence to the contrary. Yet here we are: Yesterday, Sudanese culture and information minister Ahmed Bilal Osman alleged that the previous evening, four Israeli fighter jets flew over Khartoum from the east and partially destroyed the Yarmouk munitions factory, in the city's south.

Eight paragraphs go by before the writer closes with this shocker: "Or it might have been nothing more than a fire at a munitions facility." So the reader is strung along for several hundred words under the impression that one thing happened, only to find out at the end that it's quite possible something altogether different occurred.[44]

Sometimes writers create holes because they have **misunderstood reports**, particularly medical or scientific ones. By far, the most common problem is confusing *correlation*, when two things happen at the same time, with *causation*, when one thing causes another. In one example, many media outlets were quick to pick up on a study about teens and their music. The typical article went something like this:

> A new study shows a strong, early penchant for gothic, punk, heavy metal and hardcore dance music can be a predictor of teens who will go astray.
>
> Lovers of "deviant" music by age 12 were "more engaged in minor delinquency in late adolescence," the four-year study, published in the journal Pediatrics, found.[45]

Fortunately or unfortunately, depending on the reader's perspective, that is not what the study showed. As a brilliant analysis of the study indicated, it could not prove any sort of causal relationship between listening to various types of music and acting out. For one thing, the study was based on surveys, which

> can't really show why things tend to happen together, only that they tend to happen together. If you want to find out why – that is, you want to know what causes something – you have to do experiments. ... In the end, it's probably best to see the research as showing that there's something about listening to music that's not chart pop, or highbrow music (jazz, classical) which makes teens more likely to tell researchers they act up. But whatever that something is is still a bit of a mystery.[46]

As a good rule of thumb, it's always best to seek advice from the authors of a report or another expert in the subject area if there is any uncertainty about what a report means.

In other cases, it's not the writers who are to blame for holes but in fact **overzealous editing**. This type of hole often occurs when editors are trying to drastically cut an article to a brief. So for instance, this was the entirety of one brief in a major newspaper:

A French scuba team has discovered parts of the missing warplane piloted by Antoine de Saint-Exupery, author of The Little Prince and one of France's most beloved writers, an Air Force official said Wednesday.

The French aviation hero disappeared during World War II while flying a reconnaissance mission for the Allies over the Mediterranean. Until now, nobody knew where the plane went down.[47]

Using only the first two paragraphs of what was originally a 13-paragraph story created one huge hole: Rather than giving readers the answer to a 60-year-old question, the brief ends by raising the question.

Another case was even worse. One major news outlet reduced a 17-paragraph article to just its lead:

Nine-year-old Jessica Lunsford was raped, bound and buried alive, kneeling and clutching a purple stuffed dolphin, state prosecutors said in documents released Wednesday.

As one horrified reader wrote to the newspaper that published that brief:

Why would you print the description of the way 9-year-old Jessica Lunsford died ... and why just that and nothing else? What purpose did it serve? In what way did that benefit readers?[48]

The most important question for all writers and editors: How does this information help my audience? A piece that raises more questions than it answers is likely not to be at all helpful.

Using Online Resources to Find and Verify Information

Not long ago, an editor needed access to a roomful of reference works in order to do his or her job. But since the advent of the Internet, all that and much more is readily available at a person's fingertips. That's a good thing – and a bad thing. It's good because of the breadth and ease with which information can be checked. But it's bad because people tend to be lazy and to rely on a few sources: the basic Google search and Wikipedia.

While both of those sources can offer quick answers to a multitude of questions, they also can overwhelm the searcher with far too much information, some of it wildly inaccurate. So before even turning to one of these default sources, an editor should ask this question: What is the most authoritative source for answering the question? Instead of searching for the answer, the searcher should begin with a quest for the source that should have the best answer.

So, for example, a 2013 article that referred to Natalie Portman's 20-year acting career should raise a red flag for any editor who knows she is fairly young but doesn't know the details of her career. The best bet would be to head to the definitive site on all things film-related: IMDB.com. And sure enough, her filmography there shows her first screen appearance occurred in 1994, confirming that her career had already spanned 20 years. (To be fair to Google, the IMDB.com site will likely turn up high in the results, but why not save a step and go right to the source?)

One downside to this approach is that although corporate sites might be the most authoritative sources on some topics, they also can be one-sided. Therefore, an editor has to proceed with caution when confirming information that came from such a site.

When no definitively authoritative site appears obvious, it's fine to use Google or Bing. But in doing so, a searcher needs to try a few variations on the search terms. Merely typing the terms in a different order can lead to substantially more or fewer results. For example:

Search Terms	Google Hits	Bing Hits
flu shot safety	22,200,000	34,500,000
safety flu shot	28,900,000	2,180,000
are flu shots safe	8,380,000	16,700,000
is the flu shot safe	29,700,000	35,400,000

Granted, any of these results contains way more information than anyone could ever need. Still, the results seem random and unpredictable, so it's always a good idea to try a few combinations of words and different search engines.

Limiting results to a specific type (e.g., images, videos, discussions) can help sort through mountains of returns. Another useful tool is the advanced search option. Using this option can help locate results in specific Internet domains, in specific languages, in certain types of documents, and so on. (On any Google search results page, it can be accessed by clicking on the little gear icon in the top right corner, then choosing Advanced Search. Bing has a similar feature, but finding it is difficult if not impossible.)

One emerging resource likely to become a favorite for writers and editors is VerificationJunkie.com. The site collects all sorts of tools to help journalists check photos, user submissions and many other types of content. Another great resource is the free e-book Verification Handbook (http://verificationhandbook.com/book).

And what of Wikipedia? While some studies have found the immensely popular site is about as good a source of accurate information as Britannica, not everyone is comfortable with it. In large part, that's because anyone can add and edit information in almost any article at any time, so a user has no guarantee as to the credibility of particular information. As a general rule, Wikipedia is more useful for providing a general overview of a topic or linking to primary documents than for verifying information.

Corrections

Despite the best intentions, every editor will occasionally notice an error in print or online – or be informed of the error by attentive readers. In this age of communication transparency, the best bet is to correct errors of fact as quickly as possible.

When most publishing was print-based, there was a simple rule in running corrections: Publish them as soon as possible and in a spot where readers are likely to see them. Many newspapers, for example, had – and still have – a "Corrections" box on Page A2.

Online publishing makes correcting factual errors much quicker, but it also brings with it questions about the best way to make corrections. Many editors – and readers – feel it is dishonest and a little "1984"-ish to change the content of an article once it has been published. But there's really no suitable equivalent of the newspaper Corrections box online. What most publications have ended up with is a policy of correcting the original material but appending a note to it. For example, after The New York Times confused llamas and alpacas in an article, it ran this correction (possibly paying tribute to an old Rolling Stones song in the process): "Because of an editing error, an earlier version of this article referred incorrectly to alpacas. They are bred for their wool; they are not beasts of burden."

And what if the error occurred on Twitter? The question arose in 2011 after some news outlets erroneously tweeted that congresswoman Gabrielle Giffords was killed in a Tucson, Arizona, mass shooting. The question resurfaced after false reports hit Twitter following the Boston Marathon bombings in 2013. Twitter offers no way to send out a correction other than just sending a new tweet that would be easy to overlook. However, in 2013 Slate social media editor Jeremy Stahl began using a simple but effective strategy: issuing a correction as a reply to the original tweet. With that technique, "Anyone viewing the original tweet can see the resulting correction in the stream of replies." Stahl said that Slate employs the same strategy on Facebook. Slate editor David Plotz explains: "Generally speaking, we don't want to memory hole our mistakes. … When we make an error, our readers should know that we made it, and know what it was, and they should know that the instant we make the correction, and 10 years later, too."[49] However, Craig Silverman of Poynter, one of the leading experts when it comes to verification, says that sometimes it is necessary to delete an erroneous tweet. For example, if the original posting keeps getting retweeted but the correction does not, deleting the original might be the only way to stop further dissemination.[50]

Perhaps the most promising avenue is working to prevent erroneous tweets in the first place. As Silverman writes:

> During emergencies, news organizations that might otherwise compete can work together and help spread good information, banding together to call out hoaxes and fakes. This kind of coordination can amplify the good information and help it rise above the fake and unreliable content that's frankly more appealing from a sharing standpoint.[51]

Finally, more publications are openly asking readers to report any errors they find. The Washington Post, The New York Times, the Chicago Tribune and Toronto Star are among a growing number of publications that have online forms for error reporting to ensure that errors do not stand uncorrected.

Wrapping Up

Nothing is more central to journalism than getting the facts straight. While errors have always slipped into publications, the combination of fewer editors and constant deadlines often proves toxic for the task of keeping the facts straight. With each error, journalists lose more credibility. While it will never be possible to catch every error, it's important to be on the lookout for the most common and serious types of errors, as well as to make sure that readers are not left with unanswered questions.

Key Points

- Factual errors are a major factor in diminishing a publication's credibility.
- While it is impossible to check every fact, several categories of facts call for special attention: names and titles, place names, numbers and conversions.
- Myths, hoaxes and urban legends also need special attention; at a minimum, they should be checked at Snopes.com.
- Photos and videos can be just as untruthful as text. Editors need to learn how to evaluate these visuals.
- Holes can be even harder to avoid than factual errors, as by definition a hole indicates information is missing. So the editor has to place himself or herself in the reader's seat and ask if everything needed to make sense of the story is there.
- While online resources greatly simplify fact-checking, they should be used with caution and precision. The best strategy is to seek not answers but instead authoritative sources for the information being sought or verified.
- When errors do occur, full and forthright corrections should be published as soon as possible.

CHAPTER EXERCISE

Each of the following excerpts was published by a major media outlet. Each also contains at least one factual error. After each excerpt, list the correct information and the source you used to find it. *Note: Do not try to just find the original article with a correction; instead, think about how you would have been able to check it **before** the correction was run.*

1. The debate took place on the campus of Virginia Tech, the site of a 2007 shooting by a mentally disturbed student who killed 23 people.

   Correction:

   Source:

2. Using Twitter sounds so simple. Type out no more than 160 characters – the maximum allowed in a single tweet – and hit send. That's all, right?

   Correction:

   Source:

3. On Sept. 25, 2003, a magnitude 9.1 quake struck Hokkaido, Japan's northernmost island, injuring hundreds.

   Correction:

   Source:

4. The ACL – the anterior cruciate ligament that connects the kneecap to the tibia – tears remarkably easily.

   Correction:

   Source:

5. In the movie "Bad Milo," with the help of a therapist (Toby Huss), Duncan gradually learns to control his gremlin by treating it like a maniacal puppy – with loving coos and infuriated yelling.

   Correction:

   Source:

6. Science fiction writer Bruce Sterling won the prestigious Huge Award.

   Correction:

   Source:

7. Former Washington Post reporter Jeff Himmelman sketches a vivid portrait of the legendary Post editor Bill Bradlee in his new authorized biography, "Yours in Truth."

   Correction:

   Source:

8. But at the time, Morgan Spurlock was wrapping up films about Charles Manson and Comic-Con.

   Correction:

   Source:

9. Thousands of Swiss people will soon be racking their brains for words that rhyme with Alps, cuckoo clocks and chocolate, after the country launched a search for a new national anthem.

   Correction:

   Source:

10. The chemical compound BPA potentially affects the memory gland.

    Correction:

    Source:

 # WRITE RIGHT

Using Quotations Properly

For many journalists, the facts they use most often come in the form of quotations from sources. The same rules about fact-checking apply to quotes as to all other kinds of facts, but quotations also have special demands of their own.

To begin, writers and editors need to make sure they know their publications' policies on editing quotes. While no one would argue that making substantial changes to words in quotes is ever a good idea, publications have different rules on handling things like grammatical errors and missing words.

In an era when most readers had limited sources of news, a publication could get away with cleaning up those sorts of things. But in the digital era, it's easy to find not only multiple printed versions of a quote but multiple broadcast versions, as well. So the audience can only be confused if they see multiple variations of the same statements.

The obvious way to avoid that problem is by sticking with a basic rule: "When a person's words are put inside quotation marks, those specific words should have been said in exactly that form."

But, and of course there is a *but*, some writers are uncomfortable with that rule in certain circumstances. For one thing, people do not talk as well as they write. Incomplete sentences, dangling modifiers, interrupters, and other problems mar people's speech, especially that of

(Continued)

(Continued)

people not used to dealing with the media. And those problems often are exacerbated by a speaker's cultural background, class or race or by the fact that the speaker's native language is not English. Some writers believe it's only fair to clean up quotes so that such speakers do not sound stupid.

But the more convincing argument is that a quote is a fact, and writers and editors should not change facts. Washington Post columnist Mike Wise notes:

> I just have a hard time cleaning up anyone's quotes. I just feel it robs people of their personality. And if I'm not capturing who the person is through the rhythm and cadence of their words, I'm not telling the readers who they are. I just feel people need to be portrayed as they sound, irrespective of whether you're an aging white coach or a young black athlete. Otherwise, we run the risk of homogenizing everyone.

Wise's comments came in response to a discussion of the Post printing two versions of the same quote on the same day. In his column, Wise quoted Redskins running back Clinton Portis as saying, "I don't know how nobody feel, I don't know what nobody think, I don't know what nobody doing, the only thing I know is what's going on in Clinton Portis's life." But an article by Howard Bryant had Portis saying it quite differently: "I don't know how anybody feels. I don't know how anybody's thinking. I don't know what anyone else is going through. The only thing I know is what's going on in Clinton Portis's life."

Deborah Howell, ombudsman at the Post at the time, discussed the dueling quotes in a column and came down on the side of accuracy:

> My view: Quotes should not be changed. If coaches or athletes are routinely "cleaned up," that should stop. Simply put, quotes should be and sound authentic. And The Post needs to set this particular record straight. Wise's Portis quote should be restored to its original form. The rough draft of history is still history.[52]

Beyond ensuring quotes are accurate, what's an editor to do? The following are some good ground rules for handling quotes.

- First, make sure a quote is called for. When a person says a routine thing in a mundane way, there's really no reason to use a quote. A paraphrase will suffice, but maybe that's not even called for.
- It's OK to remove words like *um*, *ah* and *like* from quotes. Such so-called **disfluencies** add nothing to a person's ideas but make it harder for readers to understand his or her thoughts.
- It's OK to cut a few nonessential words from a quote as long as the change is clearly indicated with ellipses. **Interrupters** like "if you must know" typically do not add to a quote.
- For a single change beyond such minor alterations, use ellipses (…) to indicate words removed and parentheses to indicate words substituted. If the quote needs more work than that, it's best to paraphrase the material.
- *Said* is usually the best word to indicate attribution. While dozens of English words indicate that someone has said something, most carry shades of meaning far beyond the neutral *said*. Consider, for instance, *claimed*, *admitted* and *blurted* – not quite the same as *said*. In the majority of cases, *she said* is better than *said she*. But occasionally, a long title will make the latter form the better choice: "The chemical spilled from a 40,000-gallon storage tank and breached a containment wall before flowing into the river, said Tom Aluise, a spokesman for the West Virginia Department of Environmental Protection."
- Watch where the attribution goes. Typically, it's best placed at the end of the sentence, in noun-verb form (*Sutton said*). But moving attribution to the middle of a long sentence often helps make it more readable. When speakers are changing, moving attribution to the start of the sentence helps make the change clear to readers.

Exercise

Edit the following sentences to improve the handling of quotations.

1. "What we needed to do – what we all, uh, thought was necessary – was, like, work together, uh, show that we had solidarity on the issue," Burlington said.

2. "In another," she offered, "thousand years, none of this will matter."

3. "This group of projects aren't going to go away, no matter what some bureaucrats think," Wang pointed out.

4. He said that the recognition "has given him the boost that he needed to keep going."

5. This album is dedicated to all the Tijuana Brass fans who always ask "when am I going to make another record?"

6. The chair of the company explained "Prolonged downtrending in the economy has coerced the firm to implement significant downsizing, on the magnitude of 200 positions."

7. Most people wouldn't understand "the misery this has brought her," the lottery winner said.

8. Powers answered "that all depends on who wanted to."

9. "Our house has six fireplaces, and there's always one going somewhere," she said.

10. "When she said "I love you," I thought she meant it," he cried.

EDITOR'S TOOLKIT

Choosing a Stylebook

Using a less-common spelling of a word (do you get a *guarantee* or *guaranty* with a new car?), a slightly incorrect version of an organization's name (is it the National Organization *of* or *for* Women?) or otherwise deviating from a consistent style does not rise to the level of serious factual error. However, such little errors undermine reader confidence in a publication. One recent study found that elimination of such errors "improves [reader] perceptions of news articles' professionalism, organization, quality of writing, and value."[53] Therefore, every publication should choose and use a stylebook to keep things consistent.

No one stylebook is the best. Instead, different stylebooks cater to different audiences. The Publication Manual of the American Psychological Association is mostly used for research in the social sciences. The Modern Language Association stylebook is used to write papers and cite sources within the liberal arts and humanities. And the Chicago Manual of Style offers two documentation styles: one catering to those in literature, history and the arts, and the other to those in the social sciences. In all these, a great deal of attention is paid to references and bibliographies.

While those stylebooks can be found on the desks of editors of some publications, most mass media outlets are far less concerned about references and bibliographies than about other issues. And that is what makes The Associated Press Stylebook the most common reference on media editors' desks.

The AP Stylebook offers a wide-ranging set of rules for everything from capitalization to spelling of foreign names. At first glance it might seem intimidating because of its hundreds of pages of rules. But a few hints can help make it not only less intimidating but a great resource:

- Always check on names and uncommon words and terms the first time you encounter them. The AP Stylebook does not agree with other stylebooks and, in some cases, runs counter to common usages. It even disagrees with many dictionaries. So assuming that something would be acceptable under AP style is a bad idea.

(Continued)

(Continued)

- Learn the three major sections of the Stylebook. The majority of the time, style questions center on abbreviations, capitalization and numerals. And the AP Stylebook devotes a lengthy section, with many cross-references, to each of those topics. Once you master them, you're well on your way to knowing AP style.
- Work from the specific to the general. For instance, if you come across *smart phone* and think it should be one word, look up that word in the AP Stylebook. If there is no entry for it, move on to *phone* or *telephone*. Still no entry? Think more broadly, such as *electronics*. If that fails, try another tactic. In this case, searching for the name of one particular phone (e.g., *iPhone*) might reveal the correct style for the original word.
- Don't overlook the special sections in the AP Stylebook. Each new annual edition of the Stylebook seems to add another special section with detailed information on topics such as business, fashion, food, social media and sports.
- And speaking of those annual editions, probably more than any other stylebook, the AP Stylebook is updated regularly. Some changes reflect new terminology, while others reflect a reconsideration of long-standing rules. Recent changes have included a switch from *e-mail* to *email*, the acceptance of *over* to mean *more than* (as in "Over 1,000 people …") and one that caused quite the panic in editing circles, the acceptance of *hopefully* to mean *I/we hope*.[54]

One of the advantages of the AP Stylebook is that it is available virtually everywhere. In addition to the traditional paper version, it is also offered in a searchable online version (http://www.apstylebook.com/online), as an iOS app, and as the StyleGuard plug-in for Microsoft Word. In addition, answers to style questions can sometimes be found by tweeting them to @APStylebook.

Student Study Site

Visit the Student Resource Site at **http://study.sagepub.com/lieb** to access:

- Chapter-by-chapter **web quizzes** for independent assessment of course material
- List of online web links and general resources

Chapter 4   **Polishing Writing**

Choosing material that suits the interests of an audience and making sure it is factually correct may be the fundamental components of the editing process, but they are hardly the end of the process. It's also important that copy be edited so that it is as clear and readable as possible and that it is presented in the appropriate style.

This chapter looks at the steps involved in accomplishing those tasks. No matter whether you are serving as your own editor or working with someone else's words, this part of the process is critical to successful publishing.

From Writer-Centered to Audience-Centered

Part of the reason some writers are recognized as being good at what they do is that they have developed a great deal of knowledge and expertise concerning the areas they cover. A writer who knows little about a topic not only cannot begin to ask the most interesting questions or present the most interesting information about it, but he or she easily can fall for bogus or useless information.

The downside of being an expert writer is that sometimes the knowledgeable writer fails to remember that the reader is not as knowledgeable about the topic or familiar with insider terminology. Now, this is a relative situation and depends largely on the publication. An enthusiast magazine or website may be packed with information that anyone outside the core audience could not even understand, just as many parents have little idea what their children's texting abbreviations stand for. Such specific language is fine in that context (but it still raises the question as to how a new reader would even be able to "break into the club").

For more general audiences, however, it's essential that there is little assumption of reader knowledge and expertise. Therefore, technical language and jargon should be kept to a minimum and all but the simplest concepts explained.

The best way for an editor to make sure that copy is reader-friendly is to be a voracious and critical reader. As editing guru John E. McIntyre has written:

> You [must] learn to read analytically, and the best way to start is to pay close attention to your own reactions as a reader. When you stumble over a word or phrase, you do not shrug and keep moving, like a pianist who hits a wrong note during a concert. You stop, back up, and examine why you stumbled. When you find yourself bored, you stop to ask why the text is so boring. Part of your job as an editor is to represent the interests of the reader, and your own responses as a reader will steer you toward the problem patches.[1]

Using the Appropriate Writing Style

Tailoring content to the intended audience involves not just word choice, but also a number of other variables that taken together add up to an appropriate writing style. For just one example, articles in a publication catering to high school students will have completely different style, tone and voice from those in a publication for doctors.

Writing styles vary along a continuum from the very casual to the deathly serious. But for most purposes, it's enough to distinguish between **informal** and **formal styles**. Informal style is distinguished by:

- *Colloquial language*. Informal writing is essentially conversational writing, presented as though the writer were directly addressing the reader. Contractions, abbreviations, slang and asides appear regularly in informal writing.
- *Simplicity*. Informal writing favors short sentences and paragraphs to help the reader grasp points quickly. On the Web, bullet lists are one example of informal writing style.
- *Empathy and emotion*. The writer appears engaged with the topic and presents the information in a way that helps him or her relate to the reader, particularly when it comes to understanding a topic or determining a course of action.
- *Use of first, second or third person*. The writer can use the first person point of view (*I* or *we*) and is likely to address the reader using the second person (*you* and *your*). Third person (*he, she, they*) is also used.

In contrast, the following are the hallmarks of formal writing:

- *Use of full words, jargon and terminology*. Formal writing is typically targeted toward readers with some degree of expertise on a topic, so using the language of the field and technical terms the average person would not recognize is acceptable.
- *Complex sentences and paragraphs*. These are often needed to fully explore more technical or involved ideas and topics.
- *Objective stance*. Points are stated clearly and fully supported.
- *Use of third person*. Formal writing is not a personal writing style. The formal writer is disconnected from the topic.

Informal Style	Formal Style
Colloquial language	Use of full words, jargon, and terminology
Simplicity	More complex sentences and paragraphs
Empathy and emotion	Objective stance
Use of first-, second- or third-person point of view	Use of third-person point of view

The following examples show how the same information was presented to two different audiences. In the first, the audience is biologists, and a formal style is used:

Endogenous rhythms of circalunar periodicity (~29.5 days) and their underlying molecular and genetic basis have been demonstrated in a number of marine species. In contrast, there is a great deal of folklore but no consistent association of moon cycles with human physiology and behavior. Here we show that subjective and objective measures of sleep vary according to lunar phase and thus may reflect circalunar rhythmicity in humans.[2]

The same information, presented informally to a general audience:

> In the days close to a full moon, people take longer to doze off, sleep less deeply and sleep for a shorter time, even if the moon isn't shining in their window, a new study has found.[3]

Neither is right nor wrong; both are acceptable styles for their appropriate audiences. However, using one in place of the other would be wrong, as the style would not fit the intended audience.

Offer a Unique Voice

The most serious publications (for example, those for legal, scientific and medical professionals) usually feature a writing style that gives little indication of the writers' personalities – other than that they are serious, and often humorless, people. But for many publications, writers are encouraged to have unique voices that appeal to readers. This might seem to violate a traditional rule of journalism – the requirement to maintain an objective stance – but the reality is that people have always flocked to writers, columnists and broadcasters who have distinct personalities. While that was important in the pre-Internet era, it's absolutely crucial in the digital domain where countless voices fight for an audience's attention.

However, not every writer's natural (or constructed) voice works well. Writers and their editors need to be careful that the voice used in a piece of writing does not cross the line from inviting to alienating. Among the questions writers and editors should consider are the following:

- "What inferences about my personality do I want my readers to make?
- "Given my audience and purpose, is it appropriate to express my feelings about this subject?
- "Would it be more appropriate for me to project a strong, passionate tone, or should I try to appear more objective?
- "Based on what I have written, what sense about my personality or feelings about the subject will readers be likely to infer?
- "Have I used any words or examples that are emotionally charged and likely to alienate my readers?
- "What personal examples should I add or delete to help my readers better understand me and my message?"[4]

For an editor, helping writers refine their voices while at the same time being careful not to undermine their styles is one of the biggest challenges. This is not a huge problem when dealing with new writers or nonwriters, who often need all the help they can get in developing an appealing voice and style. One freelance editor notes that "As a technical editor frequently called upon to edit the correspondence of high-level managers in a large corporation, I find it extremely difficult to [preserve the authors' voices]. The sheer number [of] grammatical errors and stylistic improprieties require a plethora of emendations that leave little of the original text – and hence the author's voice – intact."[5]

But when dealing with professional writers, an editor needs to be careful in changing words and sentence structure. As editor Erin Brenner writes:

> Once we begin editing, we have to consider how our decisions affect the author's voice. Not every change will hurt the voice, but many changes together can. The manuscript is like a bucket of clear water, and edits that change voice are food coloring. One drop of blue won't change the color of the water, but drop after drop adds up until, all of a sudden, your water is undoubtedly blue and you can no longer see the bottom of the bucket.[6]

CASE STUDY

SmittenKitchen

What is the secret to success for a food writer who never trained as a chef or even worked in a restaurant? In the case of Deb Perelman, founder of SmittenKitchen.com, the answer is her appealing voice, a voice that has attracted millions of visits to her site. In fact, her unique style and tone were enough to propel her first book – appropriately titled "The Smitten Kitchen Cookbook" – to debut at the No. 2 spot on The New York Times best-seller list for hardcover advice and miscellaneous, even though the recipes it contains are similar to those available free on her website.

As a Times article noted, "Perelman's style appears to resonate particularly with young women learning to cook. She is conversational, self-deprecating and often seems to be confessing, without ever really yielding embarrassing details."[7]

As but one example of Perelman's voice, take the introduction to her recipe for pear scones:

One of the saddest things you should probably know about me is that I'm a terrible host. I don't mean to be; in my head, I'm the kind of person who would find out you were coming over, quickly gather some wildflowers from the side of the road, put them in an old Mason jar, pour-over some coffee from a local roaster, steam cream from an upstate dairy in a spouted glass and pull out something warm and enticing from the oven right as you arrived. In my head, I understand that none of these things are terribly difficult to pull off. In reality, were you to come over right now, you'd find a plate of pears (one with a toddler mouth-sized bite removed) and mostly-empty jar of something delicious, but alas, too delicious to have lasted until you arrived, on the table. ... Also notable is the absent aroma of freshly-brewed coffee. Upon closer inspection, you might see that I don't actually own any coffee-making apparatus. And not a single warm thing has left the oven this morning; we had stove-top oatmeal for breakfast again.[8]

As a result of her style and tone, Perelman's readers feel as though she is a friend. As one fan said at a book signing event, "It's like she jumped out of the screen and is your best friend next door."[9] That's just what writers and editors love to hear.

Editing for voice should be thought of as a three-step process: First, identify the writer's voice. Second, edit carefully. And third, review the work. "While we must consider every edit as we make it," Brenner notes, "we should also review our work afterward to ensure that the voice is the same as when we began. Perhaps it's clearer, purer, so readers hear and engage with it better, but it's still unmistakably the author's voice."[10]

Avoiding Verbosity and Achieving Clarity

Part of the process of polishing a writer's style, and of good editing in any situation, is making sure that the message is as clear as possible and is expressed in as few words as possible. Doing that requires paying attention to two interrelated areas: **verbosity** and **clarity**.

Verbosity is using more words than are necessary. Even a little verbosity is a bad thing, especially online. As Web writing expert James Mathewson notes: "Brevity is important because obviously people don't have a lot of time. ... People don't really give you the time to process the information."[11]

Renowned writing coach Roy Peter Clark would agree with that. In his book "How to Write Short: Word Craft for Fast Times," he writes: "In the digital age, short writing is king. We need more good short writing – the kind that makes us stop, read, and think – in an accelerating world." To make his point, Clark rewrites a well-known passage from Strunk and White's "The Elements of Style" about eliminating verbosity. The original:

> Omit needless words. Vigorous writing is concise. A sentence should contain no unnecessary words, a paragraph no unnecessary sentences, for the same reason that a drawing should have no unnecessary lines and a machine no unnecessary parts. This requires not that the writer make all his sentences short, or that he avoid all detail and treat his subjects only in outline, but that every word tell.

Clark's revision, which coincidentally comes in at 137 characters, or just under the max for a tweet:

> Write tight. A text needs no extra words as a drawing needs no extra lines. A sentence can be long with detail. But every word must tell.[12]

The easiest types of verbosity to find are those that are simply redundancies. *ATM machines*, for example (the *M* stands for *machines*) or *Easter Sunday* (it never falls on any other day). While some of them might take a little thinking in order to catch (*a 26.2-mile marathon*? That's how long a marathon is by definition), all are worth editing as the extra words add nothing. The list of common redundancies is a long one, and all good editors should familiarize themselves with them. A few of the classics:

- (12) noon/midnight
- (armed) gunman
- (completely) destroyed
- each (and every)
- (free) gift
- kneel (down)
- (past) history
- (usual) custom

Plenty of other examples can be found at "200 Common Redundancies" (http://grammar.about.com/od/words/a/redundancies.htm) and "50 Redundant Phrases to Avoid" (http://www.dailywritingtips.com/50-redundant-phrases-to-avoid).

While redundancies present a good place to start in looking for verbosity, there are plenty of other problems, too. Perhaps the next most common problem is when writers use long and less common words in place of short ones. As writer Jonathan Crossfield notes:

> Sure, it is nice to be able to choose from a number of words to find just the right cadence or subtlety, but in most daily writing this is entirely unnecessary. Why say "expenditure" when you can say "cost"? Why use "saturated" when you can use "wet"? Of course, context is important and there will be times when it is more appropriate to use "saturated" or "expenditure." But the idea that a longer or more archaic word is preferable over short, simple language is just plain wrong.[13]

Sometimes writers use unfamiliar words to try to demonstrate their expertise. In reality, outside of specific journals, such language does nothing of the sort. Instead, it just makes it harder for all readers – experts and average – to understand the point the writer is trying to make. And platforms such as Twitter make it clear that using longer words means getting less information across in a given space than using shorter words. Again, Crossfield has thoughts worth sharing:

Yes, often big words are used as a form of egotistical boasting on the part of the writer. "I know what that means – how clever and educated do I look." What it actually says is that the writer cares more about appearing clever than conveying the message. Good writing is invisible. The moment a reader is jolted out of the message to interpret a word or reread a sentence to understand it, the writer has failed.[14]

People have waged the fight against wordiness and pretension for many years. In his essay "Politics and the English Language," in 1946, George Orwell listed six rules to help avoid the problems:

- "Never use a metaphor, simile or other figure of speech which you are used to seeing in print.
- "Never use a long word where a short one will do.
- "If it is possible to cut out a word, always cut it out.
- "Never use the passive where you can use the active.
- "Never use a foreign phrase, a scientific word or a jargon word if you can think of an everyday English equivalent.
- "Break any of these rules sooner than say anything outright barbarous."[15]

Of course, there is a difference between knowing the rules and being able to apply them. But some responses to a request to help cure a person's verbosity offer good, easy-to-apply solutions:

- "The trick, I think, is saying less than you think you need to, but choosing your words so well that your listener/reader will be fascinated enough to think about what you've said and, if applicable, ask questions."
- "One cause of verbosity is using multi-word phrases to express ideas that could be better expressed with single words. Often a multi-word phrase is the first way I can think of to express an idea, but I know there's a more precise word that I can't think of. A good thesaurus – or more than one thesaurus – helps a lot."[16]

On a more technical level, a great resource for writers and editors is "The Paramedic Method," originally developed by Richard Lanham in his book "Revising Prose." The method can be applied to any sentence by taking a series of steps:

1. Circle the prepositions (*of, in, about, for, onto, into*): This step accomplishes two things. First, it helps to highlight the number of prepositional phrases used; having too many is a common cause of making sentences hard to understand. Second, it helps to isolate the main components of the sentence, the subject and the verb.

2. Draw a box around the *is* verb forms (*am, is, are, was, were, have been, am being*): These verbs slow things down because they do not actually make anything happen in a sentence. Often the presence of such verbs signals **nominalization**, which is wordiness that occurs when nouns appear in place of verbs. For instance, *Viewers are supportive of adding the channels, even if it increases their monthly cable bill* can be shortened to *Viewers support adding the channels, even if it increases their monthly cable bill*. Editors should replace as many of these nominalizations as possible with action verbs. (In addition, all instances of passive voice, such as *is surrounded by*, should be changed to active voice, in this case *surrounds*. (See the Write Right section of this chapter for more on passive voice.)

3. Ask, "Where's the action?"

4. Change the "action" into a simple verb.

5. Move the doer into the subject: This and the previous two rules work together. Often the action in a sentence is dormant, buried in a form of the verb *is*. At first glance, it might be hard to find. But once an editor discovers the action, it's an easy task to make it more obvious and stronger. In the process, the person or thing doing the action often needs to

be moved into the position of subject of the sentence. For example, *Burning books is considered censorship by some people* works much better when revised to *Some people consider burning books to be censorship.*

6. Eliminate any unnecessary slow wind-ups: Especially online, but anywhere, really, starting a sentence slowly works against readers finishing it. In particular, removing *it is* and *there are* from the start of a sentence helps get the action moving more quickly. Almost as bad are wind-ups like *My opinion is that* and *The fact of the matter is that.*

7. Eliminate any redundancies.[17]

Following those rules, let's try an example:

> Controlling the quality and level ⊙f television shows that children |are watching| |is| a continuing challenge ⊙o parents that they |must be meeting| ⊙n a daily basis.

Here is just one possible revision:

Parents struggle daily to control the quality and amount of television that their children watch.[18]

The original included 25 words, the revision, 16, for a reduction of more than a third. More important, readers will be able to capture the idea much more quickly from the revision than from the original.

Here is one more example, from the PlainLanguage.gov website:

Before: *When the process of freeing a vehicle that has been stuck results in ruts or holes, the operator will fill the rut or hole created by such activity before removing the vehicle from the immediate area.*

After: *If you make a hole while freeing a stuck vehicle, you must fill the hole before you drive away.*[19]

Finally, an easy way to reduce wordiness is looking for words that add nothing. Perhaps the most common is *very.* Some writers reach for it routinely, even though it is

Worry About This/Not About That

The Truth About Short and Long Sentences

Ask most writers and editors what the maximum length of a sentence should be, and you'll probably get a lot of answers suggesting 25 to 30 words is the outside limit. There is sound thinking behind such a recommendation, as we will see in the discussion of limiting sentences to one idea each: Longer sentences tend to be packed full of ideas that can make readers' heads spin, as in this 62-word example:

> *As it exists now, customers wishing to procure names and addresses of association members, or association journal subscribers, or Annual*

(Continued)

(Continued)

Meeting attendees (either exhibitors or vendors), or buyers of books published by the association, or any other type of list from any of our databases, are routed to a number of different departments where varying rates, policies and procedures are in effect.

But that does not mean that any sentence longer than 30 words should automatically be cut. Capable writers can handle sentences substantially longer than that without losing readers in a thicket of clauses and ideas. For example, in his Pulitzer-winning nonfiction novel "The Executioner's Song," Norman Mailer slipped this sentence in among his typically much shorter ones:

With all the excitement, Brenda was hardly taking into account that it was practically the same route their Mormon great-grandfather took when he jumped off from Missouri with a handcart near to a hundred years ago, and pushed west with all he owned over the prairies, and the passes of the Rockies, to come to rest at Provo in the Mormon Kingdom of Desert just fifty miles below Salt Lake.

Yes, at 71 words, this sentence takes some effort to digest. But there is nothing in it to confuse or mislead the reader. Instead, it is more like a rich entrée that exhibits a wide range of tasty flavors and scents waiting to be discovered by the discriminating diner.

On the other hand, sometimes *short* sentences can cause problems, especially when every sentence in a piece is similarly short. Consider this example, slightly modified from the original news article:

Authorities will go door-to-door. They will strongly recommend residents leave. There's a possibility for more rain and more flooding. Right now, 260 homes are still without power. About 55 people aren't able to return to their homes. Many of them have gone to the local Community Center. Search and rescue teams conducted several rescues throughout the morning.

Granted, this example is a bit of a stretch. But it is not far from the work of some writers. And it is choppy and unlikely to hold a reader's attention, unless the reader's favorite book is "See Spot Run."

As with much else in writing – and in life – the key to success lies in balance. An occasional well-crafted long sentence? No problem. Lots and lots of short sentences? Problem. A combination of sentences of all shapes and sizes? Just right.

imprecise and meaningless. Just as bad are *some, a lot, a few, much, plenty* and *little*. Unless such words add to a sentence (*She has fond memories of traveling abroad when she was a little girl*, for instance), they should be deleted or replaced.

Limiting Sentences to One Idea Each

One way to help ensure sentences are easy for readers to follow is to make sure that they contain a single idea each. Some writers regard sentences as duffel bags that beg to be stuffed full of multiple thoughts. But readers' brains don't deal well with that sort of approach. Instead, sentences should rarely contain more than a single idea so that readers can absorb it before moving on to the next sentence.

This sentence fails that test: *If human fossil fuel consumption continues as projected the environmental effects will be felt for millennia, according to a new analysis that considers long-term feedback processes not usually included in climate projections.* Even though that sentence is only 33 words long and is relatively straightforward, the additional information tacked onto the end makes it harder to digest than it should be. How bad is it? One measure of clarity is the Flesch-Kincaid Grade Level test, which scores text on a U.S. school grade level. For example, a score of 7.0 means that a seventh grader can understand the document. A score in the range of 7.0 to 12.0 is recommended for general audiences. The example sentence scores a whopping 21.2, which is just on the border of what is considered graduate school level. Another common measure, the Gunning-Fog Score, places the sentence at an even higher level: 27.7. The sentence also gets a dismal rating on the Flesch-Kincaid Reading Ease test. A piece of writing that can be understood by everyone is rated 100 on a 100-point scale; this sentence gets an astounding rating of 1.6!

Fortunately, gauging the readability of a piece of writing requires little more than asking Microsoft Word to analyze it or pasting it into an online site like Readability-Score.com for an instant analysis. In most cases, cutting out extraneous ideas can go a long way in getting better scores.

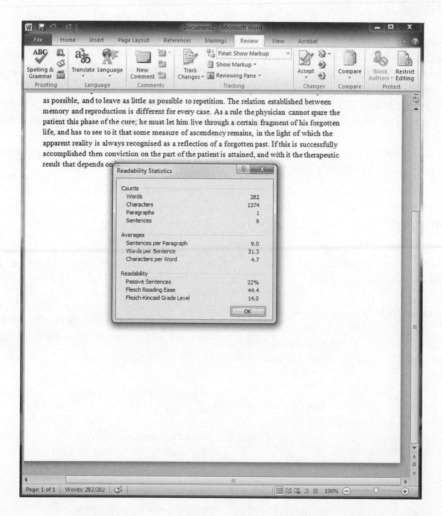

To test readability of all or part of a document in Microsoft Word, you first have to click the **File** tab, and then click **Options**. Click **Proofing**, then in **When correcting spelling and grammar in Word**, make sure the **Check grammar with spelling** check box is selected. Also check **Show readability statistics**. Click **OK**. Then choose the **Review** tab. In the **Proofing** group, click **Spelling & Grammar**. After you correct any mistakes, the dialogue box above appears with the readability information.

One warning: In their zeal to chop sentences down to just a single idea, writers and editors need to be careful that they don't end up with a bunch of short, choppy sentences. (See this chapter's "Worry About This/Not About That" for more on the topic.)

Wrapping Up

While many writers complain about how hard it is to get words down on paper or screen, doing so is only the first step of many toward making sure that readers can understand the writer's intentions. The best writing is audience-centered, written in an appropriate style that showcases the unique voice of the writer. An editor can help to achieve all those objectives, as well as to make sure wordiness is eliminated and clarity is improved. Once the entire process is complete, the writer's work is ready to reach a wide – and appreciative – audience.

Key Points

- While expertise in a topic is a desirable trait for a writer, editors must make sure that non-experts can understand everything.
- Both formal and informal writing styles have their places in publishing. The key is to match the style with the topic and audience.
- Serious publications prefer that writers do not inject their personalities into their writing styles. But many less formal publications strive to have writers emphasize their unique voices.
- Editors must strive to make every piece of writing as clear and concise as possible, being careful not to cut necessary facts and information.

CHAPTER EXERCISE

Edit the sentences below to eliminate all verbosity. Rewrite sentences if necessary.

1. If and when you would like more facts and figures on our products, simply contact us by telephone and we will send you a brochure that spells out a great deal about the uses of our products.

2. After finishing the 26.2-mile marathon in record heat, the runners were pretty thirsty.

3. The educators mutually cooperated on planning ahead to prevent fatal killings in the school district.

4. Just before 12 midnight on Thursday night, the thieves penetrated into the bank vault.

5. The group planned to repeat again their cautions about leaving deadly poisons in the vicinity of young children.

6. In the early hours of Labor Day that year – Monday, Sept. 5, 1994 – a blazing inferno broke out in the warehouse district.

7. If the past history of voters is any indication, his future plans should include writing a resignation speech.

8. They drank up to the bride and groom, drinking until they had emptied out all the champagne bottles.

9. The condo association filed a lawsuit against the builders for failure to perform the task of keeping the building secure.

10. If the State Secretary finds that an individual has received a payment to which the individual is not entitled, whether or not the payment was due to the individual's fault or misrepresentation, the individual shall be liable to repay to State the total sum of the payment to which the individual was not entitled

 **WRITE RIGHT**

Avoiding Fragments and Comma Splices

Ask any grade-schooler what makes a sentence, and the answer comes quickly: a subject and a verb. There is another name for the basic sentence, an **independent clause**. Despite the lofty sounding name, an independent clause can be as simple as *Let's eat* or *Go!*

A sentence without either a subject or a verb is known as a **fragment**. Fortunately, fragments are rare, as the basic lesson is ingrained so early and often. Everyone knows that *His brother, Joe* and *Running toward me* are not complete sentences. (However, in some publications such fragments are acceptable as long as they are made on purpose to achieve a stylistic effect.)

But sometimes fragments are more insidious. That's because the most common problems occur with **dependent clauses**: material with a subject and a verb but not capable of standing on its own. The strange thing is, sometimes just removing a word or two would make a dependent clause into an independent one, but language is funny that way. For example:

He takes the subway to work.
Whether he takes the subway to work.

The first is an independent clause (sentence). *He* is the subject; *takes* is the verb. The addition of the word *whether* in the second one makes it a dependent clause (fragment). That's because *whether* is a **subordinating conjunction**. Such words join two sentences but in the process make one of the sentences dependent on the other:

She made a steady income doing freelance software development while she was in graduate school. (sentence)

While she was in graduate school. (fragment)

Subordinating conjunctions include the following:[20]

after	if	though
although	if only	till
as	in order that	unless
as if	now that	until
as long as	once	when
as though	rather than	whenever
because	since	where
before	so that	whereas
even if	than	wherever
even though	that	while

Fortunately, remembering the basics discussed so far is all that is necessary to spot a fragment:

1. Is it missing either a subject or a verb?

2. Is it a single clause that contains a subordinating conjunction?

(Continued)

(Continued)

If the answer to either of these questions is yes, then the material is a fragment and must be corrected, usually by attaching the dependent clause to an independent clause that precedes or follows it:

Incorrect: *He decided to spend the semester abroad. Before he would be tied down by a new job.*

Correct: *He decided to spend the semester abroad before he would be tied down by a new job.*

Note that there is no comma between the two clauses, and there never should be one between a dependent and an independent clause.

A second problem is the **fused** sentence, often referred to as a run-on. A fused sentence is what the name makes it sound like: two independent clauses fused together without a proper conjunction or punctuation:

Incorrect: *He likes ice cream on hot summer days, he loves warm pie on cold winter days.*

Correct: *He likes ice cream on hot summer days; he loves warm pie on cold winter days.*

Correct: *He likes ice cream on hot summer days. He loves warm pie on cold winter days.*

Correct: *He likes ice cream on hot summer days, and he loves warm pie on cold winter days.*

As these examples show, the solution to a fused sentence is adding a semicolon, adding a period, or adding a comma and a **coordinating conjunction** (*for*, *and*, *nor*, *but*, *or*, *yet*, *so*). If there is a relationship between the two clauses, a subordinating conjunction might also work.

Exercise

In the blank before each item, identify whether the item is a sentence (S), a fused sentence (FS) or a fragment (F).

___ 1. Whether you drive to work or not.

___ 2. "In a market that's not trending up, a buy-and-hold strategy will lose relative to some market-timing strategy, we just don't know which one."

___ 3. Expanded tax credits for child care, additional funds for immunization and a provision for increasing staff-to-child ratios at day-care centers are part of the plan.

___ 4. Which brings us to influences.

___ 5. He said, "Let's go," she testified.

___ 6. A shampoo unlike any you've ever used.

___ 7. Irwin's early works were abstract paintings, he later used fabrics and metals.

___ 8. Get hooked on reading.

___ 9. What's more, the company assumes total responsibility for the project.

___10. It's part of the learning process that leads us to quality.

EDITOR'S TOOLKIT

Blogs Editors Should Follow

The great thing about the English language is that it is a living, changing organism that can accommodate new words and usages. And that also is probably the worst thing, at least as far as an editor is concerned. That's because in some ways English is a moving target, and what was correct yesterday – and maybe for a million days before then – can suddenly become incorrect.

Case in point: the use of the word *hopefully* as a floating sentence adverb, as in *Hopefully, our team will end up in the playoffs*. After decades of insisting that such usage was unacceptable, The Associated Press Stylebook welcomed it with open arms in early 2012, causing howls of protest from language purists who just know that such usage has never been acceptable. The reality of the word's historic usage tells a different story, though:

That floating "hopefully" had been around for more than 30 years in respectable venues when a clutch of usage critics, including Theodore Bernstein and E.B. White, came down on it hard in the 1960s. Writers who had been using it up to then said their mea culpas and pledged to forswear it. Its detractors were operatic in their vilifications. The poet Phyllis McGinley called it an abomination and said its adherents should be lynched; and the historian T. Harry Williams went so far as to pronounce it "the most horrible usage of our times" – a singular distinction in the age that gave us expressions like "final solution" and "ethnic cleansing," not to mention "I'm Ken and I'll be your waitperson for tonight."[21]

So for a long time, such usage was OK, and then it wasn't, and then it was again. Got that?

Fortunately, plenty of word geeks keep up with earthshaking matters such as this, and regularly checking out their blogs can help an editor stay on top of changes, debates, emerging language concerns and other issues. As a bonus, the blogs often include features such as examples of egregious editing errors and illuminating interviews with working editors.

The following list is by no means exhaustive, but it does include many of the best known and most useful blogs for editors. To make the cut, a blog had to be current as of deadline, updated regularly, and focused largely or exclusively on editing. Bloggers who focus on academic writing and book publishing were excluded, as those are niche areas.

- **Bill Walsh's Blogslot** (http://theslot.blogspot.com): While this blog is not updated all that frequently, the Washington Post editor and author of "Yes, I Could Care Less" offers good advice.
- **Charles Apple** (http://www.charlesapple.com): An emphasis on visual journalism with lots of head-slapping examples of errors.
- **Common Sense Journalism** (http://commonsensej.blogspot.com): Veteran journalist Doug Fisher offers good before-and-after examples, showing how an editor can improve weak writing.
- **Copyediting** (http://www.copyediting.com): Many interesting posts, but perhaps the most useful are the regular news roundups.
- **Copyeditors' Knowledge Base** (http://www.kokedit.com/ckb.php): Good for the basics and reference materials.
- **Editing Hacks** (http://editinghacks.wordpress.com): Recurring "Hack the Flab" section is a great resource for learning how to cut verbosity. Also features interesting interviews with editors and copyediting tutorials.
- **Grammar Cops** (http://grammarcops.wordpress.com): Plenty of examples of grammar problems. More entertaining than educational or practical.
- **Grammar Underground** (http://www.grammarunderground.com): Nitpicky but informative observations in this blog and podcast on proper word choice and usage.
- **Heads Up** (http://headsuptheblog.blogspot.com): Great examples of bad editing and word choice.
- **John McIntyre's You Don't Say** (http://www.baltimoresun.com/news/language-blog): The Baltimore Sun editor and author of "The Old Editor Says" offers lots of useful information in one of the most popular and interesting editing resources.
- **Language Corner** (http://www.cjr.org/language_corner): Merrill Perlman, formerly of The New York Times, takes on word misuse.
- **Law Prose** (http://www.lawprose.org/blog): Geared to legal writers, but with general info on grammar and usage, some nitpicky. Not that that's a bad thing.
- **Mighty Red Pen** (http://mightyredpen.wordpress.com): Lots of examples of grammar problems. More entertaining than educational or practical.

(Continued)

(Continued)

- **Pam Nelson's Grammar Guide** (http://grammarguide.copydesk.org): The most useful part of this blog are the dozens of grammar quizzes based on published errors.
- **Quick and Dirty Tips** (formerly Grammar Girl) (http://www.quickanddirtytips.com/grammar-girl): Boatloads of information including interesting stories about language and instructive videos.
- **Ragan: Writing & Editing** (http://www.ragan.com/WritingEditing/WritingAndEditing.aspx): Covers a wide range of topics including PR and training, but some good posts for editors.
- **Regret the Error** (http://www.poynter.org/category/latest-news/regret-the-error): Craig Silverman spotlights newspaper corrections, particularly the outlandish ones. A good lesson in what not to do.
- **Sentence First** (http://stancarey.wordpress.com): Written by an Irish author, not everything here will apply or be of interest elsewhere. But there are loads of links to good readings and videos.
- **Style and Substance** (http://blogs.wsj.com/styleandsubstance): This Wall Street Journal blog largely focuses on the paper's style guide rules but also offers food for thought for any editor.
- **Vocabulary.com** (http://www.vocabulary.com): A very specific site, Vocabulary.com "combines an adaptive learning system (The Challenge) with the world's fastest dictionary (The Dictionary) so that you can more quickly and more efficiently learn words."

Student Study Site

Visit the Student Resource Site at **http://study.sagepub.com/lieb** to access:

- Chapter-by-chapter **web quizzes** for independent assessment of course material
- List of online web links and general resources

Chapter 5 This One Weird Chapter Will Help You Grab Readers

No matter how much time and attention has been put into an article, no matter how good the lead is, if readers don't notice the article, all that work is for nothing. And the decisive factor in whether an article gets noticed or not often comes down to a handful of words: the headline.

Headlines have long played a major role in helping readers decide what publications to buy and what articles to read. Whether they scream from the front page of a tabloid newspaper, seduce the prospective reader from a glossy magazine cover, entice a skimmer to take the time to read a blog post, or showcase the range of news on an online site, headlines are often the most important words in any publication. By some estimates, while eight of out 10 people will read a headline, only two out of 10 people go on to read the article or post, which means that poor headlines can lead readers to skip over the vast majority of content.[1]

In the digital environment, headlines reach the height of importance. Not only do they assist readers in making decisions once they are at a blog or news site, but they also often are responsible for attracting readers to that site in the first place, through search engines or links recommended via social media. It's not surprising then, that writing a great headline can take nearly as long as writing a basic article or post or that some professionals try a dozen or more headlines before settling on one.

This chapter takes a look at the basics of headline writing. It starts with general rules of headline construction and then looks at how those rules differ in the digital realm.

Keep It Simple

It probably goes without saying that when dealing with a form of writing that allows the use of only a few words, simpler is better. Unfortunately, it is not hard to find examples of headlines that instead of enlightening readers just make them scratch their heads (for instance, *Psychics Predict World Didn't End Yesterday*). While some beginning headline writers may argue that such puzzlers will draw people to the article so they can figure out what the headline is about, very few people work that way. Instead, swimming in a constantly expanding ocean of information, readers are likely to be captivated by headlines that provide a clear idea of what is in store.

From a structural standpoint, the best way to accomplish that goal in a headline is to use the traditional **subject-verb-object** format. (And yes, that previous example did follow S-V-O, but doing so did not save it.) That format makes sense because typically a headline tells the reader that someone or some organization (the **subject**) has done something (the **verb**) to or for someone or something (the **object**). The concept of object is looser than the grammatical direct object – in a headline, it is whatever is needed to complete the idea.

Further, S-V-O is a natural way of writing and reading information. When the prospect of having a potential reader move along is on the line, it does not make sense to give him or her a push with a headline that takes work to comprehend. So while there are sometimes good reasons to use a format other than S-V-O (as we discuss later), it provides the best starting point for headline writing.

These headlines all provide good examples of the format:

Cancer physicians - attack - high drug costs

Iranian men - dress - in drag for gender equality

Earbits - brings - its indie music discovery service to Android

NBC News - looks - across the pond for president candidates

The S-V-O format at first might feel like a straitjacket, but it actually allows for a good degree of flexibility. That's because in many cases, there are multiple possibilities for the subject. For instance, in news coverage of a deadly building collapse in Bangladesh, headline writers found a variety of options:

Bangladesh factories in collapse ignored evacuations

Death toll from Bangladesh building collapse climbs to over 200

From Bangladesh: Plea to arrest building, RMG owners

Rescuers scour mangled heap after Bangladesh building collapse kills 244

Workers rescued alive from Bangladesh factory

In each case, the headline writer used a different subject. The result is a wide variety of takes on the same story, but all essentially following S-V-O format.

Headline Style Rules

Headlines generally follow the same style rules that copy follows. But they also have their own set of rules governing a number of matters. Here are the Top 10 Style Rules:

1. Headlines should not echo the lead: It's always disappointing to read a headline and then find the same words used in the lead that follows. While a good headline will summarize the news, it should feature at least slightly different wording and order than the lead.

2. Headlines should be written consistently in either upstyle or downstyle: Most publications and blogs have a consistent style of headline writing. The less common choice is upstyle, in which every word of the headline except short conjunctions and prepositions is capitalized (*Blankfein Said to Be Among CEOs Meeting Lew on Economy*). More common is downstyle, in which only the first word of the headline and proper nouns are capitalized (*B&N to add Google Play app store to its Nook HD*). This style is easier to read and gives those writing headlines for print a little more room, because lowercase letters are not as wide as capital ones.

3. Most headlines do not end with punctuation: While every sentence requires an ending punctuation mark, the only headlines that do so are those that ask a question. Periods should appear in a headline only in abbreviation.

4. Quotes, semicolons, colons and dashes are used differently in headlines than in text: Single quotes are used in place of double quotes, to save space. Semicolons take on the role of periods in headlines when there is a need to separate two independent clauses (*Europe bans bee-harming pesticides; U.S. keeps spraying*). Colons and dashes are used to show attribution without using a verb like *says* (*IDF source: Hamas working to stop Gaza rockets* and *Rat meat sold as lamb in China – USA Today*).

5. Headlines are almost always in present tense: While articles for print and electronic delivery are almost always written in past tense, headlines almost always get present tense. That's because a headline should present the latest news as the reader sees it (*Winds ease, but wildfire threat remains*). Sometimes, however, headlines appear to be written in past tense because an *is* or *are* is omitted to save space (*Gas Stations Fined for Price-Gouging After Hurricane*). In a few cases, past tense is used to help make sense, for instance, when news breaks about something that happened in the past (*Ex-State Senator Was Directed to Record Elected Officials*). And obviously, future tense is required for things that have not yet occurred (*Storms will complicate evening commute*) – although two other options are also used: the infinitive (*Sarah Palin, Rick Perry to speak at NRA convention*) or present tense with a time element (*President heads to Turkey Friday*).

6. Headlines do not typically include a time element: With the exception just noted, most headlines do not indicate when the event happened, for two reasons. First, in most cases the time element is the day of writing or the day before. Second, adding a previous time element to a present-tense headline seems clumsy.

7. Headlines may be allowed to violate style rules that apply to copy: In order to make it easier to write headlines that fit, some publications make exceptions to rules governing things like state names and numbers (*3 killed in N.H. plane crash*) and in some cases allow abbreviations to be used without periods (*US dollar, stocks rally on strong US jobs data*).

8. Multiple-line headlines should contain one thought per line: When headlines are broken over several lines, most readers find it easier to absorb them one line at a time. So the writer has to be careful with the structure. For instance, this would not be a good headline: *Savage gives first crash/course in sex on campus*. Far better would be *Sex on campus is focus/of Savage's crash course*.

9. Writers should avoid **headlinese**: When headlines were written primarily for newspapers, the tight space limits of some headlines motivated writers to invent a new vocabulary of synonyms for long words. The only problem is that most of the so-called synonyms are words that normal people never use the way headline writers use them. For instance, *Spider bite eyed in Slayer guitarist's death*. Here, *eyed* is used instead of the longer *suspected*. But like other examples of headlinese – words including *rap, nix, probe, kin* and the like – it is just awkward.

10. Headlines should not repeat words: Because a headline contains only a few words, writers should not repeat words within a headline or even between a headline and a subhead. Of course, every rule has its exceptions, so a headline as good as this one (about firefighters giving up on putting out a smoldering pile of tires) can get a pass: *Firefighters tire of fighting tire fire*.

Make It Specific

A mistaken belief of new headline writers is that headlines should not give the story away but should instead surround themselves with an air of mystery. For that strategy to work, there needs to be plenty of people who have nothing better to do than spend hours reading stories bearing headlines like *Meeting to be held*, which might or might not be of interest. Not likely. A good question to ask is: If someone were reading only the headline, would he or she know what the article is about? To accomplish that task, the best headlines summarize the key point of the article or post so the reader can decide quickly whether it is of interest. All of the examples in the previous section do a good job of this.

Another key question is: How many articles or posts could this headline be used with? The ideal headline matches up with exactly one, but more generic headlines could be used over and over. While recycling is generally applauded as a good idea, that's not the case with headlines.

Two tips are helpful in creating unique and useful headlines. First, just like the lead of an article should focus on the most important or interesting part of the story, so should the headline. That's why a headline such as *Speaker series to be scheduled* fails the test: The mere scheduling of the series is neither interesting nor unusual. Instead, the headline (and the lead, if the writer has made the same mistake!) needs to feature what's exciting about the series: *Pulitzer-winning novelist to headline speaker series*, for instance.

Second, the headline should focus on the latest news. Sometimes new headline writers get tripped up because the most important or interesting part of a story is not the latest news. For instance, when a person is finally sentenced for committing a crime, the sentencing needs to be the focus of the headline, even though some details of a long-ago crime might seem to be more interesting. The headline writer has to presume that interested readers already know some of the background of ongoing stories – but at the same time must be careful not to assume too much. A good headline in such a case would be something like *Starlight Drive-In shooter sentenced to life plus 15 years, no parole*. What makes that a good headline is it manages to combine the latest news with the most interesting aspect of the overall story. Even someone who knew nothing about the story beforehand could understand the basics from this headline.

Size It Right

This guideline is trickier than the first two, as the right size depends on the medium. Print media such as newspapers and magazines have specific dimensions and point sizes that limit the options for the size of a headline. For instance, a one-column, three-line, 36-point newspaper headline (often referred to as a 1-36-3 or just a 1-36) can at most contain two or three short words per line, as in this example: *Terror case/cleared/for trial*. While such a headline obviously puts serious limits on the writer, space constraints don't leave much wiggle room. The same is largely true for magazine covers and article layouts, where photos, text and headlines compete for precious space.

In the online environment, however, things look much different, at least on first inspection. The unlimited amount of storage available for content means that a headline writer can indulge his or her desires to try for the record books, such as this headline (accompanied by *three* subheads) does:[2]

Alleged son of Westboro Baptist Church leader attacked in publicity stunt by naked 500lb man who burst out of bathroom, sat on him and shouted: 'Who's your daddy?'

- 'David Phelps' was being interviewed when the man ran at him
- He calls himself Billy The Fridge
- Kansas-based church has caused controversy by preaching gay-hate

---

http://www.dailymail.co.uk/news/article-2300604/David-Phelps-son-Westboro-Baptist-Church-leader-attacked-naked-35-STONE-man-hilarious-publicity-stunt-video.html

But such extreme headline lengths are rare, and in fact the most common recommendation is to keep online headlines to a maximum of 70 characters. Unlike print headlines, shorter lines are OK, as things don't look messy if a headline falls short of that limit, but writers should try to get as much information into a head as possible. Why 70 characters? That's the average maximum length that search engines will show in their results, so anything longer will be truncated. (Quick tip: Write a headline in Microsoft Word, select it, then double-click the word count icon in the bottom left of the window. A pop-up window will appear with several pieces of information, including the character count.)

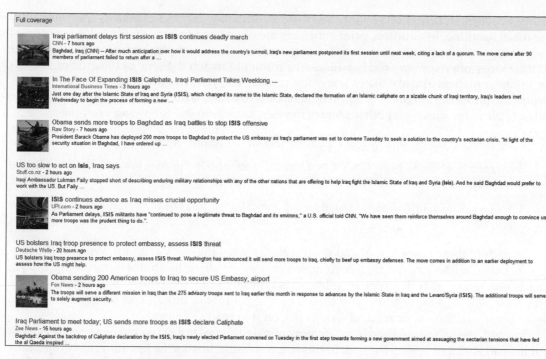

Google search results show what happens when headlines are longer than 70 characters: They are cut off, as in the second example here.

The 70-character maximum is also good for Twitter headlines, since the 140-character limit on tweets leaves room for the identity of the original poster when they are retweeted, as well as tags, retweeters' comments, and so on. Some good examples:

Your Facebook likes can help scientists track obesity trends (60 characters)

Income, education biggest predictors of political/civic involvement (67 characters)

Ask Yourself, How Secure Are Your Social Media Accounts? (56 characters)

Need a babysitter in a pinch? There's an app for that (53 characters)

And speaking of Twitter: There, too, clear and direct works better than clever or obscure. As a member of the team that runs The New York Times Twitter accounts noted:

> As social media editors, we spend a lot of our time writing headlines. And as headline writers we like nothing better than trying to outdo each other with well-placed zingers. … We love these tweets, the reader reaction to them, and the wisecracks they evoke from our peers at other companies. But readers don't click on or retweet us when we're being clever nearly as much as they respond to clearly stated tweets describing the meat of the stories they point to. … We also engage in the practice of being coy and trying to make readers curious enough to read a story. But even then we find that the best results were more direct and straight-forward about what the reader could expect after they clicked. … Ultimately, we don't always need to try so hard to write an unforgettable tweet, or one that tempts the reader too much. Clarity and straightforwardness around interesting subject matter are ultimately rewarded by substantial reader interest.[3]

When It's Time for a Subhead

Subheads mean different things, depending on whether material is destined for print or online publication. No matter the medium, they are often well worth adding.

In print, the function of a subhead is to add additional, often explanatory information to the main headline. In addition, print subheads are often used to present the S-V-O version of a story when the main headline is a more stylized one. For example, both feature stories and sports stories often use stylized headlines, the former to match the tone of the articles, the latter because readers already likely know the results. The purpose of these main headlines is largely to attract the attention of a potential reader. To do so, writers use references to popular culture, plays on words and other literary devices, such as in the following examples:

Years Underground, Hatching an Invasion (about the return of cicadas)

With Hop and Flick, Little Guys Get Upper Hand (about the teardrop shot sweeping the NBA playoffs)

A Solitary Soul Whose Pained Voice Heads Into Strange Realms (a review of a James Blake concert)

In each of these cases, a subhead should clarify what the story is about. Without the subheads, many readers might be left confused and move along to another story. And in fact, that is one reason that this type of subhead is typically not used online: Since many people find their way to a story through a search or a social media link, the main headline has to make sense on its own, or readers won't click on it to read the story.

Instead, the online subhead is a different animal. It comes not at the top of an article or post but instead is placed within the text. In this use, a subhead breaks the text into easily digestible chunks and summarizes the forthcoming section. Both of these actions help readers make their way through a longer article or blog post. As blogger Shelley Kramer has written: "With so much content coming at us from all directions, most of us read less, scan more. And that's why optimized subheads are becoming a critical component of blog posts." Kramer notes that even when a subhead does not prompt a reader to stay with a piece, it has other advantages:

Even if someone doesn't stick around to read the full piece, providing subheads gives them enough contextual clues to satisfy their curiosity – and if they discover information they find entertaining or helpful, they're more likely to return to your site for more, share your link, save your page to read later or curate your content.[4]

How Print and Online Headlines Differ

Beyond the differences in how subheads are used in print and online, other points are important to consider. The biggest is context.

A headline printed in a newspaper or magazine nestles snugly into a package that provides a great deal of context. Surrounding photos and cutlines often help the potential reader get a sense of what the story is about. Larger type sizes indicate more important stories.

But online, everything changes. More often than not, a potential reader sees a headline on a search results page, in an RSS reader or in a social media post. In most of those situations, the headlines are isolated from any context. And there is virtually no differentiation of text size in those various presentations. As one headline writer notes, "If your news sites' headlines can appear anywhere on the web and without supporting content, it's incredibly important to be able to convey the point of the story with just text."[5]

SEO and Why It Matters

And not just any text will do. Every serious discussion of online headlines (as well as post titles and page titles) inevitably includes the concept of search engine optimization, referred to as SEO. Briefly, the idea is to tweak key aspects of an online document so it is more likely to rise to the top of search results. Headlines and subheads are among the most important items to tweak, as they count highly in search results.

Even though the phrase may sound a bit techy and complex, at its essence it merely requires the headline writer to think of words that people interested in the article or blog post might enter into a search engine. The cutesy headlines often found in print publications are out; in their place are headlines containing specific words, especially ones that are unique. As one blogging advice website notes:

> Any SEO pro worth listening to will tell you that you don't go after the most popular keywords. You target the niche phrases. They may result in less traffic individually, but there's a lot more of them, and less competition. … The niche phrases are much more specific, and specificity makes for a much better headline.[6]

Resources like Google Trends (http://www.google.com/trends/explore) can help the process, but since every piece of writing is different, the most important thing to keep in mind is that an editor needs to know how readers think and what they think about in order to develop the best key words, and hence the best headlines and subheads for online use.

That can take some work. As one writer notes, it's not enough to just go with the first idea that pops up:

> Don't stop at just one or two title ideas – you might miss out on a really good one because it didn't occur to you immediately. If you get stuck, unleash yourself at the title with no inhibitions until you've practically got a page full of ideas. Then you can mix and match the best words and phrases on the page to form your final winner.[7]

One site that takes that practice to heart is Upworthy, whose mission is "to make important stuff as viral as a video of some idiot surfing off his roof."[8] To help accomplish that, the staff at Upworthy spends a great deal of time polishing headlines:

> For Upworthy, it's more akin to a science – and not one of those mushy sciences like anthropology or psychology, either. We're talking straight-up particle physics.
> For every article they publish, its writers come up with 25 headline options. They then A/B test the four most promising before settling on a winner.[9]

When it comes to writing the actual headlines, one good starting point is what Susan Steade of the San Jose Mercury News has christened the **mullet model** ("business up front, party in the back"). The idea is to start with a few keywords, so the search engines can find the heads, then use the rest of the headline to attract actual humans. Often, a colon is used to separate the two parts, as in these examples:

Google applicant's killing: Woman testifies about robbery plan

San Jose man in bank bomb plot: Terrorist or delusional wannabe[10]

Trends in Online Headlines

Just as the Internet has changed so many of the ways people do things, so has it changed ideas of what makes for a good headline. It was one thing to write a Page One newspaper headline that had to stand out from a competitor or two on the newsstand, but it is something altogether different to stand out among the millions of voices clamoring for a reader's attention online.

Not surprisingly, one of the prime advocates of breaking rules to attract readers is Upworthy.com. Site cofounder Peter Koechley offers these tips:

1. "Forget everything you know," especially traditional rules "that say headlines must be informative, objective or even grammatically correct."[11] Sites such as the Huffington Post prove daily that strange new approaches can attract online readers (Some examples: *The*

CASE STUDY

Crafting the Most Attractive Headlines

Just how much difference can a headline make in attracting readers? One blogger wondered just that and decided to conduct an experiment. As the editor in chief of the Pick The Brain blog noted:

> On Friday, January 26, I wrote a post titled "The Two Types of Cognition." I posted it to Reddit, StumbleUpon, and Del.icio.us and attracted a grand total of 100 visitors in the next two days.
>
> The average time [spent] on the post (6:11) was great, so I knew the people who read it liked it. The problem was people weren't seeing it.

The author decided to try a new headline and came up with *Learn to Understand Your Own Intelligence*. Not a single word in the article itself was changed, but in a few days the number of unique readers had soared to just under 5,000, a nearly 5,000 percent increase and many times the traffic the average article on Pick The Brain draws. In addition, many readers found their way to other articles on the site that they would otherwise never have seen, so the payoff was huge.[12]

Other examples of how rewriting a headline can increase readership are covered in "Five of Your Headlines ... Remixed" (http://www.copyblogger.com/five-headlines-remixed). While most of the examples in that piece are taken from business rather than journalism sites, several of the lessons apply no matter the content.

1 Chart That Reveals Just How Grossly Unfair The U.S. Tax System Has Become, SHE Likes HIM?!?!?!?!, and Siri, Does Apple Use Tax Gimmicks?)

2. "Overpromise and overdeliver." While one of the worst sins of headlines traditionally has been making a story seem bigger than it is, today's mavericks don't worry about that. "We write what some people would call clickbait headlines and we try to live up to that," Koechley said. Note that this is easier said than done. Take for example this headline: *Here's the Real Reason India's Yuppies Are Queuing for Up to an Hour to Get Into Starbucks*. As one critic noted: "The real reason is that the 'new Indian yuppie' wants 'a clean, quiet, comfortable, air-conditioned space, to work, meet friends or linger for hours, no questions asked.' Unlike, you know, everyone else everywhere. Which makes that headline a good bit overbuilt."[13]

3. "Create a curiosity gap." Again, while the traditional advice has been to get the most important or interesting information across in the headline, that's not always followed today. "Tell people enough to get them interested but not so much they don't need to click," Koechley said. For example, *Justin Bieber Is The Seventh Most Popular Woman On The Web*.

4. "Telegraph emotion." Totally at odds with objective journalism, this new rule aims to get readers to bite by promising an emotional jolt – a laugh, tears, whatever. For example, *This study about race and dolls will make your jaw drop*.

5. "Don't write for your audience, write for their friends." Because many people come across articles and blog posts in social media, the idea here is to create something people will feel comfortable posting under their names.[14] An example that probably pushes the envelope: *Meet The Man Who 'Made Love' To A Dolphin*.

As outlandish as those tips might seem today, soon they could be seen as archaic. Trends come and go in headline writing as in much else online. But it is clear that the rules are changing from what they long were. As one commentator noted in reference to the headline *Everyone Wants to Adopt This Adorable Three-Legged Dog Who Was Caught on Camera Stealing Pet Food from a Supermarket*:

> What's oddest about this form of headline is that it's disassociated from conveying news. Instead it conveys interaction. Headlines once were stuffed full of proper nouns. But it turns out, old-fashioned headlines don't convey things that aren't news well. "Three-Legged Dog Desirable"? Nope. It doesn't work, because there's nothing there. Nothing except "aww." And service pieces – how to do x, why not to do y – need the help for their softness too.[15]

As to whether the displacement of hard news by soft news is a good thing … well, that's another discussion.

Worry About This/Not About That

Why Headline Writers Need Dirty Minds – and Shouldn't Hesitate to Ask Questions

One of the most important rules of headline writing is to make sure a headline cannot be read in a way other than the writer intended, particularly if such a reading makes the headline and story seem sexually suggestive. Unfortunately, many headline writers and editors don't seem to have minds that are filthy enough to catch such potential problems. Among the jaw-droppers cited in a Huffington Post compilation[16] are these:

> *Tiger Woods plays with own balls, Nike says*
>
> *A-Rod goes deep, Wang hurt*
>
> *Colleagues Finger Billionaire*
>
> *Lady Jacks off to hot start in conference*
>
> *Hooker named Lay Person of the Year*

Another traditional caution for headline writers has mostly fallen by the wayside, however. In the past, headline writers tried not to break parts of a prepositional phrase across multiple lines, so constructions like this were avoided: *Teenager dies in/motorcycle crash*. That rule has been relaxed in recent years, as it rarely causes confusion among readers. It's OK now and then to have a preposition at the end of a line, although a preposition at the end of the first line of a headline would still raise some eyebrows. As one source notes, "If your choice is between a stilted headline that doesn't split and a more fluid one that does, you may be better off splitting the lines."[17]

Similarly, the prohibition against asking questions in headlines has been relaxed. As longtime headline whiz Vince Rinehart of The Washington Post says: "I think they are very appropriate for some stories and effective at drawing people in. They're also a good way to frame what the debate is about without appearing to take sides." Of course, not all question headlines are created equal. Headlines that can be answered simply *yes* or *no* invite the reader to move on to the next story. Instead, a good question headline should ask a question the reader cannot answer, at least not without reading the accompanying article. As one source notes, "In that sense, your question (like all good headlines) becomes a compelling promise to the reader that they're about to discover something they didn't know before, if only they keep reading."[18]

Captions and Cutlines

A close relation of headlines and titles is the caption. Because that term is often used interchangeably with the term *cutline*, perhaps it's best to start by defining the two terms as they are used here. A **caption** is essentially a headline for a photo or other graphic. In just a few words, it attempts to draw a reader's attention and provide a little information. Often – in reality, way too often – caption writers prize cleverness over usefulness, using puns and other wordplay that do little more than annoy many readers. Occasionally, these captions do work, however, as was the case with *Goodnight Moon*, which ran over a photo taken from the International Space Station of the moon rising over clouds.

At the same time, a caption should be more than a prosaic restatement of what the reader can clearly see. For example, a photo of a man and two children leaving the scene of some sort of devastation was topped with a caption reading *Walking away from a deadly scene*, a fairly obvious observation.

While some publications stick captions on every graphic element, others never use them. However, **cutlines** always should be used. Cutlines typically run under photos and help complete the "story" of a photo. As the Poynter Institute notes: "Photos tend to communicate in an impressionistic way; they are rarely as precise or clear as verbal communication. They beg for confirmation in words. A good cutline satisfies the reader's curiosity quickly."[19]

Cutlines do that by:

- *Identifying the main people in the photo.* Unless the people in a photo are part of a crowd scene, at least one or more of them are notable. The rule of thumb is that anyone whose face is clearly visible and is part of the main action should be identified. Some publications disregard this rule when dealing with children, however, to protect their privacy.
- *Explaining the action in the photo.* The major point of a cutline is to help the reader understand what is happening in the photo. So as much as possible, it should explain not just the action but its context. For instance, a cutline that notes that a politician "waves as she steps off a plane" does not get a passing grade. It needs to do more: Tell the reader whom the politician is waving to, what the purpose of the trip is, and so on.
- *Pointing out details that the reader might not notice.* Sometimes key elements of a photo need to be pointed out to the reader either because there is a lot of activity in the photo or a small detail is crucial. For instance, a photo of a soldier reading a letter only realizes its impact when the cutline tells the reader that he is savoring the first communication he has had from his wife in weeks.

Typically, these sorts of things are covered in the first sentence of the cutline, known as the **main descriptive sentence**. In some cases, that's all that is needed. But if information

Writing the Ultimate Cutline

Photo cutlines are often the first words read on a page or screen. The following rules and tips will help cutline writers produce the best work they can.

- *Understand what is happening in the photo.* This seems obvious, but sometimes cutline writers are not careful about describing the action in a photo. In one embarrassing case, a cutline writer described the action in a photo as a firefighter lifting a fire truck. Setting aside for a moment the impossibility of such an action, it's still hard to understand why the writer would not have taken the time to check before publishing that cutline, especially since the photo was being used in a slide show created several years after it was taken.[20]

- *Use present tense to describe the action.* Because the cutline tells the reader "This is what is happening in this photo," present tense should be used to describe that action. In most cases, a time element is included; organizations' policies differ on whether it should refer to a day of the week or a date. Many prefer the latter for online content, as there is no guarantee as to when a reader will see it.
- *Use other tenses as appropriate.* Beyond the main descriptive sentence, tense will vary with the information provided – past tense to describe earlier actions, future tense to discuss upcoming events.
- *Identify by location when necessary.* While the cutlines in a community newspaper sometimes might not have to include information for common locations, larger publications and pretty much all online outlets should tell readers where the action occurred.
- *Double-check names and identities.* This should go without saying, but unfortunately it does not. The New York Times was forced to issue a painful correction to a cutline containing two errors in just eight words: "An earlier version of the [cutline] with this photo incorrectly identified Denzel Washington's daughter as his wife and misspelled Mr. Washington's surname."
- *Don't begin with unfamiliar names.* The job of a cutline is to lure a reader to it, then to the photo, and then the accompanying story (if there is one). Therefore, starting with a name few people know is not a great idea. Instead, the first few words should focus on the most interesting or unusual aspect of the photo.
- *Don't imagine things beyond what is shown in the photo.* Cutline writers often indulge their imaginations, writing things like someone "seems to be thinking" or "is enjoying the warm day." Unless the person has said as much to the photographer, such constructions should be avoided.

about events before or after the action in the photo is important, that should follow in an additional sentence or sentences.

Wrapping Up

For all the thousands of words written daily for most publications and blogs, a select few of them are by far the most important. Giving extra care and attention to headlines, subheads, captions and cutlines will help attract readers to stories, and ultimately may go a long way in making them not just casual visitors but loyal fans.

Key Points

- Far more than any other words on a page or screen, headlines determine whether a reader will engage with a piece of writing.
- A simple subject-verb-object format usually results in the best headlines.
- While headlines generally follow the same style rules as body copy, editors should be aware of several exceptions.
- Headlines need to be as specific as possible. "Generic" headlines will never draw in a reader.
- Subheads can help add information that might attract even more readers.
- While the basics are largely similar, online headlines often differ from their print counterparts in an acknowledgement of the importance of search engine optimization and potential for sharing.
- Captions and cutlines function similarly to headlines, but instead of adding information to stories they add it to photos.
- Every photo should include a cutline to help readers make sense of it. The first sentence of the cutline should clearly indicate what is going on and should identify any people who are part of the main action.

CHAPTER EXERCISE

Write headlines from the following article summaries. Your instructor will specify the count for each headline.

1. Scientists in Liaoning Province, China, have discovered fossils of three small species that resemble squirrels but are only about the size of a mouse. They date to the time when dinosaurs roamed the Earth, indicating that mammals have existed for more than 200 million years – about 40 million years earlier than previously thought.

2. Three days after a state police trooper was shot to death, federal investigators and state authorities from two neighboring states have been brought in to help in the manhunt for his killer. So far, hundreds of interviews have been conducted. The trooper and his partner were shot during a shift change in what police believe was an ambush. His partner survived.

3. Officials of states across the U.S. report that the annual number of Americans killed in traffic accidents reached its lowest levels in more than 70 years in many places last year. The amazing drops are attributed to new safety measures and education campaigns.

4. According to a new report by the National Football League, nearly one-third of former NFL players are at risk of developing Parkinson's and Alzheimer's, and at earlier ages than average people. A proposal calls for a regulation of the NFL's fund to pay damages to former players who develop the diseases.

5. A local rapper has been charged with distributing heroin, and his music videos might be used to help convict him. A detective noted that the videos show that the rapper's songs include "raps about distributing narcotics, violence and using a firearm to commit violence." This is only the latest in a number of similar cases recently.

 ## WRITE RIGHT

Avoiding Passive Voice

One of the most common writing constructions that can lead to confusion is the use of passive voice. While virtually everyone agrees that passive voice is usually a poor choice, some people are confused about what exactly constitutes passive voice.

To begin with, the mere use of an *is* verb form does not constitute passive voice. Sentences using those verbs tend to lack the power of sentences with stronger verbs, but that's a different matter. In addition, in some cases passive voice works as well or better than active voice, so there's no blanket prohibition against it.

So what exactly is it and what's the problem? Basically, sentences written in passive voice put the object up front rather than the subject. That typically makes them harder to comprehend and sometimes leaves readers wondering what the subject is.

The presence of an *is* verb form is a tipoff that a sentence might be passive. But another element is required in order to qualify: The *is* form needs to be followed by the past participle form of a verb (usually, but not always, ending in -*ed*).

Once those elements are deemed to be present, the next question should be: "Does this sentence describe an action?" If so, where is the person or thing performing the action, at the beginning of the sentence, where it belongs, or at the end? In an active sentence, the subject performs the action; in a passive one, the subject is acted upon. Some examples of passive sentences:

The arriving forces were met with negativity by the local population.

Investors were surprised by the company's stock performance in the third quarter.

The investigation will be conducted by a group of citizens and law enforcement officials.

The exam was failed by more than 40 percent of the students who took it.

Rewritten in active voice, all of these sentences gain power:

Local citizens booed and jeered the arriving forces.

The company's third-quarter stock performance surprised investors.

A group of citizens and law enforcement officials will conduct the investigation.

More than 40 percent of the students who took the exam failed it.

A passive sentence does not always call for a rewrite. In a few cases, passive voice works well:

- When the person or organization that performed the action is not known
- When the object or person to whom the action was done is more important than the person or organization that performed the action

The following examples from news articles pass these tests:

Two bodies have been found after a small plane crashed into two homes near a Connecticut airport Friday, and authorities fear the death toll could rise.

A Bangladeshi student was sentenced to 30 years in prison after pleading guilty to trying to blow up the Federal Reserve Bank in a fake operation organized by undercover agents.

People infected with a deadly virus that emerged in Saudi Arabia last year may have caught it from one-humped camels used in the region for meat, milk, transport and racing.

Like much else in the practice of editing, dealing with passive voice is a matter of art and science. But every passive sentence that sees the light of publication should be there by choice, not by oversight.

Exercise

The following sentences contain passive voice. Rewrite those that would be better in active voice, and be prepared to explain why you did not change the others.

1. The initial edition of the classic book "The Elements of Style" was written by William Strunk Jr.

2. They were raised by a loving aunt and uncle, who loved them as though they were their own children.

3. Participants in the race were treated to ice cold watermelon at its conclusion.

4. County authorities were tipped off by an anonymous informant that the illegal dumping by neighbors was taking place regularly.

5. It was determined by the board that the cost-cutting initiatives were ineffective.

6. The passive voice should be avoided unless there is good reason to use it.

7. We were encouraged by several current members to attend the group's recruitment event.

8. There is evidence of an increasing amount of skill and knowledge demonstrated by the wine maker in his latest releases.

9. The proposed plan will be bitterly opposed by local small business owners.

10. The major points of the presentation were buried in overly complex PowerPoint slides.

EDITOR'S TOOLKIT

Resources for Writing Better Heads

One of the best ways to master headline writing is, not surprisingly, to look at lots of good headlines. A couple of online resources can help with that.

First is Google News (http://news.google.com). Right-clicking the arrows to the right of a headline brings up related articles, each with its own headline. That offers a great way to compare the efforts of dozens or even hundreds of headline writers. While many of the heads on a given story will be similar, the amount of variety and creativity is always surprising. For instance, the headlines on a story about utility operator Southern California Edison Co.'s plans to permanently close the San Onofre nuclear power took many forms:

Calif. utility to retire troubled San Onofre nuclear power plant

Edison Faces Regulatory Battle Over San Onofre Closing Costs

Workers, surfers, pols react to San Onofre

Closure of Southern California nuke plant shouldn't lead to blackouts in Northern California this summer, state says

Activists hail San Onofre nuclear power plant reactor shutdown

Another great resource is the Newseum daily archive of newspaper front pages from around the world (http://www.news eum.org/todaysfront pages/default.asp). Every day, the world's only museum of news posts close to 1,000 front pages from nearly 100 countries, ranging from small community papers to major international publications. Looking at the front pages is an education not just in how different writers and editors handle headlines, but also in how they choose news, how design varies around the world, and much more.

Finally, while "A Reader's Guide to Headlinese" (http://www.yorkblog.com/ydrinsider/ 2013/01/24/a-readers-guide-to-headlinese) is intended to help a reader cope with the crazy words headline writers sometimes resort to using, it also is a great reminder to headline writers of the words they should avoid.

Student Study Site

Visit the Student Resource Site at **http://study.sagepub.com/lieb** to access:

■ Chapter-by-chapter **web quizzes** for independent assessment of course material
■ List of online web links and general resources

Chapter 6　**Defamation**

One of the most exciting aspects of digital publishing is its instantaneous nature. Type something, hit the Publish button and it is there for the world to read. Unfortunately, as we have seen in earlier chapters, that spontaneity can cause serious problems. Tight deadlines often lead writers to publish material they cannot verify or do not fully understand, resulting in a multitude of errors.

While all errors are embarrassing, one slip-up in the realm of legal issues can lead to long trials, massive legal bills, loss of employment and other nightmare scenarios. The situation is only made more difficult by the complexity of ever-changing legal regulations governing digital publishing (the most recent edition of "Internet Law: A Field Guide" runs nearly 900 pages) as well as by the fact that laws vary significantly from state to state and country to country.

Further, the laws and privileges that cover traditional journalists do not necessarily apply to nontraditional publishers. In recent years, it has become increasingly more common to hear of bloggers running into problems over defamation, copyright and other issues. But, the Electronic Frontier Foundation notes: "The difference between [a blogger] and the reporter at your local newspaper is that in many cases, you may not have the benefit of training or resources to help you determine whether what you're doing is legal. And on top of that, sometimes knowing the law doesn't help – in many cases it was written for traditional journalists, and the courts haven't yet decided how it applies to bloggers."[1]

Adding to the problem is that unlike print media, online publications are accessible to millions of people around the globe. Courts award some damages based on the number of people who saw material, so online publishers are more at risk than their print counterparts. Throw in the fact that people and companies are more likely to find material when it's online, and things become especially thorny for the digital publisher.[2]

The goal of this and the next chapter is to help readers navigate the minefield of legal issues. These chapters will not make readers into legal experts, but they will help keep them from getting into dangerous situations they did not even anticipate.

Defining Defamation

No laws are more important to the digital publisher than defamation laws. These laws were designed to strike a balance between the right of publishers to disseminate material and the right of the public not to have their reputations unjustly tarnished.

On its face, defamation seems straightforward: Defamation is the publication of a false statement of fact that harms a person's reputation or harms a person in his or her occupation.

As simple as that seems, however, the definition demands a nearly word-by-word dissection in order to fully understand the scope of the law.

CASE STUDY

Sending a Blogger to Jail to Keep Him From Publishing

One of the fundamental principles of U.S. publishing law is that the use of prior restraint – government action that prohibits publication before it can take place – is almost never allowed. As the First Amendment Center notes: "Perhaps no First Amendment right is more secure than the news media's right to publish information free from government censorship. While public officials frequently wish they could prevent newspapers, magazines and broadcast stations from publishing sensitive or embarrassing information, their ability to censor the media is extremely limited."[3]

That's not, however, to say that officials do not try from time to time. And, in the case of one unfortunate blogger, sometimes they succeed. By late 2013, Roger Shuler had become known for his blog Legal Schnauzer, which for six years had focused on exposing political corruption. The blog's content was often questionable; as The New York Times noted, "His allegations are frequently salacious, including a recent assertion that a federal judge had appeared in a gay pornographic magazine and a theory that several suicides were actually a string of politically motivated murders."[4]

Shuler had posted a series of stories on the blog that claimed "that Robert Riley, Jr., son of former Alabama governor Bob Riley, had an affair with lobbyist Liberty Duke. Riley is an attorney who has been mentioned by news outlets in the state as a potential candidate for a soon-to-be vacant U.S. House of Representatives seat."[5]

After Riley filed a lawsuit alleging that the blog posts were potentially defamatory, a judge ordered Shuler to stop writing about Riley. Shuler ignored the order, and Alabama officials jailed him for contempt. He spent five months in jail – the only jailed reporter in the Western Hemisphere – before a judge ordered his release "after Shuler made what the court deemed 'good faith' efforts to remove content relating to the allegation." But the judge noted that the release was temporary and "that Shuler might be asked to take down additional items after full court review." In addition, the permanent injunction remained in effect, so Shuler was still prohibited from writing about the alleged affair.[6]

So how did Shuler end up spending nearly half a year in jail despite the fact that the Supreme Court has ruled that prior restraint is presumptively unconstitutional? The answer seems unfortunately simple. Shuler and his wife, who was also named in the proceedings, had no previous experience in such legal situations. "I had hoped to get outside legal representation that could get my release on lawful grounds," he told the Reporters Committee on Freedom of the Press. "But that was very slow in developing, so I just had to make a move for what I considered to be my own survival."[7]

Had Shuler still been employed by a news organization as he had been in the past (he worked for the Birmingham Post-Herald for more than 10 years), it seems unlikely he would have spent any time in jail. Unfortunately, his case indicates how perilous life can be for small publishing operations.

What's the Difference Between Libel and Slander?

When early defamation laws were written, they distinguished between material that was spoken and that which was printed. The former was seen to be transient and therefore not capable of inflicting as much damage as more permanent printed charges. The terms *slander* and *libel* differentiated the two types.

With the development of broadcast media, however, the balance shifted. Now charges that were spoken could reach millions of people, and once having reached them would be harder to correct than charges in print. So any defamation action against the media will generally be a libel suit. Slander cases are rare and typically involve individuals.

Publication typically conjures up images of newspapers, magazines and books. For the purposes of defamation law, however, publication is defined much more broadly. In fact, all that is required is that one person publishes information about a second person to at least one other person. So an email, a tweet, a Facebook post and a mailed letter are all considered publications, just as The New York Times is. In one case that should stand as a warning to journalists, a $9.2 million judgment was initially returned against a newspaper for an article it had not published. Instead, two Alton (Illinois) Telegraph reporters had sent a memo to a federal prosecutor based on a tip they had received about a contractor's possible link to organized crime. When the reporters' investigations did not find any evidence, they ended their research without writing even a single article. But in the meantime, the memo was sent to banking officials, who cut off loans to the contractor, forcing him out of business. Fortunately for the Telegraph, the initial award, which would have bankrupted the paper, was later reduced, and it was able to continue publishing.[8] But the moral is clear: When it comes to defamation, publication is very broadly defined.

Further, every aspect of a publication is considered on its own. An article, column or post might be fine, but an accompanying headline or cutline could be deemed defamatory. High-profile defamation cases have been based on a range of items:

- An advertisement was the basis of the most important case in U.S. libel law history, New York Times Co. v. Sullivan,[9] which we discuss later in this chapter;
- A photo, such as in the case of a regional television news channel in Chicago using the wrong person's photo with a story about a mass transit security guard who was charged with handcuffing a teen gate-jumper, taking him into a bathroom, removing the boy's shoes and socks, and putting his genitals on the teen's feet;[10] and
- A satirical piece, as in Hustler Magazine v. Falwell, which arose after the magazine ran an ad spoof in which it claimed that Jerry Falwell, leader of the Moral Majority, lost his virginity to his mother in an outhouse.[11]

The only exception to this broad definition of publication is when an exchange takes place within a news organization. For example, if an editor rejects a writer's material as potentially defamatory, publication is not regarded to have taken place.

Falsity is a precondition for defamation to occur. Publishing a charge that a convicted murderer has committed murder is perfectly fine. In fact, truth is an absolute defense against a defamation claim: If the material can be proved to be true, there is no case. (It's important to note that the charges have to be proved true; it's not enough to prove that someone made a charge.)

One area of particular concern in the digital environment is defamation by omission. Bloggers in particular tend to have a distinct point of view that they often buttress with selective details, unlike traditional journalists who strive to cover all aspects of a story. Sometimes, omitting facts can cause a false impression so that the actual lack of information could be considered defamatory. For example, in one classic case a newspaper reported that "a woman shot her husband and another woman after finding them together in the second woman's living room … its 'clear implication' [being] that the husband and second woman were having an affair. The report omitted the fact that the two were not alone and that several other people were in the same room during the wife's attack."[12] The best defense against such a situation is having a disinterested third party read any piece that could possibly be misconstrued.

Factual allegations are required for defamation to take place. As shown in the next section of this chapter, the United States and many other countries draw an important line between opinions and facts.

Harming a person's reputation is the basis of defamation law. Without that requirement, things would be seriously crazy for publishers. Even the most conscientious writers and editors make an occasional mistake (getting an age, date or address wrong, for instance). But while such a mistake meets the previous criteria – it's published, it's false, and it's a factual allegation – it does not meet this one. As one online legal resource site puts it, "The general

CASE STUDY

When a Blogger Is Not a Journalist – and Then Is

Since the advent of blogging, a key question has been: Are bloggers journalists? Given the many important stories that have been broken or helped along by bloggers, that question would seem to be long settled. But occasionally, a case pops up that once again raises the question, at least where legal protection is concerned.

A case in Oregon concerned a self-described "investigative blogger" by the name of Crystal Cox. In December 2011, U.S. District Court Judge Marco A. Hernandez denied a motion for a new trial after Cox was ordered to pay a $2.5 million defamation judgment to Kevin Padrick of the Obsidian Finance Group. Cox had written that Padrick and his company "had engaged in a wholesale fraud in a bankruptcy case."[13] Some observers worried that the judge's action suggested he did not see bloggers as journalists. But as another blogger wrote, "Hernandez' decision does not say that bloggers are not journalists, it merely says that Crystal Cox is no journalist."[14]

So why did Cox not make the cut? Among other things, she registered a large number of Internet domain names seemingly with the sole intention of using them to attack her perceived enemies. But there was a twist: She then offered her paid services to the people her websites were attacking to help them reclaim their good reputations.

Hernandez said his decision was not based on a belief that bloggers cannot be journalists, but rather on his belief that Cox did not function as a journalist:

> In my discussion, I did not state that a person who "blogs" could never be considered "media." I also did not state that to be considered "media," one had to possess all or most of the characteristics I recited.
>
> The uncontroverted evidence at trial was that after receiving a demand to stop posting what plaintiffs believed to be false and defamatory materials on several Web sites, including allegations that Mr. Padrick had committed tax fraud, defendant offered "PR," "search engine management," and online reputation repair services to Obsidian Finance, for a price of $2,500 per month.
>
> The suggestion was that defendant offered to repair the very damage she caused for a small but tasteful monthly fee. This feature, along with the absence of other media features, led me to conclude that defendant was not media.[15]

At that point, it appeared that the case was settled. However, in early 2014, Hernandez had another chance to reconsider the case when it reached the federal appeals court he sits on. At that time, the court ruled that there could be no distinction between bloggers and journalists. Hernandez wrote:

> The protections of the First Amendment do not turn on whether the defendant was a trained journalist, formally affiliated with traditional news entities, engaged in conflict-of-interest disclosure, went beyond just assembling others' writings, or tried to get both sides of a story. As the Supreme Court has accurately warned, a First Amendment distinction between the institutional press and other speakers is unworkable.[16]

But the ultimate outcome of the case remained up in the air. Padrick and Obsidian still retained the option to attempt to prove that Cox was negligent or acted with actual malice at a follow-up trial.

harm caused by defamation is identified as being ridiculed, shamed, hated, scorned, belittled or held in contempt by others, and lowers him/her in esteem of a reasonably prudent person, due to the communication of the false statement."[17] If the mistake is not sufficient to do that, there is no defamation.

This requirement includes two parts. First is that a specific person (or small group) must be identifiable and has to be alive at the time the suit is filed. Specific names do not necessarily have to be included, but other information would be needed that makes it easy to identify a person or persons.

Second is that the person's reputation must be harmed. Typically, defamatory statements claim one of the following things:

1. a person has committed a crime;

2. a person is dishonest or incompetent;

3. a person has a sexually transmitted disease or mental illness;

4. a person is a member of a group society holds in contempt (such as neo-Nazis);

5. a person has made racist, sexist, anti-Semitic or otherwise offensive remarks; or

6. a person (or company) has engaged in questionable business practices or is insolvent.

Harming a person in his or her occupation is an extension of the previous point. A false statement might not do much to ruin a person's reputation generally, but if it interferes with his or her ability to get or hold a job, that's a problem. In fact, it seems fair to say that in most people's eyes losing a job is at least as serious an injury as losing the respect of friends and neighbors.

A corollary of this idea is that businesses also can be harmed by defamation that lowers their profits or forces them into bankruptcy. Many lawsuits have been filed over negative restaurant reviews,[18] and key cases have included one in which the Bose audio company sued Consumer Reports for an unflattering review of its speakers[19] and another in which the beef industry sued Oprah Winfrey after she swore off hamburgers on her show.[20] (Apparently the beef industry has many beefs with the media: In an unrelated case in 2012, Beef Products Inc. sued ABC News for its coverage of a beef byproduct that came to be known as "pink slime.")[21] While the plaintiffs in such cases generally do not prevail, the proceedings can take years and cost the defendants hundreds of thousands or even millions of dollars.

Journalistic Privilege

To encourage lively discussion of important matters, the United States and some other countries afford journalists several privileges. Those privileges allow publishers more leeway under certain conditions without worrying about incurring a defamation suit.

The Opinion and Fair Comment Privilege

The first privilege covers **opinion and fair comment**. The key idea is that journalists should be able to express their opinions on matters of public importance, as well as to criticize the goods and services offered to the public.

The key difference between facts and opinion is that the former can be proved or disproved, while the latter cannot. For example, "She has done a poor job as mayor" is an opinion that cannot be proved or disproved – some people likely will disagree. On the other hand, "She has stolen city funds while working as mayor" is a factual allegation that can be proved or disproved. The first statement would not be sufficient grounds for a lawsuit, but the second could, if indeed it is false.

CASE STUDY

Truthful Blog Post Costs Subject a Job – Should Blogger Pay $60,000?

It was no secret that John Hoff, who blogged as Johnny Northside, had it in for former community leader Jerry Moore. In fact, Hoff used his blog to make a specific allegation tying Moore to a mortgage fraud case: "Repeated and specific evidence in Hennepin County District Court shows that Jerry Moore was involved in a high-profile fraudulent mortgage at 1564 Hillside Ave. N." A day after Hoff's post, Moore was fired from his new job studying mortgage foreclosures at the Urban Research and Outreach/Engagement Center at the University of Minnesota.

After Hoff blogged about the firing, Moore sued him. But not for defamation, since the charge was true. Instead, he claimed tortious interference with a contract. The jury awarded Moore $35,000 for lost wages and $25,000 for emotional distress.[22] Hoff appealed, but a district judge refused to set aside the award.[23]

Finally, more than three years after the initial blog post and Moore's firing, the Minnesota Court of Appeals reversed the decision. The court noted:

> Because truth is an absolute defense to a claim for defamation, truth should also be a defense to a claim for tortious interference with a contract arising out of an allegedly defamatory statement. …
> Hoff's blog post is the kind of speech that the First Amendment is designed to protect. He was publishing information about a public figure that he believed was true (and that the jury determined was not false) and that involved an issue of public concern. Attaching liability to this speech would infringe on Hoff's First Amendment rights.[24]

The lesson here? That bloggers can indeed be good journalists, but even when they are, their subjects can make their lives miserable.

There is no finessing this issue. A writer who tries to have it both ways by publishing a passage such as this one will find it offers no protection: "While he has denied all the allegations and has not been charged with any crime, I still believe he is guilty." Guilt can be proved or disproved, so this is not an opinion. (And as an important side note: There is a not-subtle distinction between writing that a person has been *arrested for committing a crime* – which implies he or she did it – and writing that the person has been *charged with committing a crime*.)

Now here's where things become a little complicated. In most cases, a writer should offer facts to support his or her opinion. Doing so establishes that there is a good reason for holding that opinion, and it's not just something the writer came up with out of thin air. (Of course, the supporting facts have to be true.) So returning to the example cited a few paragraphs ago ("She has done a poor job as mayor"), the following is preferable:

> Young has done a poor job as mayor. In her three years on the job, she has been indicted for misconduct and repeatedly has failed to follow through on promises she made to upgrade essential services in the city.

Another area of concern is opinions that imply false underlying facts. While labeling someone an "idiot" would clearly seem to be an opinion, labeling the person a "psychopath" might not. The former is a common insult that few people would take seriously, whereas the latter refers to a specific personality disorder that would require professional diagnosis.

In close calls, one of the factors used in determining whether material is fact or opinion is the context. A statement on a blog, for instance, will more likely be found to be opinion than would a similar statement in a news magazine. At the same time, however, the online environment can make it difficult to judge context, since different sites have different social conventions. So it is best not to count on any presumptions.[25]

Note that these guidelines apply no matter what section of a print or online publication material appears in or how it is categorized. While context is considered in determining whether the opinion privilege applies, just labeling an article "Opinion" or putting it in an Opinion section of a news site or blog does not make it exempt from a defamation suit if it contains false factual allegations.

The Fair Report Privilege

A second type of privilege is called **fair report**. This offers journalists the privilege to report on any material that took part in an official governmental proceeding, such as a trial, a city council meeting or a police report, even if there are mistakes or falsehoods in that proceeding. So if witnesses lie on the stand or errors arise in the arrest report, a publisher is shielded from being sued because of those issues.

However, to take advantage of this privilege, a publisher must stick to material arising from such proceedings or statements from government officials acting in their official capacities. Information that comes from a conversation with a detective in a coffee shop is not likely to be privileged.

It's also a requirement that the material reflect a full accounting of the proceedings (a writer cannot just pick and choose details that he or she likes while ignoring conflicting information) and that the material be presented as free of opinion and editorial content as possible. Finally, clear and accurate attribution of all material is vital.[26]

The Neutral Report Privilege

The third and final type of privilege is called **neutral report**. (*WARNING: This privilege is not observed everywhere, and even where it is, it may not be honored for nontraditional media. So it is best to check before counting on it.*)

Under certain circumstances, neutral report privilege protects a journalist who relays a charge someone else has made. For instance, in a 1996 case, it was applied to a "newspaper report that a state auditor accused a town trustee of faking a snow emergency to gain access to emergency funds."[27] In most cases, doing that provides *no* protection for a publisher. However, when the charge concerns a matter of vital public interest, this privilege *may* cover its publication. According to the Digital Media Law Project:

In those states that do recognize the privilege, it will generally apply where

- a responsible, prominent organization or individual
- makes a serious charge on a matter of public interest
- against another public figure or organization, and
- the charge is accurately and disinterestedly reported.[28]

If a publisher feels a charge is so important that it must be run, the publisher should run quotes in full, being careful to attribute quotes and fully identify the title of the speaker. In addition, it is important to "Be fair in your coverage of the accusation or controversy. The neutral report privilege is not available if you provide a biased view of the situation."[29]

Differences in Status

To make matters even more complicated, laws differ depending on the type of person who believes he or she has been defamed. There are two basic categories (and one subcategory) that publishers should be aware of.

CASE STUDY

Courtney Love's Costly Tweets

Many celebrities have warmly embraced social media as a way to engage and enlarge their fan base. But one celebrity is better known for using Twitter to defame people.

That celeb is Courtney Love, actor, former leader of the band Hole and widow of Nirvana leader Kurt Cobain.

Love's first brush with Twitter defamation began with a 20-minute burst of tweets in 2009 when she was disputing a $4,000 payment for clothing owed to fashion designer Dawn Simorangkir. As The Hollywood Reporter notes: "Love argued that her rantings were merely an expression of opinion and that Simorangkir could not prove how they damaged her. The fashion designer, on the other hand, pointed to Love's influence as an entertainer and the power of social media to disseminate damaging comments, including that Simorangkir was an 'asswipe nasty lying hosebag thief.'" Those tweets ultimately led to a settlement of $430,000. Love attorney James Janowitz said he believed she had given up Twitter at that point, "But I could be wrong."[30]

Turns out, he was. In a later case, Love was sued for $9 million over comments made on Twitter about Rhonda Holmes, a lawyer who had initially represented Love in a case involving money allegedly stolen from Cobain's estate. At one point, Love dropped Holmes' firm, then asked it to represent her again. Citing Love's substance abuse issues, Holmes refused to take Love on as a client again. Somehow, Love took that refusal to mean that Holmes had been bribed. So Love tweeted that "I was fucking devestated [*sic*] when Rhonda J Holmes esq of San Diego was bought off. I've been hiring and firing lawyers to help me with this."[31] Love insisted that the public tweet was meant to be a private message, and she deleted it quickly. In early 2014, a jury found that while the tweet was false and harmful to Holmes, "They were not convinced that Love didn't believe it to be true." Therefore, Love was off the hook.[32]

Private Figures

The first category of people is the **private figure** (or **private person**), the average person just minding his or her own business. In order for a private figure to win a defamation case, all that he or she needs to prove is that the charge is false. In other words, a publisher will lose even when there has been only **negligence**. However, the extent of negligence required varies by the location. In some states, simple negligence (in other words, just making a mistake) is the standard. Other states, however, "have required a showing of 'gross negligence' or some greater standard of liability. Still others specifically have defined a professional standard – 'journalistic negligence.'"[33] It's therefore vitally important that every writer and editor understand local laws.[34]

A private figure can establish negligence by showing that the publisher did not act with a reasonable level of care in publishing the statement at issue. The Digital Media Law Project notes that factors the court might consider include the following:

- "the amount of research undertaken prior to publication;
- "the trustworthiness of sources;
- "attempts to verify questionable statements or solicit opposing views; and
- "whether the defendant followed other good journalistic practices."[35]

Public Figures and Public Officials

The second category of people is the **public figure**. Within this category are two subcategories. The first consists of people classified as **pervasive public figures**. All aspects of these peoples' lives are considered public. Many entertainers fall into this category, as do some business and religious leaders, elite athletes and others who exercise pervasive power and influence in society.

The second subcategory contains people classified as **limited purpose public figures**. Members of this group are considered public figures for only a portion of their lives. Most of those in this subcategory are people who have thrust themselves to the forefront of public controversy; many people who would not consider themselves public figures would indeed be seen that way by the courts. As an analysis of one recent case notes, "In today's world of instant news and celebrity, average citizens can be converted into public figures in an instant."[36]

An interesting aspect of defamation online is that some private people who believe they have been defamed are sometimes ruled to be limited purpose public figures simply because they have engaged in online discussion before the defamation occurs:

> The Internet has developed a reputation as a free-wheeling environment in which the unrestrained comments of one speaker may well be met with vigorous rebuttal. Arguably, anyone who regularly posts electronic messages, whether on a bulletin board or in a chat room or other online forum, may be deemed to have "invite[d] attention and comment" about himself or herself and thus to have voluntarily assumed an increased risk of being defamed.[37]

Some people are classified as *involuntary* limited purpose public figures. This group includes those who through no design of their own have played a role in a major public occurrence, such as an air traffic controller who was working at the time of a fatal plane crash.[38]

Often grouped with public figures are **public officials**, politicians and employees who have responsibility for or control over the conduct of government affairs.[39] Because they are chosen by and/or paid by the public, they continue to be considered public figures even after they leave governmental positions.

Unlike private figures, public figures and public officials have to clear a higher bar to win a defamation case. Negligence is not enough. The courts have held that because public figures and public officials *are* public, they invite discussion of their actions, often to promote themselves and their activities (an election campaign, a product launch, a new movie, and so on). Sometimes, those discussions contain factual errors. When that happens, the courts have ruled, the public

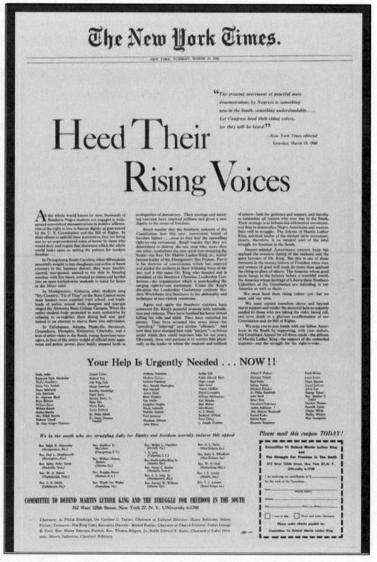

A lawsuit over this ad in The New York Times changed libel law in the United States.

http://www.archives.gov/exhibits/documented-rights/exhibit/section4/detail/heed-rising-voices.html

figures and public officials have to roll with the punches, unless they can prove the errors were published with **actual malice**. This requirement for a public figure in the United States to prove actual malice stands in sharp contrast to laws in other countries, where the actions taken before publication have no bearing on a publisher's liability.

The concept of actual malice originated in the New York Times Co. v. Sullivan case. In that instance, a group of concerned citizens bought a full-page ad in The New York Times in which they sought financial support to defend Martin Luther King Jr. against a perjury indictment in Alabama. The ad took to task the police force of Montgomery, Alabama, for the way in which civil rights protesters were being treated. L. B. Sullivan, the Montgomery Public Safety commissioner, was not named in the ad. However, the ad contained factual errors that he believed defamed him as supervisor of the police, so Sullivan sued the Times. (Even though the ad was created and paid for by outsiders, the Times published it. Today in the online environment, things would be different, as we'll see shortly.)

The case made it all the way to the U.S. Supreme Court, which unanimously found in favor of the Times. In doing so, the court defined actual malice as *knowledge that a statement is false*, or *acting with reckless disregard for the truth of the statement*. Sullivan was unable to prove either condition was true at the time of publication, and few other public plaintiffs in the decades since have been able to do so, either. So more than any other U.S. media law case, this one was a huge leap in expanding freedom of the press.

Worry About This/Not About That

The Risks of Relying on *Allegedly* and Inference, and the Safety of Publishing Online Comments

Many people think attaching the word *allegedly* to a defamatory statement makes it OK to publish that statement. That idea is wrong and dangerous. All *allegedly* means is that someone made the charge. If the statement is false and is not covered by any type of journalistic privilege, publishing it with the word *allegedly* is the same as publishing it without.

Similarly, some publishers think that as long as they don't come right out and make an explicit charge, they are in the clear. Again, this is mistaken and dangerous. For most intents and purposes, courts make no distinction between outright defamation (known as *per se*) and implied defamation (*per quod*). As one source notes,

Defamation per quod depends on context and the interpretation of the listener. It means that a person would have to have what's called extrinsic knowledge to understand the statement as defamatory. For example, a former employer wrongly says he saw you drinking whiskey in a bar, a statement that could be problematic if the person

the employer is talking to knows you were court-ordered last year to stay sober.[40]

Not so worrisome, however, is material contributed to an online publication by outside sources. One of the twists of defamation law in the digital realm is that the traditional definition of publisher has in some ways been turned upside down. In the pre-Internet days, any material appearing in a newspaper would be considered to have been published by the newspaper, even if the material were a letter to the editor or an advertisement (such as the Sullivan case turned on). But online, a special provision of the Communications Decency Act (usually referred to by its section number, 230) immunizes publishers "from liability for freelance content, bulletin-board postings, and other third-party content."[41]

There are important caveats associated with Section 230 immunity. As the Digital Media Law Project notes:

You will not lose this immunity even if you edit the content, whether for accuracy or civility, and you will be entitled to immunity so long as your edits do not substantially alter the meaning of the original statements. However, if you alter someone else's statement so that it becomes defamatory (e.g., changing the statement "Bob is not a murderer" to "Bob is a murderer"), you would be responsible for the content of the edited statement; and if it turns out to be untrue, you could be liable for defamation. In addition, if you add your own commentary along with the user-submitted content, you will only be shielded from liability for the material created by your user, not for your own statements.[42]

In addition, Section 230 "does not apply to federal criminal law, intellectual property law, and electronic communications privacy law."[43] Therefore, it's vital that publishers carefully monitor user contributions for material that runs afoul of those laws and remove it as soon as possible.

Satire and Parody

When they're looking for a laugh, millions of readers turn to The Onion (http://www.theonion.com). With headlines such as "Trump Announces He's A Very Sad Man" and "Nation Did Not See Mark Wahlberg's Sex Change Coming," The Onion routinely mocks the rich, the famous and the powerful – and pretty much everyone else. Satire might seem like all fun and games, but the Reporters Committee on Freedom of the Press, a nonprofit association dedicated to providing free legal assistance to journalists, points out that it plays an important role:

> Satire and parody are important forms of political commentary that rely on blurring the line between truth and outrageousness to attack, scorn and ridicule public figures. Although they may be offensive and intentionally injurious, these statements contain constitutionally protected ideas and opinions, provided a reasonable reader would not mistake the statements as describing actual facts.[44]

Even though some individuals and news organizations occasionally *do* mistake The Onion's articles for real news, the staff does not have to worry about being sued for defamation because it is clearly satire. But the distinction between satire and fact is not always so clear, especially for less skilled writers. When a reasonable reader confuses the two, a defamation suit might not be long behind.

The Reporters Committee on Freedom of the Press suggests several steps to help minimize the chances of such confusion:

- "Use an unorthodox headline to alert readers from the beginning that the story is not straight news and use an irreverent tone throughout the piece;
- "Consider your web site's history, or lack thereof, of publishing satire or parody. If you generally publish only financial reports, for example, you should be more careful than a blogger or other online content provider who regularly publishes stories like those in The Onion;
- "Choose carefully the parody's location on the site, making sure to avoid posting it among several straight news stories;
- "Include in the story unbelievable or outrageous items, experts or groups with ridiculous names or silly acronyms and quotes that are incredible, illogical or over-the-top;
- "Substitute fictitious names that are close to or suggest real people for the names of actual people;

- "Publish the parody soon after the actual incident while it is still in the public's mind and, if possible, explicitly refer to that event in your commentary on it; and
- "Post a disclaimer but keep in mind that it will not necessarily avoid liability, especially if it is written in small print at the end of an otherwise believable story."[45]

Publishing Anonymously

Some new publishers think they don't have to worry about things like defamation as long as they remain anonymous. (And just one more reminder: *Everyone* who even sends an email or comments on a blog post is a publisher.) As "Internet Law: A Field Guide" notes:

> Anonymity and the freedom to speak one's mind that comes from that anonymity are attractive to many Internet users. Increasingly, those who are the subjects of unflattering anonymous speech are turning to the courts to try to identify their detractors. They bring libel suits against "John Doe" defendants and subpoena the message-board hosts in an effort to obtain identifying information about the authors of the allegedly libelous remarks.[46]

Such unmasking is usually easy and straightforward. Many Internet service providers include a provision in their terms of service that specifically states they have the right to supply personal information about users when ordered to do so. So unless a person takes great pains to ensure anonymity, it is not hard to unmask him or her.

Fortunately, an emerging standard offers anonymous publishers protection from many unwarranted requests to reveal their identities. According to the Reporters Committee for Freedom of the Press,

> Because many of the demands issued are attempts to silence critics or whistleblowers, courts have started to settle on a standard that tries to tell the two types of claims apart: If the one demanding the unmasking can show he's got a credible libel claim, and the anonymous speaker is given an opportunity to defend himself, courts will allow the unmasking.[47]

However, this standard does not provide any protection for truly defamatory material; no one should publish such material anonymously if he or she is not ready to accept responsibility for its publication.

SLAPP Suits

Just as people sometime request the identities of anonymous publishers to stifle criticism, others will file a strategic lawsuit against public participation (commonly referred to as a SLAPP suit) for the same purpose. Typically, SLAPPs are used by corporations, real estate developers, government officials and others when they want to stifle individuals and community groups who oppose them. "SLAPP filers frequently use lawsuits based on ordinary civil claims such as defamation, conspiracy, malicious prosecution, nuisance, interference with contract and/or economic advantage, as a means of transforming public debate into lawsuits," notes The First Amendment Project.

Most SLAPPs are not successful in court. However, they often accomplish their users' objectives, because "Defending a SLAPP, even when the legal defense is strong, requires a substantial investment of money, time, and resources." Therefore, these suits tend to quash public debate on important issues. "This 'chilling' effect is not limited to the SLAPP target(s): fearful of being the target of future litigation, others refrain from speaking on, or participating in, issues of public concern."[48]

The good news for many publishers is that approximately 30 states have enacted anti-SLAPP statutes. As "Internet Law: A Field Guide" notes, those statutes are "designed to dispose promptly of meritless libel suits complaining of speech on matters of public interest.

CASE STUDY

Getting SLAPPed for Calling Someone a Dumb Ass

While political candidates generally are glad for any publicity, two candidates for public office in California, John Vogel and Paul Grannis, could not have been happy to see themselves listed in the No. 1 and No. 2 spots on a compilation of the "Top Ten Dumb Asses." So they sued Joseph Felice, the owner of the website on which the list appeared. Their charges included libel, false light invasion of privacy, intentional and negligent infliction of emotional distress, and negligence.

Felice saw the suit not as a serious defamation case, but instead as an attempt to shut him up (and down) – in other words, as a SLAPP suit. So he requested that the complaint be struck down, citing California's anti-SLAPP statute, which requires the dismissal of any suit "arising from any act of [the defendant] in furtherance of [his or her] right of petition or free speech under the United States or California Constitution in connection with a public issue … unless the court determines that the plaintiff has established that there is a probability that the plaintiff will prevail on the claim."

While the trial court denied Felice's request, the court of appeal sided with him. That court found that Vogel and Grannis had failed to establish a probability of success because they had failed to show that Felice acted with actual malice. The court also concluded that being called a "dumb ass" was not defamatory because it was a statement of opinion and could not be proved true or false.[49]

… Under these laws, a libel suit will be dismissed promptly on motion by the defendant if the speech complained of is on a public issue and the plaintiff cannot show that it is likely to prevail on its claims."[50]

In the remaining states, defendants might still be able to swat down a SLAPP suit, but doing so takes some work. The Reporters Committee for Freedom of the Press publishes a guide titled "How can I oppose a frivolous lawsuit?" (http://www.rcfp.org/browse-media-law-resources/digital-journalists-legal-guide/how-can-i-oppose-frivolous-lawsuit-anti-0) offering suggestions in those circumstances.

The Importance of Corrections and Clarifications

Despite the best efforts, defamatory material does sometimes get published. When a publisher realizes defamatory material has been distributed, it is usually a good idea to publish a correction or clarification.

Most states will reduce the amount of damages a publisher may be assessed provided the publisher runs a correction or clarification upon request of the plaintiff. It's important that *corrections and clarifications do not repeat the defamation* and are displayed as prominently as the original material. In cases in which there is a print and an online version of a publication, the correction should be run in each. In all cases, the Reporters Committee for Freedom of the Press warns, publishers should not "rush to 'clarify' something without thinking about what you're saying about the truth or accuracy of your original article."[51]

Even in states with retraction statutes, it's not certain they will apply to online media. "Internet Law: A Field Guide" notes that in many places "retraction statutes designate only newspapers or other traditional printed matter as falling within their protections." In those locations, online sites that are tied to print publications are probably covered. However, "While in theory retraction statutes should equally protect publications that exist only online, it is less clear that such publications are covered."[52]

Another problematic area for online publications is defamatory material that appears in archives. Many publishers are rightly reluctant to "rewrite history" by changing material in archives. At a minimum, uncorrected archived material should be time-stamped and clearly indicated as part of the archive. "A more elaborate disclaimer might specifically inform users that material in the online archive is presented in its original form, has not been updated since the original date of publication, and does not reflect information subsequently obtained by the publisher."[53]

Wrapping Up

As the material in this chapter should make clear, navigating defamation law requires knowledge of local laws and ongoing vigilance. While the ground rules covered here are a good starting point, it's always best to seek legal guidance in any situation that is not completely clear.

Key Points

- Defamation is one of the most important topics for publishers to understand, to prevent harm to their readers and themselves.
- While some basic guidelines apply in most cases, the rules governing defamation vary from place to place and change over time. In addition, not all the rules governing print media apply to online media.
- For the purposes of defamation law, anyone who writes something about a person and causes it to be seen by another person is regarded as a publisher. However, third-party comments published online are the responsibility of the commenter, not the publisher.
- Journalists have several privileges – opinion and fair comment, fair report and neutral report – that allow them to print material that could otherwise lead to a defamation suit.
- Private figures can win a defamation suit in some cases just by proving a factual statement is incorrect. Public figures and public officials must prove actual malice in order to win.
- Whenever a correction or retraction of potentially defamatory material is requested, a publisher should fully investigate the material and take appropriate action.
- It is almost impossible to publish anonymously.
- SLAPP suits are sometimes used to mimic defamation suits when really all they are intended to do is shut down discussion. Most states have anti-SLAPP laws that make dismissing meritless SLAPP suits easier.
- Satire and parody are important forms of expression, but publishers need to make sure they are obvious to avoid defamation actions.

CHAPTER EXERCISE

Read the following article excerpts and underline each instance of potential defamation. After each excerpt, list the type of defamation; the defense that allows you to publish the defamation (if there is no defense, write ``None''); what action to take (publish the material as is, edit the material or delete the material). If you have decided that the material must be edited, write in the edited version on the last line.

1. Elena Williams was found guilty today of being an accessory after the fact of murder in trying to cover up the death of 19-year-old Anna Spaulding.

Type:

Defense:

Action:

Edited Version:

2. (From a column) The chief of police of this town is clearly schizophrenic and corrupt. It is not surprising that he was thrown out of a local pizza parlor recently for his behavior.

Type:

Defense:

Action:

Edited Version:

3. Byron Jones of Columbia Road told police earlier today that for the past week, his neighbor, Kenneth Johnson, had had a steady stream of men and women visiting his home every night. "It's pretty clear he's running a drug business in there," Jones said.

Type:

Defense:

Action:

Edited Version:

4. Pettiford testified that her ex-husband forced his way into her house, knocked her unconscious and then dragged her to his car. "The next thing I knew, we were in the wooded area where he raped me."

Type:

Defense:

Action:

Edited Version:

5. (From a column) It's unfortunate that he has chosen television news as a career, because his is a face best suited to radio. But his tendency to mispronounce words would be a liability in that field, too.

Type:

Defense:

Action:

Edited Version:

6. She announced her withdrawal from the race because, she said, "It's clear my opponents have rigged the election."

Type:

Defense:

Action:

Edited Version:

7. The detective told reporters that Simmons undoubtedly would be charged with child abuse after police questioned him.

Type:

Defense:

Action:

Edited Version:

8. (From an editorial) While the governor has served his state well, his ideas are simply tired and he is no match for his challenger. Hawes, on the other hand, promises to get this state out of its budgetary quagmire and is easily the better man for the job.

Type:

Defense:

Action:

Edited Version:

9. The funds for the medical school scholarship come from alumnus William Lee. He

(Continued)

donated $1 million to the university last year, shortly after rumors surfaced that he is dying of AIDS.

Type:

Defense:

Action:

Edited Version:

10. Before the previous speaker could finish her comments at the public meeting on changes in the zoning laws, Calder jumped to his

feet and yelled, "You think you have problems? You should live next door to junkies like I do! Ever since the Nash family moved in, we've had nothing but trouble."

Type:

Defense:

Action:

Edited Version:

 # WRITE RIGHT

Using Commas Properly

Commas are without a doubt the most commonly used mark of punctuation, as well as the most commonly misused. While some of the most common uses are easy to understand, even then conflicting style rules can cause confusion. What follows are the basics for correct comma usage.

- When used in a series, a comma is not placed before the *and* or *or* according to Associated Press style: *As an active person, she loves to bike, hike and ski.* However, most other styles, including the American Psychological Association and the Chicago Manual of Style, require a final comma in those situations. In addition, Associated Press style requires a comma if the series contains any items that include words like *and* and *or: The breakfast options were ham and eggs, pancakes and sausage, and waffles and bacon.*
- Use a comma and a coordinating conjunction to join independent clauses. When the major parts of a sentence can stand on their own, they are referred to as independent clauses. Two or three can be joined together with a comma but only when a coordinating conjunction (words such as *and, but, for, or, nor; either … or; neither … nor; both … and; not only … but also*) is also used: *Two of them headed into the building, and the other three went around the back.* Failure to use the conjunction results in a fused sentence (often referred to as a run-on sentence).
- Do not use a comma if part of the sentence cannot stand on its own (known as a dependent clause): *His sentence was reduced because he expressed great remorse for the crime.*
- Use a comma to set off introductory phrases of more than a few words. Doing so helps the reader digest the information: *To help first-time home buyers, the builder offered a buy down on the mortgage rate for the first three years.*
- Use commas to set off nonessential material. Material is considered nonessential when there is only one item in a category: *Her husband, Michael, worked for years as a radio talk show host.* Do not use commas when there is more than one item in a category: *The class Abnormal Psychology was her favorite among all those required for her minor.*
- Use commas to set off nonessential adjectival clauses. Typically, these include the word *which,* while essential clauses include the word *that,* but just because the writer has used one of those words is no reason to conclude that the material is essential or not. The test is the same as in the

preceding rule: Does it narrow down choices or just add information? *He ate almost every meal at fast-food restaurants, which are not known for their healthful menus. She ate only food that she prepared herself from raw ingredients.*

- Use commas to separate equal adjectives. If the comma could be replaced by the word *and*, it should be used. If not, it should not. *It was a typical hot, humid day in Atlanta. Her last clothing purchase was a dark blue blazer.*
- Do not use a comma to separate the subject from the verb. When subjects are even a little complex, writers sometimes put a comma after the subject. But that is never correct.

Exercise

Add commas as needed to the following sentences.

1. Military officials had identified the two sailors who died as crewman Petty Officer Brian Collins 25 of Truckee California and pilot Lieutenant Wesley Van Dorn 29 of Greensboro North Carolina.

2. According to experts in Houston it surely is shaping up that way in Texas— and as a guy who right now has a barking cough low-grade fevers some chills and sweats as well as an insatiable urge to sleep 23 hours a day I suspect it is widespread here in Manhattan as well.

3. "We don't teach music in school to make everyone a concert violinist" says Clive Beale director of educational development at the Raspberry Pi Foundation a nonprofit organization based near Cambridge England that promotes computer studies in schools.

4. A warning to mariners issued by the Coast Guard said portions of the Houston channel and its offshoots to Texas City and Galveston Texas along with a portion of the Gulf Intracoastal Waterway could be closed through March 29 2014 or longer depending on the requirements of a cleanup.

5. According to SpaceX Dragon is a spacecraft designed to deliver both cargo and people to orbiting objects such as the ISS.

6. You're in pain after surgery and your doctor prescribes you Vicodin or maybe Percocet.

7. Uriel Estrada 41 his wife Maria 40 and their children Isabel 12 and Alejandro 7 were pronounced dead at local hospitals after a fire swept through their home around 4:30 a.m. Monday according to family members and hospital officials.

8. The Korea CDC specifically cited a spike in the cases of scrub typhus an illness that causes fever headaches rashes and scabbing as one example for the increase.

9. Patty McKibben a clinical dietician at Fletcher Allen Health Care confirms that her department is seeing more patients with food allergies and celiac disease in part because she says "A lot more people are aware of it."

10. Armed with one liners a few digs and a broad smile President Barack Obama welcomed the 2013 NBA Champions the Miami Heat to the White House Tuesday afternoon and congratulated them on winning the world championship for a second year in a row.

EDITOR'S TOOLKIT

Resources for Free and Affordable Legal Help

Writers and editors working for established journalistic institutions usually have immediate access to knowledgeable experts when legal questions occur. But smaller operations and individual bloggers can hardly afford to keep lawyers on retainers – or in some cases, even to pay for a quick consultation. Fortunately, a host of free resources is available to aid those in need.

(Continued)

(Continued)

Overviews

A good starting point is the Digital Media Law Project's guide to Nonprofit Legal Assistance (http://www.dmlp.org/legal-guide/nonprofit-legal-assistance). This page links to several organizations that provide assistance or advocacy on First Amendment issues. Additionally, the page links to a list of nonprofit legal assistance organizations by state (http://www.dmlp.org/legal-guide/nonprofit-legal-assistance-organizations-state).

Also helpful is Jeremy Kaplan's "Practical tips, resources for entrepreneurial journalists with legal questions" (http://www.poynter.org/how-tos/leadership-management/entrepreneurial/164826/practical-tips-resources-for-entrepreneurial-journalists-with-legal-questions). This short article includes sections on finding forms for legal proceedings, determining the best legal structure for a journalism entity and creating contracts.

Finally, the American Bar Association Consumer Guide to Finding Legal Help (http://apps.americanbar.org/legalservices/findlegalhelp/home.cfm) lists resources available in each state.

Pro Bono Programs

One of the organizations Kaplan cites in his article is well worth bookmarking: the Online Media Legal Network (http://www.omln.org). OMLN is an initiative that offers to "connect lawyers and law school clinics from across the country with online journalists and digital media creators who need legal help."

Blogger and journalism professor Jay Rosen, who is also a CMLP advisory board member, notes: "This network is trying to level the playing field for independent online producers. That's why it matters. That's why I support it."[54]

OMLN provides some services free, while others are available at a reduced rate. OMLN offers help with issues that include

- business formation and governance;
- copyright licensing and fair use;
- employment and freelancer agreements;
- access to government information;
- prepublication review of content; and
- representation in litigation.

Another useful resource is the Society of Professional Journalists Legal Defense Fund (http://www.spj.org/ldf.asp), which supports litigation that enforces public access to government records and proceedings.

Legal Hotlines

When all that's needed is the answer to a simple question, a legal hotline might be the best option. The nonprofit Reporters Committee for Freedom of the Press (http://www.rcfp.org) offers free legal assistance to journalists 24 hours a day, seven days a week: 1-800-336-4243.

Those working on student media can get free help from the Student Press Law Center (http://www.splc.org/legalhelp.asp) on topics including censorship, libel law, copyright law, and freedom of information law. In addition to offering a Legal Hotline at 703-807-1904, the organization offers help via email or a virtual lawyer (http://www.splc.org/virtual_lawyer).

Student Study Site

Visit the Student Resource Site at **http://study.sagepub.com/lieb** to access:

- Chapter-by-chapter **web quizzes** for independent assessment of course material
- List of online web links and general resources

Chapter 7 Privacy, Copyright, International Regulations and Other Legal Issues

W hile defamation clearly represents the area of most concern for those who publish in print or online, it is far from the only legal issue with which they need to be concerned. This chapter looks at several other issues of importance, some of which are unique to the digital age.

Those issues span a wide range. In an era in which people's every movement and transaction is recorded by some company or agency, it is probably not surprising that one of the most common areas of concern is privacy. The ease of cutting and pasting online content makes copyright infringement a more important issue than it has been in the past. Allowing readers to comment on articles can create liability when they post links to copyrighted material. Bloggers can unknowingly run afoul of the law by failing to disclose relationships with those whose products and services they endorse. Journalists can also run into problems when they record conversations. In addition, publishers must cope with other issues related to new technologies, employment, publishing material that a governmental body considers secret, and dealing with foreign legal threats. While no editor can possibly keep track of the latest developments in each of these areas, having a basic knowledge of all of them is essential.

Privacy Issues

Concerns about privacy of information arose long before the Internet – and before radio and television, for that matter. Shortly after the emergence of the telegraph in the mid-19th century, with the Civil War in full blaze, "The Union and Confederate armies tapped each other's telegraph communications to ascertain battle plans and troop movements. Rival press organizations tapped each other's wire communications in order to be the first to report major news items."[1]

Not long after, another new technology raised fresh concerns about privacy. As small cameras joined their slow, bulky brethren, worries arose that candid photographs threatened to undermine privacy – well over 100 years before the word *Instagram* was first uttered.[2]

In the coming sections, we look at five main aspects of privacy law:

- false light;
- public disclosure of private facts;
- intrusion into seclusion;
- misappropriation; and
- right of publicity.

A common issue in media privacy cases is **false light**. The definition of that **tort** (a civil wrong recognized by law as grounds for a lawsuit) is simple, as legal definitions go:

One who gives publicity to a matter concerning another that places the other before the public in a false light is subject to liability to the other for invasion of his privacy, if

(a) The false light in which the other was placed would be highly offensive to a reasonable person, and
(b) The actor had knowledge of or acted in reckless disregard as to the falsity of the publicized matter and the false light in which the other would be placed.[3]

As simple as it seems, though, false light is a slippery concept. To begin with, false light very closely resembles defamation. Because of that, about one-third of the states do not recognize false light claims, lumping them in with defamation. Among the states that do recognize both defamation and false light, there is often a fine line. As the Reporters Committee for Freedom of the Press explains:

Perhaps the most significant difference between false light and defamation is the nature of the interests protected by each; defamation protects the objective interest of reputation while false light protects the subjective interest of emotional injury that includes personal feelings like embarrassment, helplessness or mere hurt feelings. Accordingly, false light plaintiffs need not show reputational damage caused by publicized information, only that the material would be highly offensive to a reasonable person – a vague standard that potentially chills speech.[4]

The truly chilling aspect of false light is that it can occur even when all the facts are true. One example would be a photo that inadvertently gives the impression that someone is engaged in criminal activity, even though there is no information in the accompanying caption or story that would reinforce that impression.

Because some states' laws allow false light claims to be based on such implications, editors should carefully check every piece of copy as well as every headline, photo, caption and cutline. The Reporters Committee for Freedom of the Press warns, "Always be cognizant that statements that seem completely benign to you may be offensive to more sensitive, 'thin-skinned' people and could give rise to false light claims if also false or create a false implication."[5]

In addition, online writers and editors need to "be particularly mindful of the formatting of your site. Be sure that your website doesn't get reformatted in such a way as to create an unwitting juxtaposition of images and stories that creates a connotation that you had not intended."[6]

The second major privacy issue is **public disclosure of private facts**. Also sometimes known as the **embarrassing-facts tort** or **private-facts tort**, this one also seems simple: the widespread dissemination of information that "(a) would be highly offensive to a reasonable person and (b) is not of legitimate concern to the public."[7] (How wide is "widespread"? In at least one case, sexual photos emailed to a small group of people were ruled to have met that test, as those people could forward them easily to many others.)[8]

As with false light, truth is not sufficient to avoid a lawsuit. However, newsworthiness is a defense. Of course, as discussed in Chapter 2, newsworthiness is not always an easy concept to nail down even for journalists, with other stories and factors affecting the value of any given story. To assess newsworthiness, courts consider several factors:

- the social value of the facts published;
- the depth of the publication's intrusion into ostensibly private affairs; and
- the extent to which the person about whom private facts were revealed voluntarily assumed a position of public notoriety.[9]

In addition, it is usually safe to publish information that comes from a public record. So the Reporters Committee for Freedom of the Press suggests using such sources whenever possible. But writers and editors still need to be careful, as some information, including Social Security numbers, is not likely to be covered.

Finally, consent from a source also may prove critical in deflecting a lawsuit under this tort. But it's important "for bloggers and other online content providers to identify themselves and clearly state to the interviewees that the information they provide may be published or broadcast. That's because the general rule that people who talk to a reporter give implied consent for use of their names because they should anticipate publication does not apply if the people do not understand whom they are talking to and how their statements may be used."[10]

The third of the four major privacy issues is **intrusion into seclusion**. Unlike the previous two privacy issues, this one is not based on published material but rather on the manner in which the information was gathered. In some cases, there is physical intrusion – sneaking into an office, for instance – but the same issue occurs when private material is gathered through physical, electronic or mechanical means, including eavesdropping, wiretapping and other activities. Such cases require proof that the intrusion caused anguish and suffering and the person suing for intrusion must show that he or she had a reasonable expectation of privacy.[11] In most public places, that is hard to prove: "The general rule is that people may photograph, film and record what they can easily see or hear in public places, provided they do not harass, trespass or otherwise intrude."[12] In addition, a person claiming he or she has been wronged must prove that the intrusion is "highly offensive to the ordinary reasonable [person], as the result of conduct to which the reasonable [person] would strongly object."[13]

That said, journalists can cross the line even in public places by conducting overzealous surveillance of a person:

> These activities could include the constant monitoring of a subject's comings and goings from a vehicle parked near his or her home, following subjects to and from their home and places they visit and using video cameras, binoculars or "shotgun microphones" capable of picking up conversations from long distances. These tactics, often the hallmark of celebrity journalists, led many states to enact anti-paparazzi laws, which create statutory liability … for newsgathering activities that involve such harassment.[14]

Undoubtedly, the most infamous case of media intrusion occurred in the mid-2000s, when the British tabloid News of the World regularly hacked into people's voice mail to get scoops for publication. The victims included the British royal family, a murdered schoolgirl, relatives of dead British soldiers, victims of the 7/7 London bombings, and possibly thousands of other people. The revelations led to a wave of resignations and arrests and ultimately proved so disgusting that advertisers boycotted the paper, causing it to shut down after 168 years of publication.[15]

To avoid such serious consequences, editors need to know not only what is in a story but how that information was obtained, as publication is not required for a lawsuit to succeed. Editors asked to sign off on intrusive news gathering techniques should carefully examine what is being proposed and seek legal counsel if there are any gray areas.

The next major privacy issue is **misappropriation**, defined as using a person's name or image for commercial purposes without permission. Generally speaking, it is not something that writers and editors often need to concern themselves with; most cases are in the realm of advertising or promotional activities. But misappropriation can be costly: In 2013, singer Rihanna won a $5 million judgment against British retailer Topshop after they used her image on their T-shirts without permission. Early the next year, actress Katherine Heigl sued the Duane Reade drugstore chain for $6 million for improperly using "the star's name and likeness on Twitter and Facebook, without authorization, to promote their brand."

The case is an interesting one, as all Duane Reade had done was post a paparazzi image of Heigl shopping in New York City. In the photo, Heigl is holding two Duane Reade shopping bags. The company added the caption, "Love a quick #DuaneReade run? Even @KatieHeigl can't resist shopping #NYC's favorite drugstore." A confidential "mutually beneficial" settlement included Duane Reade contributing to a foundation focused on animal welfare, established after Heigl's brother was killed in a car accident.[16]

Very occasionally, a news organization might run afoul of the misappropriation statutes by using a news photo, which it has every right to use in routine reporting, to promote subscriptions or for some other commercial purpose. The easiest way to avoid problems in this area is by using common sense: Never use a person's name or image for commercial purposes without first obtaining consent. This is particularly important for bloggers, who might not be covered by the protections afforded traditional media outlets. It's not enough to rely on oral consent. As the Reporters Committee for Freedom of the Press notes:

> Consent to use a person's name or likeness for commercial purposes should be in writing. Oral consent may be unsatisfactory. Consent agreements, signed by competent adults, should state the parties to the agreement and the scope and duration of the terms and should provide for payment. A name or photo should not be used commercially after such consent has expired.[17]

Closely related to misappropriation is the **right of publicity** – that is, the right to control the commercial use of one's identity. Such cases do not necessarily need an implication that the celebrity has endorsed the product or service. For example, in a case involving Los Angeles magazine, Dustin Hoffman initially was awarded more than $3 million over publication of a photo that no reasonable person would take to imply an endorsement. The photo was part of a feature that included still photos of celebrities in various movies, with the images updated to show them wearing modern designer clothing. The photo of Hoffman was from the movie "Tootsie," in which he dressed as a woman; the magazine's update of the photo showed him wearing a designer gown. Even though the award was overturned on appeal, the cost of defending it had to put a dent in the magazine's budget.[18]

Because these two issues are complex and vary from state to state, writers and editors should be careful that they understand the relevant laws before doing anything that could lead to a suit. A good primer on the topic can be found on the Digital Media Law Project's website at http://www.dmlp.org/legal-guide/using-name-or-likeness-another.

Copyright Infringement

An area of law that has become more problematic in recent years is copyright infringement. The amount of material floating on the Internet and the crush of constant deadlines have led some journalists to make poor decisions about using others' material.

The law is actually simple: In most circumstances, it is illegal to take someone else's work – words, photos, audio, video, or anything else except basic facts – without the permission of the person who created the work or holds the copyright. (Why the distinction? For one example, while a journalist creates the work, if he or she works for a news organization, that organization will hold the copyright.) So finding a photo in a Google search, for example, does not convey permission to use it. Neither does attributing the material or linking it to the original. Only the copyright holder can grant permission to reuse material. Reusing another's copyrighted material can be a serious and costly offense. In late 2013, photographer Daniel Morel was awarded $1.2 million in damages from Getty Images and Agence France-Presse, both of which had used his photographs of the 2010 Haiti earthquake without permission. (At the time of this writing, Getty and AFP were appealing the award).[19]

There is, however, one important exception. Copyright law contains a provision to allow **fair use** of copyrighted material to "promote the progress of science and useful arts." As the Digital Media Law Project notes, "Fair use will not permit you to merely copy another's work and profit from it, but when your use contributes to society by continuing the public discourse or creating a new work in the process, fair use may protect you."[20] Some examples:

- quoting passages from a book in a review of it;
- quoting from a speech, address or position paper in a news article; and
- using elements of a work in creating a parody of it.

Unfortunately, there is no quick and simple checklist to determine whether material passes the fair use test. Instead, the person thinking about using the material should examine it in light of four considerations to determine whether the use is fair:

1. The purpose and character of the use, including whether such use is of a commercial nature or is for nonprofit educational purposes;

2. The nature of the copyrighted work;

3. The amount and substantiality of the portion used in relation to the copyrighted work as a whole; and

4. The effect of the use upon the potential market for or value of the copyrighted work.[21]

Fortunately for writers and editors, the first of these considerations (**the purpose and character of the use**) allows journalists some leeway. Using another's work for the purpose of criticism, news reporting or commentary – the key functions of journalists – is viewed favorably in determining whether fair use applies. But just copying material without adding to it is not enough.

The second consideration (**the nature of the copyrighted work**) is probably the least important of the four. Two main factors are considered under it when looking at use of another's text: First, whether the material is fiction or nonfiction – the former is typically given more protection – and second, whether the work has been published or not. The second factor is mostly important when copying an unpublished work, for reasons to be discussed shortly.

The third consideration (**the amount and substantiality of the portion used**) examines how much of the original work is being used. The best bet here is to use as little of the original work as is necessary. Book reviews and news articles about speeches get possibly the widest berth under this consideration; even substantial excerpts from either are likely to be covered.

The fourth consideration (**the effect of the use upon the potential market**) builds on the previous one and is in some ways the most important. Courts considering potential copyright infringement are more likely to find it if the new publication causes severe financial harm to the original creator. Note, however, that negative criticism that might persuade potential readers to skip purchasing a book is not considered problematic.

Fair use is a broad defense with many intricacies. The best bet is to avoid possible infringement by using original material or finding material available through the Creative Commons license, such as photos on Flickr (http://www.flickr.com/creativecommons). Even then, it's important to read the rules governing use and follow them exactly.

CASE STUDY

When Using 99 Percent Is Fair Use

With the United States threatening military action in response to Syria's use of chemical weapons in late 2013, Russian President Vladimir Putin wrote an op-ed for The New York Times urging President Obama not to strike Syria.

The Washington Post's Max Fisher read the op-ed with interest and decided it was worth fact-checking and annotating. In a column he wrote for the Post, Fisher used 992 of Putin's 1,074 words. Surely, that would not be covered by fair use, right?

In actuality, it probably was, because Fisher also added 1,349 words of his own. Therefore, his column met the standard of being *transformative* – that is, it transformed the original work into something new and intellectually valuable. An intellectual property fellow at Columbia Law School's Kernochan Center told the Poynter Institute that "increasingly decisions turn on whether derivative use is transformative."[22]

For more information about fair use issues, a great resource is Stanford University's Copyright & Fair Use site (http://fairuse.stanford.edu/index.html), "a clearinghouse for information on copyright and fair use, featuring primary source materials, articles discussing fair use issues, and commentary and analysis on current issues."

Responsibility for Publishing the Statements and Content of Others

As we saw in Chapter 6, Section 230 of the Communication Decency Act protects publishers from being sued over defamatory material posted by users. Similarly, Section 512 of the Digital Millennium Copyright Act offers protection from copyright claims based on user-submitted material as well as on links to online material posted on other sites.

The first of these two **safe harbor** provisions covers materials posted to a blog or website by a user who is not part of the staff. The coverage depends, however, on several conditions:

- The publisher does not know that infringing content has been posted.
- The publisher does not receive financial benefit from the infringing activity.
- The publisher must promptly remove or disable access to infringing material when he or she is made aware of it.[23]

The second provision covers situations in which links go to an outside site that might be infringing on copyright. The conditions for this coverage are nearly identical to those governing the first provision. The only distinction is that the first condition requires that the publisher does not know that the material linked to is infringing.

Publishing Product or Service Endorsements

The Federal Trade Commission issued guidelines in 2009 that in certain circumstances require bloggers and social media users to disclose any relationship with a company that pays them or otherwise compensates them for writing positive reviews or otherwise commenting favorably on products or services. While that might seem to be a problem for anyone who receives occasional sample products and reviews or otherwise writes about them, the law was aimed at specific types of publishers.

Based on cases so far, the law "is primarily concerned with those getting paid in cash, those participating in network marketing programs, and those receiving a steady stream of products from a company or group of companies."[24] If one or more of those conditions apply, it's important to include a disclosure on affected material, and in the interest of transparent journalism, adding a disclosure is always a good idea.

A disclosure does not have to be detailed or long, but it should be as prominently displayed as the review or mention itself. On video-sharing sites, it is recommended to put the disclosure in the video content and the description alongside. On social networks it is recommended to put the disclosure in status updates and descriptions of photos or videos and create a "disclosures and relationships" section on your profile.[25]

One other area of concern: The FTC guidelines also say that publishers may be held liable for making misleading or unsubstantiated claims about a product or service. While the tenets of good journalism prevent such claims, the FTC rules are a good reminder to stick to provable facts in discussing or reviewing a product or service. As the Digital Media Law Project notes:

> Common sense should take you a long way here: stick to your own experience with a product or service and don't make any factual claims you can't support. If you're unsure about something, contact the company to see if it can provide you with guidance and/or factual support.[26]

CASE STUDY

When Copyright Meets Privacy

Some of the most challenging scenarios involve combinations of media laws. Perhaps one of the most instructive recent cases involved a Texas teenage girl named Alison Chang. Her youth counselor, Justin Wong, took a photo of Alison (and a friend), in which Alison is making the "V" peace sign with her hand. Wong posted the photo to his Flickr account under a Creative Commons attribution license that allows others to use the photo in many ways, including for commercial purposes.

Not long after Wong posted the photo to Flickr, Chang discovered that the portion of it showing her was indeed being used commercially, on billboards to promote free text messaging on Virgin Mobile phone service in Australia. In the billboards, the photo was superimposed with the words "Dump Your Pen Friend," implying that those with Virgin phones could find "better" friends than her. (See the billboard at https://www.flickr.com/photos/sesh00/515961023/in/photostream.)

The billboard was one of many in the Virgin Mobile campaign featuring photos taken from Flickr, but Alison was the only minor featured in the photos. Once the billboard image of her made its way across the globe, Alison found herself humiliated and embarrassed.

While Virgin's action was fine from a copyright perspective, the question remained: What about from a privacy perspective? After all, Alison's image was being used to sell a product without her consent – or that of her parents. So Alison's parents sued Virgin Mobile for misappropriation of her likeness. We will never know if they might have won the case, as it was dismissed for lack of jurisdiction over Virgin Mobile Australia. But the case "highlights the fact that somebody seeking to use a photograph needs to worry not just about copyright law, but also misappropriation and rights of publicity."[27]

Laws Affecting Recordings

Cautious journalists often use audio or video recorders to capture interviews, giving them the opportunity to make sure their recollections match up with the actual words and circumstances. Sometimes recordings and videos are used to supplement a text story online or, in the case of 2012 presidential candidate Mitt Romney's "47 percent" remark, they may become the story. But using recordings in any of these ways can lead to legal problems. Wiretapping and eavesdropping laws vary from state to state; in some states, simply recording without the consent of *all* parties violates the law. Such violations may lead to criminal penalties and civil suits. Some states also have specific laws governing use of hidden cameras.

In addition, nearly every state imposes penalties for **disclosing or publishing** information obtained in violation of that state's laws. For instance, Massachusetts law "prohibits the disclosure or use of the contents of an illegally recorded conversation, when accompanied by the knowledge that it was obtained illegally. ... Distributing videos or photos in violation of the state's hidden camera laws is also prohibited."[28]

The takeaway: It's important for everyone involved in publication to know federal and state laws and proceed appropriately when gathering or publishing photos, recordings or information obtained from them. Fortunately, the Reporters Committee for Freedom of the Press has compiled a state-by-state list at http://www.rcfp.org/reporters-recording-guide/tape-recording-laws-glance.

New Technologies

Journalists are always looking for new tools to help them gather and report the news. So it is no surprise that inventions such as Google Glass and drones have created a great deal of buzz in the journalistic community, with some seeing drones – in essence, flying cameras – in particular as being as useful as smartphones. But being on the cutting edge has not kept pace with current realities.

One advocate of using drones to get images from news scenes is Lewis Whyld, a British journalist who has built drones for years. In 2013, he used one to capture the aftermath of Typhoon Haiyan in the Philippines. Whyld said his drone "was able to fly over impassable roads and get to places others couldn't." Whyld has since used his drone to cover flooding in Britain and wild wolf hunting in France.[29]

Journalists have had similar success using drones in other parts of Europe and Latin America. But in the United States, Federal Aviation Administration regulations and other legal obstacles remain an impediment to using drones in journalism. Pedro Rivera, an on-call reporter for a CBS affiliate in Hartford, Conn., went on his own time with a drone he owned to cover a fatal car crash. Police ordered him to leave the scene, and shortly thereafter he was terminated from his CBS job after police had complained the drone "compromised the accident scene's integrity." Rivera subsequently sued the local Police Department for violating his First and Fourth Amendment rights, alleging that one of the officers "was inspired by an improper motive: to prevent the public from seeing video reports of what police officers do in an investigation." The outcome of his lawsuit could help set future drone policy in the United States. In the meantime, Steve Coll, dean of the Journalism School at Columbia University and an expert on technology, offers perhaps the best advice for journalists thinking about using drones. Before doing so, he says they should ask themselves, "What can you use a drone for, that you can't achieve by other means, that really matters, that is in the public interest, and is not just for the sake of doing it?"[30]

Employment Issues

Posting content on a blog or to social media can take on dangerous new dimensions if it's done at a workplace – or if the posts discuss workplace matters. In the most serious cases, people have been fired and seen their entire careers effectively ended over workplace-related blog posts. While the First Amendment offers protection from government censorship, there is no similar law that applies to companies, and that is very clear in states with "at will" employment laws, which give employers the right to fire someone for any reason they wish.

The obvious first step to avoiding problems is finding out what an employer's policies are before posting about the company or on the employer's premises. If the posts will involve the employer, the next step should be obtaining clearance from a supervisor.

Even if all indications are "go," it's still good advice to refrain from posting negative material. As one expert notes:

> Put your best face forward. Refrain from writing things that are nasty and meant to hurt others and in all other ways behave in words as you would in any public venue, which is to say, don't embarrass yourself or make a fool of yourself. We all harbor opinions that are uncharitable, and we spend a good amount of time filtering our comments about others for public consumption. It should be no different with a blog or any other writing venue.[31]

Some writers – and online commenters – think they can get away with anything if, for instance, they publish anonymously. But that is just wishful thinking. As noted earlier, companies often can find out who wrote material by sending a subpoena to the blog, hosting company or Internet service provider.

One topic of special concern is that of trade secrets. Posts about matters such as new products and innovations can harm companies in multiple ways, including direct financial loss. Perhaps no company has been more aggressive in going after bloggers and other online publishers than Apple, which has been the target of many breaches of information in recent years. In one well-known case, in 2005 Apple sued the website Think Secret, which since its founding in 1998 had published rumors and reports about Apple. In late 2004, the site published news about a new Mac Mini computer and new software, shortly before those items were announced at MacWorld 2005. Interestingly, the editor of the site – Harvard freshman Nicholas Ciarelli, who had written under the nom de plume Nick dePlume – did not work for Apple, but instead had gathered the information from knowledgeable sources. Ciarelli filed a motion to dismiss the lawsuit on First Amendment grounds and appeared to have a good chance of having his motion granted, but at the end of 2007, it was announced that the lawsuit was finally settled, and the site was shut down shortly thereafter.[32]

Governmental Risks

Most editors never have to give a thought to governmental repercussions of the work they handle, but some areas require careful attention. Particularly in the area of national security, scrutiny has been ratcheted way up in the era of WikiLeaks (which among other things was responsible for releasing thousands of documents about the war in Afghanistan) and the Edward Snowden case (which is largely known for the release of thousands of documents about global surveillance programs, many connected to the National Security Agency). Some in government – and, amazingly, even in the media – would like to see those who publish such sensitive information stand trial for treason. For editors handling such material, the only safe course of action is consulting with knowledgeable legal counsel before publishing material that might be construed as exposing national secrets.

Editors also have run into problems with publishing other material that governmental authorities would prefer be kept secret, such as the location of red light cameras and military drone flights in the United States. As a general rule, however, if the material is available through public records or through a Freedom of Information request, it can be published without fear.

The topic of requiring bloggers to be licensed or registered is another governmental matter that has appeared in a few locations in recent years. Technically, a blogger working in any city that requires a business license should obtain one. Major cities including Philadelphia, Boston, Los Angeles and Washington, D.C., charge as much as $50 a year for business licenses. While most cities do not go after bloggers who are working more for love than money, Philadelphia made headlines when it sent letters to several bloggers in the city demanding they submit the required paperwork and fees. Editor Joey Sweeney of Philadelphia nightlife and gossip blog Philebrity.com already had a license when the requests rolled out. "Since our business model relies on advertising sales," he told the New York Daily News, "it makes complete sense that we'd need a business license, as we're in business every bit as much as a corner store. However, where people who mostly blog as a hobby and are making little to no money at all via their online pursuits, it doesn't really seem fair."[33]

Worry About This, Not About That

"Borrowing" Copyrighted Material Is Never OK, but Naming Minors Can Be

One common and seriously mistaken belief is that individual bloggers, nonprofits and other small publishers don't have to worry about occasionally "borrowing" copyrighted images and other materials. The thinking goes along the lines of "It's not going to hurt anyone, and how would anyone ever know, anyway?" As it turns out, chances are good that the owner will find out and that the party being hurt will end up being the infringer.

One cautionary tale comes in the story of Righthaven LLC. The copyright holding company worked with many

(Continued)

(Continued)

publishers to find infringing content, and then filed suit against the sites where the content was used. While ultimately Righthaven itself was sued and went out of business, the fact that it filed multiple lawsuits over a single image and routinely went after individuals and nonprofits means that no one is free to take others' materials without permission.[34]

As to the question of how anyone would know, one common technique is to embed metadata into photos that is then searchable via Google and other engines. That information not only can be used to find images that were used without permission but even images that a publisher has licensed to use for a certain length of time once that period expires. As one source notes, "Large companies like Getty have the means to track usage, often outsourcing to firms that search for digital fingerprints across the web to make sure that images are properly used, both visually and legally."[35]

On the other hand, many journalists wrongly assume that publishing the name of a minor who has been charged with a crime is illegal. That is a mistaken impression. In fact, in 1979 the U.S. Supreme Court ruled that journalists may use the names of minors in articles as long as the information is "lawfully obtained" and "truthfully" reported (the decision was Smith v. Daily Mail, 443 U.S. 97).[36]

So why aren't names routinely published? Most news organizations believe that youthful offenders deserve special protection because of their age. "News outlets are generally reluctant to name juveniles involved in or alleged in crimes because 'the publicity may stigmatize them throughout their lives,'" New Mexico Gallup Herald Editor and Publisher Joseph J. Kolb has noted. Kolb is one of many journalists who have argued that the practice should end: "If media sources stick to the facts of the story rather than the ramifications of using a juvenile's name, they can find solace in the old-fashioned social value of the media – to inform the community, advocate for the victims, and possibly even prevent future incidents."[37]

Outside of the United States, licensing is often used to control what bloggers write about and to prevent them from writing at all about some topics. In early 2011, Saudi Arabia began requiring all bloggers to be licensed and "'include the call to the religion of Islam' and … strictly abide by Islamic sharia law. The registration and religion requirements are also being coupled with strict restrictions on what topics Saudi bloggers can write on – a development which will essentially give Saudi authorities the right to shut down blogs at their discretion." In addition, only certain people are allowed to blog on news topics – Saudi citizens, at least 20 years old who have a high school degree. That effectively prevents a large percentage of the population from blogging: "At least 31% of Saudi Arabia residents do not possess citizenship; these range from South Asian migrants living in poor conditions to well-off Western oil workers. All of them will find their Internet rights sharply curtailed as a result of the new regulations."[38]

Similarly, the government of Singapore announced a new licensing requirement for "news websites" in mid-2013. The new law requires publishers to register if they "report an average of at least one article per week on Singapore's news and current affairs over a period of two months, and are visited by at least 50,000 unique IP addresses from Singapore each month over a period of two months."[39] Under those rules, many individual blogs would be required to be licensed. Once licensed, sites would have to remove any content that the government does not like.

Fending Off Foreign Legal Threats

Many digital publishers would likely be shocked to realize they don't know the answer to this simple question: Where is your blog or site published? The answer is not an office, town, state or even country. Instead, it's wherever a reader calls up the material. That's why the Singapore law discussed in the previous section applies to publishers far from its shores as well as those in the country. As The High Court of Australia noted in its decision in an early key case involving online defamation: "If people wish to do business in, or indeed travel to, or live in, or utilize the infrastructure of different countries, they can hardly expect to be absolved from compliance with the laws of those countries. The fact that publication might occur everywhere does not mean that it occurs nowhere."[40]

Given the widely differing legal standards around the world, that realization is boggling. But it's not the only worrisome issue. The Digital Media Law Project provides a list of some of the other issues that might occur from publishing content outside North America:[41]

- Standards for defamation vary and are generally not as media-friendly as in the United States.
- Requirements that the publisher must prove defamatory statements are not false, unlike the situation in the United States, where plaintiffs typically must prove the material is false.
- Defamation may be considered a criminal offense, with fines and imprisonment common, even for merely "insulting" a public official or state institution.
- Some countries "have laws criminalizing speech that incites hatred on the basis of characteristics such as race, religion, ethnicity, and national origin," and others forbid denying historical genocides and/or displaying Nazi-related materials.
- Many countries have broader notions of privacy than does the United States, restricting what publishers can disclose – even about celebrities, and even in public circumstances. "For example, in 2004 a British newspaper was found to have violated the privacy rights of model Naomi Campbell by publishing a photograph of her leaving a drug treatment clinic on a public sidewalk."
- Prohibitions on covering material that would be legal in the United States, such as certain types of hearings, can be found even in open countries like Canada.
- Copyright presents tricky issues, as foreign countries that have signed the Berne Convention might be able to sue for copyright enforcement in the United States, even if the material is not copyrighted there. Conversely, "In some countries other people may be able to use material that is copyrighted in the United States and posted to a U.S.-based web site in ways that would not be legal in the United States."

Fortunately for smaller publications, however, these differing laws are largely irrelevant. U.S. District Court Judge Jeremy Fogel made that point in ruling that "Yahoo was not subject to liability in the United States from a lawsuit filed by French students over World War II memorabilia offered for auction on the company's U.S. site." Fogel wrote in his opinion, "Although France has the sovereign right to regulate what speech is permissible in France, this court may not enforce a foreign order that violates the protections of the United States Constitution by chilling protected speech that occurs simultaneously within our borders."[42] Further, since that decision, the U.S. Congress passed a **libel tourism** law (known as Securing the Protection of our Enduring and Established Constitutional Heritage Act or SPEECH Act)[43] that prohibits "the enforcement in the United States of a foreign libel judgment if the speech at issue would not constitute defamation under U.S. law."[44] Therefore, Web publishers who do not have assets or business operations outside the United States likely do not have anything to worry about, at least not unless they are planning to travel to the country in which the judgment was enforced. Nevertheless, even the smallest news site or blog would be foolhardy to ignore such threats without first seeking legal advice.

Bigger companies, however, especially those that are multinational, need to take such actions seriously. The Digital Media Legal Project's basic guide for responding to foreign claims can be found at http://www.dmlp.org/legal-guide/dealing-foreign-legal-threats. The DMLP also offers information about obtaining insurance (http://www.dmlp.org/legal-guide/media-liability-insurance) and finding legal help for domestic cases (http://www.dmlp.org/legal-guide/finding-legal-help).

Wrapping Up

A wide range of legal issues affect publishing, and the advent of digital distribution has increased the challenges an editor must navigate. The best writers and editors understand the basics of privacy, copyright and other legal matters and keep on top of emerging issues in other areas of the law.

Key Points

- A common area of legal concern is privacy, which encompasses five main issues: False light, public disclosure of private facts, intrusion into seclusion, misappropriation and right of publicity.
- Copyright infringement is a serious problem that has been made harder to monitor because of the ease of getting information and images from online sources.
- As a general rule, publishers do not have to worry about material that infringes the copyright of others if it has been posted to a site without the publisher's knowledge, does not provide any financial gain to the publisher and is removed by the publisher upon notification.
- FTC rules require bloggers and others to disclose any relationships with companies whose products or services they review or promote.
- Editors should learn the laws affecting the legality of audio and video recordings before posting material that comes from any such recordings.
- First Amendment coverage does not offer protection from private employers. Publication of negative workplace-related material, as well as of trade secrets, should be carefully scrutinized.
- Local and national laws place limits on material that can be published without fear of legal action, and in some cases licenses are required to publish.
- Foreign laws also may effectively limit what material can be published safely, particularly if a publisher has holdings outside the United States.

CHAPTER EXERCISE

Determine whether the following cases would be grounds for privacy actions by the people mentioned.

1. The local university recently became a smoke-free campus. Yet while visiting the campus, a writer for your site notices that many students – and even faculty – are ignoring the rules. She manages to snap some photos surreptitiously. Can you publish those to show the lawbreakers?

2. A writer for a university student news site has discovered that the woman who recently was elected president of the Student Government Association was once a man. The woman has changed her name and moved since having the sex change 10 years ago, and she apparently has kept the information from everyone. The writer had a hunch, though, and checked old police records and found a traffic ticket in her old name. The writer argues that this is obviously important news; do you publish it?

3. A teen has been charged with killing an elderly couple as they slept in their home. He told police he did it "just to see what it would be like." Police are not releasing the name, but one of your newspaper reporters has obtained it through a friend who works at the courthouse. "This is a horrendous crime," the reporter says, "and we ought to let our readers know who this monster is. What a scoop it will be!" Do you use the name?

4. A profile of a successful local business woman notes that she got off to a late start because it took her 10 years to graduate from college. The article doesn't explain why she took so long, so you ask the writer. He says that he heard that

she could take only a class or two each semester because she had to work to help support her family. Deadline is approaching; can you add that information without further verification?

5. One of the writers for your magazine has turned in a short piece about a local man who has quit his job so that he can protest at abortion clinics every day. While the man refused to be interviewed, your reporter spent a great deal of time learning about him from family members and close friends. You're satisfied the information is accurate, but the subject has called the magazine threatening to sue for invasion of privacy if the piece is published. Do you run it?

 ## WRITE RIGHT

Using Apostrophes Properly

Many people seem to consider apostrophes as a form of seasoning, like a spice: Toss one in here and there, with little regard for how well it blends in. It's not a coincidence, then, that three of the Top 10 Common Word Errors in Chapter 1 involve apostrophes.

Fortunately, using apostrophes correctly requires learning only a relatively small number of rules, and most people already know many of them.

- Use an apostrophe in a contraction, taking the place of a letter or letters that have been omitted: *"We're coming along for the ride," she said.*
- Use an apostrophe to show possession: *Mary's kitten plays almost nonstop.* This includes cases where a following noun is implied: *It is the police chief's problem, not the mayor's* (problem).
- Use an apostrophe and *s* after only the second name when two people jointly own an item: *Bill and Brian's apartment is crammed full of books.* However, use apostrophes after each word if the items are owned individually: *Bill's and Brian's books have taken over their apartment.*
- Do not use an apostrophe to create a plural of a proper name: *The Brands own four Hondas.*
- Do not use an apostrophe with the possessive pronouns *his, hers, its, theirs, ours, yours, whose.*
- Add an apostrophe and an *s* to singular common nouns ending in *s* unless the next word begins with *s*: *The waitress's customers thought she could be more efficient. The waitress' shift would not be over until midnight.*
- Make the noun plural and follow it with an apostrophe when a plural noun has possession of an object: *The senators' budget plan included both tax increases and spending cuts.*
- Do not use an apostrophe when using a group of capital letters or numbers as a noun: *Learning her ABCs came easy to his daughter.*
- Add an apostrophe followed by an *s* after the last word of a compound word: *His mother-in-law's generosity was widely admired.*
- Check the Apostrophes entry in the Punctuation section of The Associated Press Stylebook for rules on double possessives (e.g., *a friend of John's*) and quasi possessives (e.g., *three days' pay*).

Exercise

Add apostrophes as needed in the following sentences.

1. Samuel Wiseman had many great memories of attending high school in the 90s.

2. The primary in the states 13th Congressional District sets the stage for a March special election that some political pundits are billing as barometer for Novembers midterm elections.

3. There were reports that the teachers union was about to undertake a retaliatory action.

(Continued)

(Continued)

4. Democrats also blocked GOP-sought curbs on the Environmental Protection Agencys power to regulate utilities greenhouse gas emissions.

5. During Tuesdays hearing, Brian Mathews then-girlfriend, Asha Smythe, walked the court through the calls.

6. While learning HTML might not be as easy as learning the ABCs, it is a task even kindergarteners can accomplish.

7. The civilian suspect approached the destroyers quarterdeck, and the ships security personnel confronted him, Navy officials say.

8. The partnership with Luxottica is expected to help broaden Google Glass appeal.

9. The Supreme Courts female justices dominated questioning in the first half of Tuesdays oral arguments challenging the health laws contraception requirement.

10. The hostess sister said she was a friend of Kevins.

EDITOR'S TOOLKIT

Online Sites for Editing Practice and Learning

Like many other worthwhile skills, learning to edit well takes lots of practice. That's why this book is bundled with exercises. But once you've completed them, you might want to polish your skills further. Fortunately, there are plenty of resources online that will help you do just that.

One of the best sites has been referred to throughout the Write Right sections of this book: The Purdue Online Writing Lab (OWL). While the name might suggest it is available only to people affiliated with Purdue University, its wide range of lessons and practice exercises is open to anyone with Internet access. The OWL Exercise Page (https://owl.english.purdue.edu/exercises) is a good starting point, with links to exercises on grammar, punctuation, spelling and other topics.

Another great resource is EditTeach.org. Among many other assets is a collection of grammar and style exercises (http://www.edit teach.org/tools?tool_cat_id=17) as well as plenty of ideas for teaching editing to others once you have mastered it.

At first glance, the Society of Professional Journalists' Journalist's Toolbox is overwhelming. Even the page devoted to copy editing resources (http://www.spjvideo.org/jtb/archive/copy-edit ing) contains dozens and dozens of links. While all are worth checking out (as is the section on fact-checking/hoaxes on the same page), several connect to good practice material. As the list is updated regularly, it's best to search it for words like *quiz* and *practice* to find those exercises.

Perhaps the most helpful resource is Newsroom 101, a wide collection of quizzes for editors. While most users are teachers and students enrolled in specific classes, individuals can sign up for access on their own (http://news room101.net/students/working-on-your-own). Access requires paying a small fee, but the site is well worth the cost.

If all of that is not enough practice, there's always Google and Bing to help you find exercises. A sample search for *AP style exercises and answers* yielded more than 100,000 hits. Not all will be useful, but there are likely some gems in that bunch.

Student Study Site

Visit the Student Resource Site at **http://study.sagepub.com/lieb** to access:

■ Chapter-by-chapter **web quizzes** for independent assessment of course material
■ List of online web links and general resources

Chapter 8 Handling Matters of Ethics, Fairness, Taste and Sensitivity

The previous two chapters have covered what journalists have *the right to do* – or inversely, what they are prohibited from doing by law. But many situations journalists find themselves in are not so clear-cut, and they need to proceed carefully to make sure they pick *the right thing to do*.

Journalists in the free world are, fortunately and unfortunately, left more to their own devices in making good choices than are most professionals. Doctors, lawyers, psychiatrists and many other professionals are bound by a **code of ethics**. A doctor cannot perform unnecessary surgery, a lawyer cannot divulge damaging information about a client, a psychiatrist cannot have sex with patients – such actions would cost them their licenses.

But having an enforceable code of ethics for journalists would entail licensing them, and that raises serious free press concerns. As a 2010 report by the Center for International Media Assistance notes:

> Licensing journalists continues to thrive as one way (among many) used by governments to control the press. An examination of regulatory practices in more than 100 developed and developing countries found that at least one out of every four governments have a role in licensing – that is, in approving who can work as a journalist and who cannot. Government policies that restrict the independence of journalists – including licensing – should be examined closely. This report concludes that organizations of journalists themselves are best equipped to regulate the ethical and professional standards of journalism and recommends that laws on licensing in developing countries be brought into line with international conventions on free expression.[1]

That concern is at the heart of a long-running debate about who is a journalist, which for years had bloggers and other independent Web publishers pulling out their hair. Though by and large the independents today have the same rights as establishment journalists, even the U.S. government often reignites the fire by giving preferential treatment to some journalists over others. One case in point was the release of guidelines on investigations involving the news media in the wake of the fallout from leak scandals involving the monitoring of AP and Fox News reporters in 2013. In the guidelines, the Justice Department "effectively exclude[d] bloggers and freelancers from protection," according to the Electronic Frontier Foundation. The EFF added, "The report is part of a broader legislative effort in Washington to simultaneously offer protection for the press while narrowing the scope of who is afforded it."[2]

Given such fundamental disagreements, the best that U.S. journalists can hope for is a nonenforceable ethics code. And fortunately, there are a few of those. But we start by considering the range of ethical issues editors are likely to encounter.

Ethical Issues

The range of ethical issues that journalists face is vast. And many of the situations that arise can lead to serious differences of opinions on the best way to proceed. But we begin our discussion with a few issues that are mostly cut and dried.

Fabrication

The first of these is fabrication, that is, making up information. This is a slam dunk: No journalist should ever do it. As we will see when we look at ethics codes, the fundamental rule of journalism is to tell the truth. And yet from time to time, cases of journalists fabricating information pop up in the news. Some of the most famous include:

- Washington Post reporter Janet Cooke, who was forced to return a Pulitzer Prize she won for her fabricated story about an 8-year-old heroin addict;
- New York Times reporter Jayson Blair, whose "widespread fabrication and plagiarism represent a profound betrayal of trust and a low point in the 152-year history of the newspaper,"[3] according to an unprecedented Page One apology to readers;
- Detroit Free Press reporter (and renowned author) Mitch Albom's advance story about two former Michigan State basketball players attending a Final Four game (the players' plans changed, and they did not attend); and
- Stephen Glass, who fabricated more than 30 articles for The New Republic as well as others for George and Rolling Stone magazines, and one for Policy Review. (Glass's transgressions were so noteworthy that they became the subject of the film "Shattered Glass.")[4]

As Steve Buttry, former digital transformation editor for Digital First Media, has noted:

Journalists must be able to vouch for the facts in their stories. … Under no circumstances should a journalist fill in even the slightest gap in a story, even with a logical presumption. Fabrication is fabrication. It is and should be a firing offense. Fabrication does not come in degrees any more than virginity or death come in degrees. Make up a tiny fact that probably is close to the truth to fill a small gap in a story and you've taken the first step on a path that will lead to bigger lies and eventual discovery and disgrace.[5]

Plagiarism

Closely related to fabrication is plagiarism, that is, using someone else's work and claiming it as one's own. It's nearly impossible to make the case that this is ever acceptable; plagiarism is theft, plain and simple. But it seems that barely a week goes by without a report of a journalist plagiarizing someone else's work (and politicians, historians, preachers and others often fall prey to the same temptation). The problem is so common and widespread that trying to excuse a case of it as "a careless mistake" just does not cut it. No matter where non-original material comes from, it needs to be attributed, and any exact phrases or sentences need to be enclosed in quotes. Steve Buttry suggests a good method for avoiding unintentional plagiarism:

If you ever copy a passage electronically directly from an Internet source, another newspaper or an electronic document for use in a story or an electronic notes file, type quotation marks and the source name before you paste the passage into your story. Paste the passage inside the quotation marks so that no faulty memory or confusion later results in presenting it as your own. You may end up cutting the passage down or paraphrasing it, but you will have the attribution right there and you will know whether you are using someone else's words.[6]

CASE STUDY

Printing a False Story to Prevent Murders

While there seems to be no room in journalism for fabrication, at least one newspaper does not regret its decision to publish a false story.

The Seattle-area newspaper Eastside Journal (now called the King County Journal) agreed to publish a made-up story about an arson to help police bust the man who was trying to get a cellmate to commit a real arson. The story had many twists: The man was already in prison for the murder of his wife; the house he was trying to have torched was the home of his son as well as the slain woman's mother. Just to make matters more interesting, the convict had tried to have his son and mother-in-law killed previously. And that arson was just the first step of a revenge plot he hoped to pull off: If it was successful, he also wanted the four children of the deputy prosecutor who tried his murder case to be killed.

Officials were tipped off by a prison informant, and they grabbed the cellmate as soon as he was released. He agreed to cooperate, but he told officials the convict demanded a newspaper article about the arson as proof that he had completed it.

So officials approached the local paper. While many publishers would not even entertain the notion of publishing a totally fabricated story, Journal Editor Tom Wolfe said, "Journalistically, we'll probably take some heat for it, but we have a responsibility to the community and that weighed heavily in our decision."

Ethics experts unanimously weighed in against such practices. Michael Parks, director of the Annenberg School of Journalism at the University of Southern California, said: "There's no room in a news report for a false, made-up story. [Doing so] violates the canons of journalism."[7]

The only possible gray area concerns how much material a writer can use from his or her previous work or the archives of his or her publication without giving credit. Such a case occurred in 2006 when The Baltimore Sun dismissed Michael Olesker, a columnist for nearly 30 years, for borrowing language from The Washington Post, The New York Times and the Sun itself. On the surface, that firing sounds reasonable, but a closer look at the material Olesker was accused of lifting makes the case somewhat murkier. According to the Post, Tom Rosenstiel – at the time working for the Project for Excellence in Journalism, more recently at the American Press Institute – said that the case did not seem clear-cut, in that most of the examples involve "background factual material rather than descriptive narrative that is in the author's voice," and that Olesker's language was "not identical." Rosenstiel added that it is "not uncommon practice to take background material from clippings." In addition, the Post noted, there was speculation that Olesker's dismissal was his punishment for being engaged in a long feud with the governor's office over his reporting. Olesker told the Post that his editors "needed to show they're not going to allow even the slightest error."[8]

A similar type of plagiarism was the focus of a more recent case, when a summer intern at the Toronto Star submitted an article on vanity license plates that "contained six paragraphs that were plagiarized 'in form and substance' from the work of another Star journalist." While the paper's public editor acknowledged that it was not uncommon for reporters to recycle some material from its archives, "This was not a matter of grabbing a couple of paragraphs of background information from the Star's archives, as I expect every journalist here has done. This was indeed a clear case of plagiarism."[9] The intern owned up to his action in a blog post:

Yes, I felt pressured to clean up, analyze and convert a data set I'd just received into an online database to accompany the story.

Yes, I was feeling burned out after spending a month of evenings and weekends working on code that would scrape the city's lobbyist registry.

But frankly, I can't make excuses for the inexcusable. No matter how much pressure there is in a newsroom, no matter how tired you may be, there's no justifying plagiarism.

In one moment I committed professional harikiri and – more importantly – I let down my editors, my Star colleague Dale and the Star readers.[10]

For further reading on the topics of fabrication and plagiarism, download the free e-book "Telling the Truth and Nothing But" (http://www.rjionline.org/sites/default/files/aces_telling_the_truth_1.pdf). The invaluable book is the result of a project undertaken by a host of companies, institutions and organizations, including the Poynter Institute; the American Copy Editors Society; the American Society of News Editors; the Online News Association; the Radio, Television, Digital News Association; and the Society of Professional Journalists.

The good news for honest journalists today is that search engines and social media make it easier than ever before to catch plagiarists. Using Google or another search tool to find a suspect phrase speeds things up in a manner unimaginable not long ago. In fact, it was a simple search by an alert copy editor at CNN that led to the dismissal of an editor who had plagiarized parts of more than 50 stories.[11]

And even when journalists themselves are not suspicious, readers and sources can take to social media to point out similarities between pieces, acting as de facto editors/detectives in the process.

Image Manipulation

Another area that has little wiggle room is the manipulation of images. Retouching and removing details from news photos was common for news organizations as recently as the 1980s. But with the introduction of powerful computer image editing programs like

The Associated Press severed its working relationship with photographer Miguel Tovar after he cloned dust in a photo and used it to obscure his own shadow.[14]

http://www.poynter.org/latest-news/mediawire/138728/ap-drops-freelance-photographer-who-photoshopped-his-shadow-out-of-image/

Photoshop since then, an ethos has emerged that regards photos as facts – and just as with all other facts, they should not be changed. Despite that, major news organizations have made some unbelievable changes to photos in the recent past. Notable cases include:

- Time magazine making a mug shot of suspected killer O.J. Simpson appear darker and more threatening looking for a cover;
- National Geographic moving the Egyptian pyramids closer together so they would better fit in the vertical format of the magazine's cover; and
- Newsweek magazine placing Martha Stewart's head on a slimmer body – belonging to someone else – for a cover article about her release from prison.

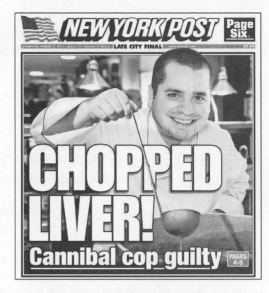

Such major manipulations are becoming rarer. But even minor changes to photos are taken seriously. The Code of Ethics of the National Press Photographers Association clearly states that photographers should "not manipulate images or add or alter sound in any way that can mislead viewers or misrepresent subjects,"[12] and many news organizations are even stricter than that. For instance, former Pulitzer Prize–nominated photographer Allan Detrich was forced to resign from the Toledo Blade after it was found that he made minor edits to photos. As another photographer noted: "His edits by most standards would seem minor. The removal of distracting elements; someone's legs behind a sign, the removal of a wire passing through his image or the addition of a basketball. … As a photographer that makes minor edits to my photos from time to time it's amazing to think that such a small edit can have such detrimental impact to [one's] career. The result of these edits by Allan Detrich has resulted in painful consequences including suspension of publication of his photos by the Toledo Blade, Reuters and AP, and his ultimate resignation."[13] (For the record, a subsequent investigation of Detrich's work revealed dozens of similar cases.)

Beyond minimal retouching for technical purposes, the best guideline is to leave photos alone. The only exception is when they are used for illustrative purposes, such as on feature articles, in food sections, and so on. But even in those instances, they clearly must be labeled as illustrations unless readers could not possibly mistake them for the real thing. And the labels must be obvious, not hidden in the photos themselves.

When a New York City police officer was found guilty of conspiracy to kidnap and eat women in early 2013, the New York Post decided to make it the cover story. The front page headline "CHOPPED LIVER – Cannibal cop guilty" ran over a picture of the smiling officer dressed as a chef and holding a soup ladle. Only it wasn't really the officer: His head had been digitally inserted into the picture. The Post barely acknowledged its alteration by burying a tiny note in the picture itself: "Post photo composite." Critics complained that most readers would not notice the disclosure (See http://www.imediaethics.org/News/3814/Nypost_photoshops_front_page_photo_of_cannibal_cop_gilberto_valle__discloses_in_tiny_print.php for more). As for the officer, in mid-2014 a federal judge overturned his kidnapping conspiracy conviction.

http://www.poynter.org/latest-news/mediawire/207002/new-york-post-quietly-acknowledges-its-cannibal-cop-front-page-is-photoshopped/attachment/newyorkpost-cannibalcop/

Getting Information via Deception

Things become a little murkier when the topic turns to using deception to gather information. While on the surface doing so would seem to be a clear violation of the journalist's first rule of truth-telling, in some cases news organizations have argued that using deception was the only way to break important stories. The use of deception in journalism has a long history. A review of a book on the topic highlights some of the cases:

A reporter for Horace Greeley's New York Tribune used a variety of cloaking strategies while covering the American South just before the Civil War, including lying to sources about where he was from and changing "names, places, and dates" in his dispatches to avoid detection. In 1887, New York World reporter Nellie Bly became famous for impersonating a lunatic to gain admittance to a madhouse so she could report on its awful conditions. Between the 1960s and the 1990s … a variety of mainstream newspapers exposed housing discrimination by having black and white reporters pose as home buyers or prospective tenants. Gloria Steinem scored a cultural exposé in the early 1960s when she used her grandmother's name and Social Security number to get a job as a Playboy bunny and wrote about it for Show magazine. In 1992, ABC News exposed substandard meat-handling practices at Food Lion, but told a raft of lies to get its reporters inside as employees.[15]

Cases can be much subtler than those. For example, a reporter concealing his or her identity on social media, listservs or in discussion groups would generally be seen as employing deception, as would someone publishing information obtained from those settings without first obtaining permission. Similarly, most people would see the publication of information from private communication – emails, direct Twitter messages, Facebook conversations – as a form of deception if the writer has not obtained permission.[16]

No less an authority than Bob Steele, the Poynter Institute's former ethics scholar, notes: "I'm not an absolutist on these matters of truth versus lies. I believe there are some situations – rare, exceptional cases – when deception may be justified."[17] Steele lists several criteria for when deception – and, similarly, hidden cameras – can be justified; all of the criteria must be met:

- "When the information obtained is of profound importance;
- "It must be of vital public interest, such as revealing great 'system failure' at the top levels, or it must prevent profound harm to individuals;
- "When all other alternatives for obtaining the same information have been exhausted;
- "When the journalists involved are willing to disclose the nature of the deception and the reason for it;
- "When the individuals involved and their news organization apply excellence, through outstanding craftsmanship as well as the commitment of time and funding needed to pursue the story fully;
- "When the harm prevented by the information revealed through deception outweighs any harm caused by the act of deception; and
- "When the journalists involved have conducted a meaningful, collaborative, and deliberative decisionmaking process on the ethical and legal issues."[18]

Using deception for any other purposes – e.g., saving time, winning a prize – does not meet this test and in actuality may bring more harm than good.

Funding Issues

While the issues addressed so far are all important ones, some would argue that the fundamental ethical issue for publishers in the digital era concerns funding. As longtime journalist Gene Foreman noted in a lecture in early 2013, the need to fund "is fundamentally an ethical issue because news organizations have a moral obligation. Their social responsibility is to give their communities accurate, reliable information that enables citizens to intelligently make governing decisions. That kind of journalism costs a great deal of money."

Foreman went on to enumerate some of the more serious ethical lapses he has seen as publishers look for new ways of making money:

- "Embedding advertising messages in the text of news stories on the web;
- "Displaying an advertiser's coffee cups in front of TV anchors as they delivered the news;
- "Naming a radio newsroom for an advertiser, so that the introduction to each newscast would be a plug for that advertiser; and
- "Staging television interview shows that were really promotions for advertisers."

But the worst problem in the eyes of Foreman and many others is "a trend toward advertising that blurs the line between news and ads – if not removing that line entirely." Such intrusions are not new to the digital age. As Foreman notes, the battle over how to properly designate **advertorials** in magazines and newspapers is ongoing:

> We editors argued that these ads are rooted in deception – namely, the suggestion to the reader that the message is not advertising but news content. It appears to be the newspaper's endorsement of the product being sold. We pointed out that advertorials erode credibility of the real news and thereby diminish the brand, which in the long term reduces our value as an advertising vehicle.

In print, publishers made minor concessions such as using disclaimers and different typefaces than they used in the news columns. But, Foreman notes: "On the web, even those distinctions are under attack. The current buzz phrase in advertising circles is 'native advertising.' That is, advertising that not only resembles editorial content but specifically resembles the editorial content 'native' to the website in which the advertising appears."[19]

Foreman cites two examples of this problem. First was the controversial move by The Atlantic Monthly to publish an advertorial by the Church of Scientology that was labeled "sponsor content."[20] The site found itself in the center of a storm, and the advertorial was pulled. For his second example, Foreman cites Forbes.com's push to add **marketer content** that would routinely be mixed with editorial content. "If schemes like these prevail," he notes, "news consumers will be confused about whether an article they are reading was written by a journalist or a marketer. And that's a crucial difference."[21] The issue of sponsored content is widespread in the news industry: Many reports of the dismissal of New York Times Executive Editor Jill Abramson noted that she had clashed with management over the issue before her firing. "She was morally opposed to that," an executive told New York Magazine. "She told me it would not happen on her watch."[22]

Some observers believe the breakdown of the traditional wall between editorial and business departments – known in the news business as **the separation of church and state** – can lead to an even bigger ethical problem: self-censorship. That is, whether stories are written, or certain aspects are played up or down, is based on perceptions that acting otherwise could lead to financial penalties. Sometimes self-censorship is a response to direct advertiser pressures, but in many other cases more subtle forces come into play: for example, a publisher steering a reporter away from one story and to another or suggesting that an event staged by a major advertiser is worth a story.[23]

It might appear that there is good news on this front as some news publishers move to a nonprofit model. But as longtime broadcast reporter turned journalism professor Adam Hochberg told Columbia Journalism Review, "Moving from a for-profit to a nonprofit funding model doesn't always take pressure off journalistic outlets, because foundations often want more input than advertisers simply seeking eyeballs."[24]

Transparency

The digital era has opened journalists to more thorough and more rapid scrutiny than ever before. Readers have at their fingertips access to a seemingly limitless pool of information on every topic imaginable. In that environment, it is vital that journalists do not try to hide information – or how they get their information, who their sources are, what they do and do not know, and how they make decisions on choosing and reporting stories. Failing to disclose any of those things means a journalist has failed in his or her obligation to be truthful with the audience.

Such transparency also seems only fair given what journalists expect of their sources. As openness advocate Jeff Jarvis notes: "It is our turn to open the shades, to reveal our process and prejudice, to engage in the conversation, to join in the community – to be transparent. Shouldn't we, of all people and professions, be the most transparent?"[25]

As much as possible, such information should be included within stories or, if not practical, in a sidebar. But journalists also should link to source materials whenever possible so readers can examine them for themselves and assess the journalists' performance. Such

CASE STUDY

Stopping the Presses

A man kidnaps his ex-wife and takes her back to her home where he holds her hostage. The neighborhood is evacuated while authorities ramp up an emergency response. And then he makes a demand: The media must stop covering him and the story.

The 2009 case in Hartford, Connecticut, tested just how far media would go to comply with the demands of a criminal. Local TV station WFSB and local paper The Day both acquiesced to the demand, but set strict limits for how long they would agree to the blackout: four hours for the former and two for the latter. But another news outlet, the Hartford Courant, had already published a story on its website, and the hostage-taker demanded it be deleted or he would blow up the house he was in. The editors of that publication decided that they would not unpublish the story.

Which of the media acted ethically and which didn't? It would be harder to find a better illustration of the tension between informing the public and protecting people, and obviously the editors making the calls differed on how best to do that. WFSB and The Day both had contact with the hostage-taker, and therefore probably had an advantage in that they could get a sense of how likely he was to follow through on his threats. In addition, they had not already committed to the story – ethically, it seems far easier to support holding off on a story than taking down one that's already out there. The Courant had no contact with the hostage-taker, so it had no easy way to assess what authorities were saying about him. A review of the case by Columbia Journalism Review takes The Courant's editors to task for not backing down, suggesting they should have taken it down "until they did all they could to satisfy themselves that publishing the story would not endanger lives."

Fortunately, the story itself had an ending that, while not happy, was not as tragic as feared, either. The hostage managed to escape from the house, her ex-husband set it on fire, and he was arrested. It turned out he had no weapons or explosives, but for at least a little while, he had possessed the power to stop the presses.[26]

information can include the full data set for stories about poll results, audio and video interview clips, official documents, maps and more.

While transparency is most important for the biggest stories, it should be practiced whenever possible. For instance, on a CNET consumer guide to the best Blu-ray discs for showing off a home theater, the author included this note:

> Though my face is at the top of the column, the list was compiled with input from editors John Falcone, Matthew Moskovciak, and David Katzmaier, who look at a lot of video content in their day-to-day testing of products. We also keep an eye on AVS Forum's Blu-ray picture quality and audio quality threads, and have always appreciated the site's tiered rating system.[27]

Working to be transparent is often a balancing act. Journalists might not have ready access to some source material, and opening up in that way invites reader criticism about missed sources, interviews, and so on. At least one media attorney opposes reporters sharing their notes. "It is very common to take notes about things you might forget, but not take notes about things you would not forget," he said. Therefore, it might seem to readers that reporters have neglected to check important matters.[28]

Balance and Fairness

Closely related to the idea of transparency are the concepts of balance and fairness. While the well-known phrase advises that "there are two sides to every story," good journalists know there are often more than that. So stories should contain enough information to give readers a thorough understanding of the issues at hand. Doing less than that is neither fair nor balanced.

At the same time, good journalists also know that not every side – or opinion – is equally valid. So their job is to weigh the evidence at hand and present their reasoned conclusions. This has been a hard change to make for many traditional journalists, who have come up in an era of "he said, she said" reporting, where all sides are given equal weight, no matter how much stronger or weaker they are. But with reporting on issues such as climate change – with 97 percent of climate scientists agreeing that trends over the past century are very likely due to human activities – some news organizations have begun to back off the practice of giving equal coverage to the tiny but vocal opposition. Clinging to traditional ideas of fairness in such cases merely obscures a settled issue and argues against the need to address it, a point that the BBC acknowledged in 2014 when it began sending journalists to courses to train them to avoid airing the "marginal views" of nonexperts.[29]

But there is a catch to this shift away from adhering to the traditional standard of balanced reporting. It has been driven in part by a move to more partisan journalism, which tends to draw a lot of online traffic and television viewers. In some cases, there is no attempt to find balance. Opposing facts are left out and minor points are played up, and audience members end up knowing less about an issue than if they had just tuned out.

Further, such journalism can lead to a slippery slope that ultimately diminishes the audience's respect for the reporter and publication. As Gene Foreman notes, journalists traditionally have kept their opinions to themselves to avoid the perception of bias. But many bloggers pride themselves on disclosing their opinions. Some journalists think that is a good idea: "They say that we can build credibility if we disclose our opinions," Foreman writes. But doing so "ignores the reality that citizen bloggers are all about expressing opinion, while professional journalists should be all about seeking truth."[30]

Finally, fairness includes not jumping to conclusions about people's involvement in unsavory activities. Setting aside possible legal repercussions from doing so, such actions plant a seed of doubt in the minds of the audience that will linger long after a person might be cleared of any such association. One tragic example of this involved the New York Post in the follow-up of the Boston Marathon bombings. The Post used a picture on its cover showing two young men who had watched the race but left before the bombings, with a huge headline labeling them "Bag Men." A secondary headline added "Feds seek this duo pictured at Boston Marathon." Inside the paper, another headline read "Feds Have 2 Men In Sights."

When the two men in the picture were cleared of any association with the bombings, the Post defended its action by saying it was merely following up on an email from the FBI. But that email was only a request for help identifying people in photos, and did not make any charges against them. The Post's lawyers said it should be clear to anyone who noticed this passage in the story: "There is no direct evidence linking [the two men] to the crime but authorities want to identify them." Ultimately, the Post's legal defense was as follows:

> In the final analysis, all that plaintiffs ultimately have to say by way of complaint is that the Post printed a large headline that brought more attention to them than they believe was warranted, and that readers who jump to conclusions might have jumped to a wrong one – at least until they realized a day later that they were wrong.

As one media critic responded: "[One] couldn't ask for a purer distillation of the New York Post's ethic: How dare those readers reach the very conclusion to which our suggestive headline and photograph led them? And sorry if our publication showers on them more attention than they expected for attending a marathon."[31] Ultimately, the men sued for defamation and won an undisclosed settlement from the Post.

Conflicts of Interest

Closely related to the issues of balance and fairness is the issue of conflicts of interest. Essentially, this refers to factors that would compromise a journalist's independence and judgment, typically but not only because of a likely financial benefit.

Among the most common problem areas are accepting tickets and other types of gifts from a source, taking part in press junkets, engaging in political activities, writing about friends or family members, writing anonymously or under a pseudonym for other publications, and having financial dealings with people and companies being covered.

One recent high-profile case involved AOL and Michael Arrington. In 2010, AOL bought the TechCrunch blog for $30 million. A large appeal of the blog was "its outspoken, controversial and well-connected founder, Michael Arrington." But a year later, Arrington founded CrunchFund, "a venture capital fund backed by AOL that invests in start-ups like those that TechCrunch covers." A tug of war ensued, with AOL initially saying that Arrington would remain at TechCrunch, but then deciding that he could not maintain an editorial presence. So two weeks after CrunchFund's launch, Arrington left AOL.[32]

Reflecting on the case, journalist and tech guru Amy Webb wrote:

> As far as conflicts of interest go. … Where are all of the conversations? Can someone who's a business journalist count startup founders as their weekend buddies? Because I know a whole bunch of folks who get early access to lots of companies over Saturday night beers and poker games. (Hell, I host some of them.) Is it OK for someone like NYT blogger Brian Stelter to date someone in the industry he's covering? Can editors and publishers serve on advisory boards to any startups in the tech space?
>
> I think that people assume everyone's on the same page, and I know that HR departments have employees sign lengthy documents spelling out policies. But in practice – as we think about our day-to-day interactions – more journalists should be asking this question: is what we're doing professionally acceptable?[33]

Anonymity and Confidentiality

Another practice long the subject of debate is the use of anonymous sources. In some cases, anonymous sources are the key to breaking an important story – such was the case with "Deep Throat," the source of a great deal of information on the Watergate break-in, ultimately bringing down a president. In other cases, sources request anonymity because they fear retribution for sharing vital information, or doing so puts their lives at risk. But more often, anonymity is granted for less worthy ends. Especially when it comes to reporting on government and politics, the cloak of anonymity has led many people to float information – true or not – that could harm their opponents, with little fear of being exposed as the source of that information. Those types of stories are "lazy and counter-productive, because the story becomes little more than propaganda dressed-up with a byline," says Antony Loewenstein of the Guardian.[34]

Audience members have no way to judge the worthiness of information provided by anonymous sources. If a source's motives and status are unclear, it's impossible to judge the quality of the information he or she provides. At a minimum, writers should provide enough information about anonymous sources to give readers a sense of their motivations for talking. Doing so may well help prevent cases like the one involving the aforementioned Jayson Blair, who invented confidential law enforcement sources in the Beltway sniper case. Not only were his anonymous sources unreliable, they did not even exist.

Further, the issue of anonymity can lead to legal problems for journalists. As the Society of Professional Journalists notes: "Keep your promise not to identify a source of information and it's possible to find yourself facing a grand jury, a judge and a jail cell. On the other hand, break your promise of confidentiality to that source and it's just possible you might find yourself on the receiving end of a lawsuit."[35] And the NPR Ethics Handbook advises reporters that

> Courts can compel journalists to testify or reveal information even when confidentiality has been promised, and refusal to reveal the information can result in jail time or fines. Judith Miller of the New York Times, for example, spent three months in jail for refusing to identify the source of the leak that Valerie Plame worked for the CIA.
>
> To make matters worse, if we have promised confidentiality to a source but disclose the source's identity, we could be liable for breach of contract.[36]

Because of all those concerns, most publishers enact strict guidelines governing when anonymous sources can be used and for what purposes. At a minimum, those guidelines require that all anonymous sources be verified. In many cases, such guidelines are enough to motivate reporters to dig deeper or press their sources to go on the record. But despite that kind of encouragement, the widespread and unwarranted use of anonymous sources continues. For example, the Anonymous Source Tracker catalogued nearly 300,000 examples of anonymous sources in 11,614 English-language news outlets from early 2010 through the end of 2013.

In recent years, controversy has arisen over another form of anonymity, that offered to those who comment on articles posted online. While encouraging online comments is a great way to engage the audience, many online publications have found that allowing readers to post anonymously leads to spam, name-calling and general vitriol. As the American Journalism Review noted:

> News sites must strike a delicate balance when deciding whether to allow those who comment to remain anonymous: To attract users, sites want to make it as easy as possible for people to participate, and anonymity allows users to feel less inhibited when they comment. ...
>
> At its best, the removal of inhibitions can lead to a lively but civil exchange of ideas. At its worst, it can mean profanity, and sites are loath to alienate potential community members, tarnishing their brands in the process.[37]

Those factors and the sheer volume of comments have led some publications to reconsider a policy of allowing anonymous posts. In 2013, for instance, The Huffington Post announced it would no longer allow anonymous comments. As founder Arianna Huffington told a conference:

> Trolls are just getting more and more aggressive and uglier and I just came from London where there are rape and death threats. ... I feel that freedom of expression is given to people who stand up for what they say and not hiding behind anonymity. We need to evolve a platform to meet the needs of the grown-up Internet.[38]

It's still too early to tell what such changes mean for the future of anonymity. Some sites have reported that the number and quality of comments increased after restrictions were imposed.[39] But at least one study suggests the opposite. Over a four-year period, commenting laws in South Korea were tightened. But the tightening ended after a Korean Communications Commission study found that malicious comments dropped by less than 1 percent. In addition, hackers swarmed the sites, most likely trying to steal users' identities. And a follow-up study "found that the policy actually increased the frequency of expletives in comments for some user demographics."[40]

Withholding Information That Could Lead to Harm

Sometimes a journalist must grapple with whether publishing certain information is likely to needlessly harm a person. For example, even though it is legal to publish the names of sex crime victims, most mainstream news organizations do not. Their thinking is that doing so will victimize those affected for a second time. Therefore, most reputable publishers don't reveal the names of sexual assault victims unless they grant permission. But with news spreading through myriad means today, it usually requires little effort to find the identity and picture of a rape victim. Even before the Internet arrived, some were arguing that it was time to change that policy. Probably the best known advocate of naming sexual assault victims is University of Southern California journalism professor Geneva Overholser. As she told The Atlanta Journal-Constitution:

> We value name identification in journalism for all kinds of reasons – accuracy and verifiability prime among them – and we should not exempt only these adult victims of crime. ... Second, we are not in a position to judge guilt or innocence, which we imply when we "protect" one party ... but name the other. ... Third, it has become virtually meaningless in the digital era to offer this "protection" since facts will out.[41]

In other cases, information has been withheld to protect lives or for reasons of safety. For instance, in recent years a sad fact of journalism has been that many reporters and photographers have been held captive by militants, rebels, criminals and paramilitary forces. And, notes the Committee to Protect Journalists, "At any given time, a small handful of these cases – sometimes one or two, sometimes more – have been purposely kept out of the news media."[42]

The thinking in such cases is that "a frenzy of questions and attention can make a quick negotiation for release tougher, either by spooking captors, or by raising their perception of the financial or propaganda value of their captive." But sometimes that plan backfires: "In some cases too much silence can be dangerous. If kidnappers know they've got someone high profile … and then there's no news, they can get to wondering if their captive is actually a spy working under journalist cover. In others, obviously, publicity can be very dangerous. Every situation has its different particulars."[43]

Decisions about withholding coverage in such situations rarely are easy. But editors requested to make them would be well served by following this advice from the Committee to Protect Journalists: "The key tests are whether press coverage will work for or against the captive individuals (whether they are news personnel or not) and how the captives' interests are balanced against the public's right to information."[44]

Matters become even more complicated when the source of a request to withhold information is a government agency. For instance, the Obama administration requested U.S. news media not to report the information that Raymond Davis, a Special Forces soldier who had killed two Pakistanis, was in fact a contractor working for the CIA. For several weeks The New York Times and other major U.S. news organizations obliged, finally breaking the news only after the Guardian in England published it. Glenn Greenwald of the Guardian noted of the incident:

> It's one thing for a newspaper to withhold information because they believe its disclosure would endanger lives. But here, the U.S. Government has spent weeks making public statements that were misleading in the extreme – Obama's calling Davis "our diplomat in Pakistan" – while the NYT deliberately concealed facts undermining those government claims because government officials told them to do so. That's called being an active enabler of government propaganda. … Moreover, since there is no declared war in Pakistan, this incident – as the NYT puts it today – "inadvertently pulled back the curtain on a web of covert American operations inside Pakistan, part of a secret war run by the C.I.A." That alone makes Davis' work not just newsworthy, but crucial.[45]

Taste and Sensitivity

Occasionally, editors are confronted with the question of whether something is too gruesome or otherwise offensive to be published – or even linked to. Standards of acceptability have definitely changed over time. In 1963, after Jack Ruby shot Lee Harvey Oswald, the assassin of President John F. Kennedy, Ruby told police, "I hope I killed the son of a bitch." At the time, no general newspaper would print such language. Even the few that substituted "S.O.B." surely raised eyebrows. But when Vice President Dick Cheney told Sen. Patrick Leahy to "Go fuck yourself" in 2004, some publications saw nothing wrong with printing the comment. But many editors remained uncomfortable with such strong language, substituting a strategic dash or two.[46]

Around the same time, more graphic images from the wars in Iran and Afghanistan began making their way to some publications. Disturbing images of dead and severely wounded troops and civilians made many editors question their appropriateness. Web publications found a solution in setting up warning screens that made viewers click before they could see the images and videos. But in print, it's impossible to create a comparable kind of opt-out. So in most cases a good deal of debate goes on before deciding to publish. The key questions always should be, "How does publishing this serve the public interest?" and "What harm could come from publishing this?"

The issue was the subject of hot debate in connection with the 2013 Boston Marathon bombings. For instance, one of the images showed a victim being taken away in a wheelchair, with his lower legs blown off and only splintered remains visible. Some of the news media used the photo as it was taken, others cropped it to hide the gruesome lower half, and still others ran the entire photo but blurred the victim's face.[47]

In another case a few months earlier, debate arose over the use of the New York Post's cover photo of a man who had been pushed onto the tracks in front of an approaching subway train. Freelance photographer R. Umar Abbasi shot photos of the man as he struggled to pull himself up. Some wondered whether Abbasi could have saved the man if he hadn't shot the scene. But Abbasi said that he wanted to use the flash on his camera to alert the oncoming train, and that he was afraid to get closer to help the man because his attacker was

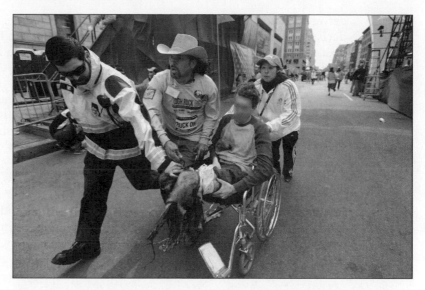

Graphic images can test the boundaries of good taste and privacy. This photo of a victim of the Boston Marathon bombing was handled differently by various news outlets. Some blurred the man's face, others did not, and some put it behind a warning screen on their websites.

AP Photo/Charles Krupa

The New York Times' graphic photo of a victim of a shooting at the Empire State Building generated controversy.

http://www.thewire.com/national/2012/08/new-york-times-says-graphic-empire-state-shooting-photo-was-newsworthy/56186/

between them. While all of that might have been true, there was still outrage over the Post's decision to run the photo on its cover. As David Carr of The New York Times wrote, "The Post cover treatment neatly embodies everything people hate and suspect about the news media business: not only are journalists bystanders, moral and ethical eunuchs who don't intervene when danger or evil presents itself, but perhaps they secretly root for its culmination." (Interestingly, the Times chose not to include the photo with Carr's column, with him noting that "We chose not to reproduce it here because tut-tutting about a salacious photo while enjoying the benefits of its replication seems inappropriate.")[48]

Similar controversy raged over The New York Times' photo of the victim of a shooting at the Empire State Building a few months earlier. As one article noted of the discussion surrounding the "startlingly graphic photo of a victim in this morning's Empire State Building shooting lying next to a vivid, red pool of blood," reader reaction was strong – but mixed. One Twitter user praised the paper for showing the "bloody consequences of gun violence." According to Dean Baquet (then the Times' managing editor for news and now its executive editor), the paper decided to run the photo because it was newsworthy:

> It was a graphic image, of course. But it is a running news story and we thought it was a newsworthy image. We have heard from many people who found it jarring, and we understand that. We have also heard from some who thought it important to show the results of public acts of violence.[49]

Making the Right Decisions

Recognizing the many types of ethical issues is a good starting point for any editor. Unfortunately, the hard part comes next: making good decisions. In all but the most straightforward cases – such as plagiarism and fabrication – there often seem to be two, three or even more reasonable alternatives.

Some people believe the answers always can be found in classical ethical theories. Based on the work of Plato, Aristotle, Immanuel Kant, John Rawls and others, these theories offer fundamental guidance with any types of ethical problems.[50] Unfortunately, they often offer competing guidance, so the "right" decision might vary from one theory to the next.

Codes of professional ethics often prove more useful, as they are designed to deal with journalism in particular and include certain blanket prohibitions. But as the Editor's Toolkit at the end of this chapter makes clear, there is no shortage of ethics codes, which inevitably means the potential for conflicting advice, even within a given code. For example, a rule requiring that journalists must always tell the truth clearly will not always mesh with another rule that says journalists should not cause avoidable harm. And no code is exhaustive, covering all potential situations.

Perhaps the best attempt at creating a workable model was developed by Thomas Bivins, an ethics scholar at the University of Oregon. In an article in Journalism Educator, Bivins outlined a 13-step model that incorporates the classical theories as well as professional rules. His model culminates with the instruction to write up a defense of the decision that even someone who does not agree with that decision can understand.

In a nutshell, Bivins' steps involve answering these questions:

1. "What is the ethical issue/problem? (Define in one or two sentences.)

2. "What facts have the most bearing on the ethical decision you must render in this case?

3. "Are there any other external or internal factors to be considered? (Economic, political factors, etc.)

4. "Who are the claimants and in what way are you obligated to each of them? (List all affected by your decision.)

5. "What are the operant ideals? (For you, for the profession, for other affected parties)

6. "Do any of these ideals conflict? In what order would you honor them?

7. "What are your options, and which would be favored by each affected party? (List at least 3.)

8. "Which options could cause harm to any claimant?

9. "Would honoring any of the ideals listed above invalidate any of your options?

10. "Are there any rules or principles (legal, professional, organizational, or other) that automatically invalidate any of your options?

11. "Which classical ethical theories support or reject which options?

12. "Determine a course of action based on your analysis.

13. "Defend your decision in writing to your most adamant detractor."[51]

Is It Time for New Ethics Codes?

Some would argue that the biggest problem in trying to resolve ethical problems is that existing professional ethics codes generally share a fundamental flaw: Most predate the digital era, in some cases by decades. That also means they predate the era when anyone with access to a smartphone or public computer could become an online publisher. So some of the central ideas of media ethics in the past – such as the need to be objective – do not always apply today.

This disconnect raises ethical tensions on two levels, according to Stephen J.A. Ward of the University of Wisconsin Center for Journalism Ethics:

> On the first level, there is a tension between traditional journalism and online journalism. The culture of traditional journalism, with its values of accuracy, pre-publication verification, balance, impartiality, and gate-keeping, rubs up against the culture of online journalism which emphasizes immediacy, transparency, partiality, non-professional journalists and post-publication correction.
>
> On the second level, there is a tension between parochial and global journalism. If journalism has global impact, what are its global responsibilities? Should media ethics reformulate its aims and norms so as to guide a journalism that is now global in reach and impact? What would that look like?

Ward continues: "Media ethics must do more than point out these tensions. Theoretically, it must untangle the conflicts between values. It must decide which principles should be preserved or invented. Practically, it should provide new standards to guide online or offline journalism."[52]

Further, many argue for a need for ethics codes that actually address specific situations rather than just provide general advice. While that might be far in the future, one interesting step toward addressing that need turns up in the bios of the staff of Re/code, an independent tech news, reviews and analysis site. Each member of the editorial staff includes a personal code of ethics, with details about his or her potential conflicts in terms of their partners and families, investments, and consultancies (http://recode.net/about). Having the staffers do this forces them to think about where they might run into ethical problems and decide how they would deal with them – not a bad idea.

Diversity as an Ethical Concern

While not everyone would list it as an ethical problem per se, the lack of diversity in some publications means they fail to fully represent their audiences – and are likely going to pay a financial price for that failure.

It's no surprise that the population of the United States has grown increasingly diverse in recent decades. While whites are still a majority in nearly all states, a growing number of those who identify as white also identify as Hispanic (the largest ethnic minority). Black and Asian-Americans together make up more than 15 percent of the U.S. population. In addition, a sizeable number of others fall

(Continued)

(Continued)

into the remaining U.S. Census categories of American Indian and Alaska Native, Native Hawaiian and Other Pacific Islander, and people of two or more races. Further, women have for some time outnumbered men, and the numbers of senior citizens, people with disabilities and those identifying as LGBTQ have also increased in recent decades.

Yet many publications do not reflect those changing demographics. That became clear in a controversy over an article published by ESPN's Grantland.com in early 2014. To keep a long story short, a reporter investigating a super golf putter and its inventor gained access to her by agreeing to "focus on the science and not the scientist." But while researching and writing the piece, the author discovered that the inventor was a transgender woman, "a piece of information he found so interesting that he broke his agreement to focus on the science and not the scientist."[53] The author then proceeded to share that information with one of the company's investors, initiating a series of missteps that ultimately led to the inventor taking her own life before the story even was published. While more than a dozen editors and others read the piece before it was published, Grantland Editor-in-chief Bill Simmons admitted to "one massive mistake. … Someone familiar with the transgender community should have read [the] final draft. This never occurred to us. Nobody ever brought it up."[54] So the lack of diverse backgrounds and insights proved fatal in this case.

Not surprisingly, ignoring large segments of a potential audience or treating them poorly is not the best business strategy. When people don't feel included, they are likely to head elsewhere. A good editor works to make diversity a routine focus not only for the financial reason, but simply because it is the right thing to do. In particular, two areas call for critical evaluation:

- *Invisibility*. The first problem is a simple one: In many areas, coverage focuses nearly exclusively on members of one demographic group. That demographic more often than not is straight white men, and it's always worth asking whether others outside that group would not be worth talking to, if for no other reason than to add a unique perspective.
- *Stereotyping*. When traditional minorities are covered, the focus tends to be in one of three areas:

  a. "Problem" stories. Coverage often focuses on the problems caused by a group: crime, costs to society and so forth. Eric Deggans of The Tampa Bay Times has said, "When something explosive involves race, that's when we talk about it."[55] That's true of stories about many groups.

  b. The exception to the rule. Seemingly positive coverage sometimes highlights a successful individual as though he or she is an exception to the rule.

  c. Athletes and entertainers. Members of these groups tend to be covered at the expense of coverage of minorities in general.

While editors have a great deal on their plates, diversity is one task that cannot be ignored. In fact, every day it grows in importance.

Worry About This, Not About That

Using Public Social Media Posts Is OK, but Private Ones Probably Are Off-Limits

As a large percentage of the population has taken to posting information online, new ethical questions have arisen. As Alfred Hermida of the BBC has noted: "This content is both private and public at the same time. It is private in the sense that it was intended for a specific audience of friends. But it is also publicly available online. This is a new ethical area for journalists."[56]

The issue broke out in the wake of the 2007 shootings at Virginia Tech University. As students turned to Facebook to deal with their emotions and connect with others, journalists used Facebook to connect with the posters. As an article in the Guardian noted: "The tragedy may have been the moment when mainstream American news channels woke up to the immediacy and power of personal accounts on Facebook, Flickr, MySpace and Twitter. But it was also the moment many Web 2.0 users first encountered digital doorstepping."[57]

Since then, the issue of which social media posts are fair game for reporters' use has grown into a wide-ranging debate. On one hand, many believe that even private citizens' social media posts that do not have any privacy restrictions can be quoted in a media report. For instance, by its very nature, Twitter is a public forum (aside from tweets sent by people who have made their accounts private), so there is no prohibition from quoting from someone's feed (linking to the original tweet, of course). The same would seem to apply to any Facebook posts that can be accessed by anyone. (But the line is generally drawn at photos, because using them without permission would violate copyright. Still, that has not stopped news organizations from republishing Facebook photos of people involved in sex scandals and other sensational stories.)[58]

But what about posts that are intended to be more private? The consensus is that those are off-limits. If a person who is *not logged into a social media site* (such as Facebook) cannot access a post, that material is considered private. That point is critical, as some people set their privacy so that even friends of friends can view their posts, and some unscrupulous reporters might try to circumvent their intentions by sending friend requests to intermediaries.

There is one big *but*. If someone has posted information that points to his or her involvement in or planning of a crime,

many editors would argue that it is permissible to use that material no matter how it is obtained.

Overall, it's a fuzzy area, and one that is generally well worth worrying about. In one classic case, an independent news site did a remarkable job of covering the story of the murder of a Yale University student. To get some of its material, the managing editor got on Facebook and friended a former girlfriend of the suspect, someone who had also reported that the suspect had once assaulted her. While initially the editor did not identify herself as a journalist – a point she later regretted – she quickly did so, and the former girlfriend let her remain a friend.

But once the editor had discovered important information from the ex-girlfriend's posts (as well as from an interview), things became cloudier rather than clearer. Even though the editor decided she would not name the ex-girlfriend, questions were plentiful:

> Bailey [the editor] had another scoop in her sights, but was she on ethically safe ground using this information? On the one hand, it was difficult to consider the postings private given that Del Rocco [the ex-girlfriend] had some 350 Facebook friends. Moreover, even if they were private, hadn't Del Rocco granted Bailey access to them by not removing her as a friend once she'd learned she was a reporter? But on the other hand, was giving a reporter access to information the same thing as allowing it to be used in an article?[59]

Ultimately, the best advice is to seek the fine line between informing the public and not harming innocent people. As the reporter working under Bailey noted: "We were charging hard for this story. But we [didn't want] to be snakes."[60]

Wrapping Up

The range of ethical issues an editor confronts is wide, and in many cases there is no quick and ready solution. But being familiar with the most common problem areas and professional codes of ethics as well as knowing some classical ethical theory can go a long way toward helping make decisions that can be lived with.

Key Points

- Unlike many other professionals, U.S. journalists do not work under an enforceable code of ethics, because such a code would require licensing of journalists, something that conflicts with the idea of a free press.
- The range of ethics issues editors might confront is broad. Some, such as fabrication and plagiarism, are always wrong. But many others cover gray areas.
- As news media continue to look for new revenue sources to assure their future, that quest raises many ethical concerns.
- Lack of diversity in many news organizations can cause ethical problems, including lack of coverage of some groups or stereotypical coverage of them.
- Lacking an enforceable code of ethics, editors should be sure to inquire with their employers about any in-house codes. Independent journalists might want to pick one to follow or create their own.

CHAPTER EXERCISE

Using the guidelines discussed in this chapter, justify how you would act in each of the following cases.

1. The police reporter of your daily newspaper has found out that the 15-year-old daughter of the county sheriff has been arrested for possessing a small amount of marijuana. While the newspaper typically would not report on such a minor arrest, the reporter argues that this case is different: The girl's father is the embodiment of law and order, and here she is breaking one of the laws that her father has repeatedly vowed to enforce. Do you publish it?

2. You are planning to run an article that will have a tremendous effect on your audience. Just before deadline, the person who wrote the article comes to you and says, "There's something I'd better tell you." She proceeds to explain that she got her juiciest information by looking in a confidential file while conducting an interview for the article. She defends her snooping by noting that the person she interviewed left the file on his desk while he was out of the room for several minutes. "I'm sure he expected me to read it," your writer says. Do you publish the article?

3. One of your student reporters at the campus newspaper tells you that she has taken a part time job at a local balloon delivery shop. When she applied, she was astonished to find that she was expected to deliver balloons topless, but she agreed because the pay was good. Now she says she's being pressured to perform sex with her deliveries, and she believes the delivery company is a major prostitution ring using local college women. She wants to write an article for the paper on her scoop. To finish her research and "nail the sucker," as she puts it, she has agreed to work with local police and wear a wire to record incriminating statements by her boss. As her editor, will you allow her to wear the wire?

4. A man recently broke into a home during daylight hours and raped a woman at crossbow point. Your newspaper has reported the case, but now you find that there have been four such rapes in the past month. Police have tried to suppress the

information so they can pursue the rapist quietly; now that you know, they're asking you to keep quiet until they can complete a sting. In the meantime, though, more women may be raped who could have avoided the tragedy if they had known about the series of attacks. Do you print or withhold the information?

5. A long-time source has given one of your reporters a good story. But later in the day, the source calls back and asks that the material not be run. Do you run an article on the information at the risk of losing the source? Or do you kill the article to please the source, in the process denying your readers information they could use?

 ## WRITE RIGHT

Avoiding Dangling Modifiers

After a long hot walk, a beautiful shade tree came into view.

Walking trees? That's just one example of the grammatical problem that's often good for a laugh: the dangling modifier. Most modifiers – words that change, alter, limit or add more info to something else in the sentence – cause no problems. But sometimes it is not clear what is being modified. While those sentences are often amusing, the writers did not set out to amuse the readers, so dangling modifiers need to be tracked down and eliminated.

Under the rules of grammar, the noun or pronoun following a phrase or clause is modified by that phrase or clause, such as in this example: *Having studied the proposals, the CEO made his selection.* In this case, the CEO is indeed the one who had studied the proposals. However, substituting a different noun would cause a dangling modifier, as in this example: *Having studied the proposals, his selection was made.* That sentence literally says that his selection had done the studying, which makes no sense.

The Purdue Online Writing Lab offers three suggestions for eliminating dangling modifiers. One of them should work in any instance:

1. Name the appropriate or logical doer of the action as the subject of the main clause.

2. Change the phrase that dangles into a complete introductory clause by naming the doer of the action in that clause.

3. Combine the phrase and main clause into one.

Let's try putting those suggestions into action:

Sitting on the steps of the bakery, the cakes in the window looked delicious to the hungry child.

Following suggestion 1, we see that the doer of the action is obviously not the cakes but is the hungry child. So the main clause should begin with those words:

Sitting on the steps of the bakery, the hungry child thought that the cakes in the window looked delicious.

Another somewhat different example:

Stranded 30 feet above the ground in a tree, the cat's owner called the local fire department for help.

(Continued)

(Continued)

Following suggestion 2, we see that unless this is one of the "too weird to be true" stories, it is not the owner who is stranded in the tree but her cat. So just telling the reader what or who is in the tree eliminates the confusion:

With her cat stranded 30 feet above the ground in a tree, the cat's owner called the local fire department for help.

And one final one:

To increase the mileage of his hybrid car, a variety of "hypermiling" techniques were used.

Following suggestion 3, we can combine the parts of the sentence into a simple clause:

Otaki used a variety of "hypermiling" techniques to increase the fuel economy of his hybrid car.

While cakes sitting on steps and pet owners stranded in trees are amusing concepts, it's critical that editors correct such dangling modifiers to make sure readers get the intended messages.

Exercise

Rewrite the following sentences if necessary to eliminate danglers. If no change is necessary, write "No change."

1. The cookbook includes a recipe for cooking eggs for a crowd in the oven.

2. An owner of a Greenwich Village barbershop survived being shot in the neck as he slept by a gunman who broke into his house in Queens.

3. Glancing to her right was an assortment of shops.

4. Conveniently nestled in a handy storage box, you'll have access to each of 16 popular colors of paper.

5. The driver in front of him jamming on the brakes, Juan realized he had no room to maneuver.

6. She watched as her father returned home with the horses all dressed in cowboy attire.

7. Struggling to pass the class, he prepared a cheat sheet for the exam.

8. Swallowing quickly, the pill went down before I could taste its bitterness.

9. The baby sleeping, her parents at last could rest.

10. Bent out of shape, the police officer tried using the coat hanger to open the lock.

11. While adjusting her binoculars, a red-winged blackbird landed on a branch.

12. When 3 years old, Bob's mother took a job outside the home for the first time since she was married.

13. A large selection of flowers is available for inspection by customers in the refrigerated showcases.

14. With his left arm severely injured, Cortes was forced to leave the game.

15. Beating fiercely against the windshield, he watched the hail as he continued driving down the interstate.

EDITOR'S TOOLKIT

Journalism Ethics Codes

There's good news and bad news for editors looking for guidance on ethical decision-making. The good is that plenty of news organizations have crafted codes of ethics. The bad, as alluded to earlier, is that in most cases the advice is by necessity general, so it might leave the seeker unsatisfied. Still, something is better than nothing, and the following guides offer a great deal of food for thought when tackling the stickiest issues. (The Pew Research Journalism Project collection of Ethics Codes – http://www .journalism.org/resources/ethics-codes – was helpful in compiling this list.)

- The American Society of Business Publication Editors B2B [Business to Business] Journalist Ethics (http://www.asbpe.org/guide-to-preferred-editorial-practices)
- The American Society of Magazine Editors Guidelines for Editors and Publishers (http://www.magazine.org/asme/editorial-guidelines)
- The American Society of News Editors Statement of Principles (http://asne.org/content.asp?pl=24&sl=171&contentid=171)
- The Associated Press Media Editors Statement of Ethical Principles (http://www.apme.com/?page=EthicsStatement)
- The Associated Press News Values and Principles (http://www.ap.org/company/News-Values)

- Gannett Company Ethics Policy (http://asne.org/content.asp?pl=236&sl=19&contentid=332)
- Los Angeles Times Ethics Guidelines for Reporters, Editors (http://www.latimes.com/news/local/la-na-ethics15jul15,0,519646.story)
- The National Press Photographers Association Code of Ethics (https://nppa.org/code_of_ethics)
- The NPR Ethics Handbook (http://www.npr.org/about/aboutnpr/ethics/ethics_code.html)
- The Online News Association Mission Statement (http://journalists.org/about/mission/)
- The Radio Television Digital News Association's Ethics Code (http://rtdna.org/article/rtdna_code_of_ethics)
- The Society of American Business Editors and Writers Code of Ethics (http://sabew.org/about/codes-of-ethics/sabews-code-of-ethics)
- The Society of Professional Journalists Code of Ethics (http://www.spj.org/ethicscode.asp).

In addition, codes of ethics for European journalists can be found at EthicNet's Databank for European Codes of Journalism Ethics (http://ethic net.uta.fi). Other principles for those outside of North America can be found at the International Federation of Journalists' Declaration of Principles on the Conduct of Journalists (http://ethicnet.uta.fi/international/declaration_of_principles_on_the_conduct_of_journalists).

Student Study Site

Visit the Student Resource Site at **http://study.sagepub.com/lieb** to access:

- Chapter-by-chapter **web quizzes** for independent assessment of course material
- List of online web links and general resources

Chapter 9 **Managing Engagement**

So far, we've covered a wide range of topics and skills that a good editor needs to master for success. But to some extent, all of that is just the first part of a process. Without one more step, everything up to now might be for nothing.

That final step is creating **engagement**. At its simplest, engagement means using the best tools and platforms to share content and encourage audience interaction. At a time when many readers' initial exposure to a headline or news summary might be through one of many social media platforms, editors *must* engage their audiences. In the digital age with its limitless sources of information, it is not enough to offer appealing content and expect readers to stop by regularly. Instead, editors must work to create a community around their news operations. As Josh Stearns of Freepress.net put it, "Many leading journalists have made the case that news outlets need to engage communities to survive."[1]

While the process of engagement has revolved largely around the use of social media, each year it becomes more important to consider the role of mobile news consumption when planning engagement efforts. As Liz Heron wrote when she was at The Wall Street Journal and announcing that the social media editor and mobile media editor positions were being combined (she has since become head of news partnerships at Facebook):

> There are a couple of good strategic reasons to merge social and mobile. The obvious one is the audiences are beginning to overlap quite a bit. A big part of our social traffic comes from mobile devices. We recently launched a responsive site for mobile and we're seeing tons of traffic come from social to that mobile site. Social media has really revolutionized the way we do journalism in the last few years and mobile is completely on the rise now and will require the same sort of approach, with editors who are very analytical and who aren't afraid to experiment and try new things, and sometimes fail.[2]

Effective engagement needs to occur both internally and externally. We'll start by looking at the former, then move on to the latter.

Internal Engagement

While the point of engagement ultimately is connecting with the audience, any successful attempt at doing so begins in-house. The importance of this might be hard to imagine for younger journalists who have had a foot in the digital world all of their lives. But the reality is that many older journalists – and even some narrow-minded younger ones – are reluctant to give up the role of lecturer in favor of taking part in a conversation.

In some newsrooms, specific people hold the positions of **social media editor** or **engagement editor**. But even if there is such a designated person on staff, engagement has to be a team effort. As Steve Buttry, former digital transformation editor for Digital First Media, has noted:

> Community engagement must be a priority throughout the newsroom, not just one person's job. In the same way that having copy editors does not mean that reporters don't need to worry about clean copy, having an engagement editor doesn't mean that other journalists in the newsroom don't need to engage the community. The engagement editor leads, guides and stimulates the newsroom's engagement efforts.[3]

Therefore, a key job for engagement editors is to help cultivate a supportive culture for accomplishing that task. That process generally can be broken into three steps:

- *Getting buy-in.* More and more, every staff member of a news organization is expected to use social media, blogs, live chats and other tools to connect with the audience. A social media editor should help other staffers understand the value of those efforts. Without such a push, many people will feel social media duties are just one more chore on an already full "to-do" list. But when they become aware of the payoffs of effective engagement, they are more likely to embrace it.

- *Training.* Just getting others excited about engagement is not enough, however. All staffers need to become familiar with the range of tools available as well as with the best practices for using those tools. Therefore, a social media editor must continuously keep abreast of trends and help colleagues understand how best to move with the times. Specific training sessions are one way of doing this, but there are plenty of other possibilities – sharing information about new tools and techniques via lunch discussions, newsletters, and so on.

- *Mentoring and monitoring.* For people who just "get" technology, the previous two steps might suffice. But those more intimidated by technology need more help. And even the most tech-savvy staffers can use someone to check in with them occasionally to make sure they are using engagement tools effectively and not doing anything that could hurt the publication's reputation. As one example of such monitoring and mentoring, Buttry notes that if multiple people share a social media account, "The engagement editor's job is to train those people in how to use it, reminding them of the voice of the account, making sure that stories don't fall through the cracks or that the flow isn't too heavy or too light."[4] When other writers and editors use social media inappropriately, the social media editor should privately discuss the issue in hopes of heading off future problems. Mary Hartney Nahorniak, social media editor for USA Today, adds: "It's also important that the top brass continually emphasize the expectations and wins in this area. The engagement editor needs a solid backing from the organization's highest ranks, or s/he will be fighting an uphill battle."[5]

External Engagement

Once the staff is on board with the need to engage the audience, it's time to put the tools and practices to use. Doing so initially might be a foreign concept not only for staffers, but also for many in the audience. Buffy Andrews of the York (Pennsylvania) Daily Record has written about the need to explain her job to people she meets. She says that many think of the Daily Record solely in print terms. So they are therefore surprised to hear about the multiple social media accounts her staff manage as well as the e-newsletters, magazines, weekly newspapers, mobile apps and more. "Whenever I have this conversation," she adds, "the person is surprised, not only by the wealth of technology we use to do our jobs but also by the variety of platforms through which we deliver the news and information we gather."[6]

Andrews's experience is growing less common with time, as in many cases the audience is getting ahead of publishers, forcing them to play catch-up to learn about the latest technologies and think about how they might be used in journalism. But no matter, her point is an important one. Katherine Viner, editor-in-chief of the Guardian Australia, echoed a similar sentiment in a lecture at the University of Melbourne: "The web has changed the way we organize information in a very clear way: from the boundaried, solid format of books and newspapers to something liquid and free-flowing, with limitless possibilities."[7]

In a comprehensive blog post about community engagement, Steve Buttry defines community (external) engagement this way: "Community engagement = News [organizations] make top priority to listen, to join, lead & enable conversation to elevate journalism." Buttry cites Joy Mayer, a University of Missouri journalism professor and Reynolds Journalism Fellow, as defining "three primary types of engagement: outreach, conversation and collaboration." Buttry notes:

> You pursue those three approaches with a wide array of tools and practices. Whichever approach you take to analyzing engagement, it's important to realize that all these categories are overlapping circles, not distinct silos. The best engagement will use all these practices (and develop some new ones) to achieve outreach, conversation and collaboration.[8]

Buttry enumerates more than a dozen techniques for achieving such engagement, many of them low- or no-tech. For instance, one technique that addresses all three objectives is soliciting content created by users. "As blogs, cellphone cameras and social media put the tools of news-gathering and publishing in more hands," Buttry writes, "people have started reporting news themselves, taking in many cases the first photographs of disasters, crimes, accidents, fires and festivals. They also are creating content about community life in countless ways. Invite people to share their content with your audience."[9]

Not surprisingly, Facebook and Twitter are central to most news organizations' engagement efforts. While at The Wall Street Journal, Liz Heron noted that those platforms had become as important to the operation as any other part of its coverage. Heron suggests having "editors write all your social content and make sure you're replying to tweets and regularly asking questions of your audience based around the news," joining the conversation on Twitter when it seems appropriate. "What we try to do is come up with an intriguing, interesting question that's designed to inspire conversation," she notes. "Usually that does pretty well for us."[10]

Mary Hartney Nahorniak of USA Today agrees. "To me, this is the cornerstone of engagement. Conversation is simply talking to readers (and non-readers) about a variety of topics. A brief chat can go a long way toward engaging a person around the news or a news brand – and for a social media editor, is often the most fun part of the job. USA Today does a #DailyChat every day on Twitter, and we reply back to commenters on our Facebook post. It surprises them – in a good way."[11]

The New York Times social media team has found that one method of creating compelling conversations is by organizing Twitter Q&A sessions with reporters when the audience is showing widespread interest in a developing news story. In those sessions, an editor – considering the news values discussed in Chapter 2 and looking for patterns of interest – selects and filters questions from the audience, then relays the reporter's responses to them.[12] (For an example of how The Times used this feature in coverage of the political crisis in Egypt, see http://www.nytimes.com/2013/08/22/world/middleeast/twitter-chat-with-the-timess-cairo-bureau-chief.html?_r=0.)

The Times example illustrates perhaps the most important ingredient in creating engagement: paying attention to what people are showing interest in. Lindsay Gabler, the one-woman social media "team" for the Grammys, notes that "A huge part of what we do is making sure that we're tracking the conversation, so we can be fluid and adjust to what people are talking about, what's trending, what kind of content we should be putting out. … It's definitely a challenge."[13]

The best news organizations carefully consider the platforms they use to engage with their audiences. "We are very active on Instagram and Vine," Mary Hartney Nahorniak of USA Today says, "because that's where users are active. We want to be where people are spending their time, talking to them in a way that feels organic and natural."[14]

The entries in a Digital First Media companywide winter engagement competition reflect the many different platforms that can be used to create engagement:

- The Chambersburg (Pennsylvania) Public Opinion held a Christmas cookie challenge, posting readers' best recipes on a Pinterest board.
- To mark the 50th anniversary of the assassination of President John F. Kennedy, The Marin (California) Independent Journal issued an online call for people's memories of the event. More than 100 emails, letters and online comments came in during the following two weeks. An editor chose the best to feature in an online article, which generated further comments.
- For Thanksgiving, The Chico (California) Enterprise-Record used Scribble Live to host an online chat with three local chefs. Dubbed "Thanksgiving 411," the chat let readers ask questions of the chefs. The chat was promoted on the website, Facebook, Twitter and the mobile video publishing platform Tout, and a chat recap was published the next day, with a link back to the full chat transcript.
- In another Christmas project, The Pottstown (Pennsylvania) Mercury asked readers to share old photos of the holidays in Pottstown. The best were shared via a Christmas Past blog.
- The four Colorado Front Range newsrooms set out to create the ultimate package to help readers find the best holiday light displays. The staff "used a new, free smartphone app, TrackMyTour, to produce a giant regional holiday map with HUNDREDS of points, all photographed and automatically plotted using smartphones onto an embeddable Google Map. … We also solicited reader submissions and photos, which we simply added to our map using latitude/longitude coordinates. We solicited submissions via the web, print, Twitter and social media (including a chat room for a local mom's group, which proved very helpful). We added comments to many of the photos to provide additional information to readers."[15] In addition, the package included several articles, a Prezi presentation, an interactive image of one of the best displays using ThingLink and an online slide show. Not only was the package a hit with readers, but it also won the Digital First competition.

But engagement does not have to be all fun and games. Another Digital First Media employee, San Bernardino (California) Sun editorial writer Jessica Keating, took the occasion of her city's bankruptcy filing to engage the community into rethinking the city's problematic political structure. Keating launched a yearlong engagement project, Beyond Bankruptcy, which "looked at some of the underlying problems in the city's governance and pointed the way to start fixing them. This was achieved not just in editorials but also in a series of related public events in which residents helped shape the paper's editorials." Public turnout at the meetings exceeded expectations and "showed not just that people cared, but that they were desperate to find ways to help fix their city." Judges who voted to extend an award to Keating for the project noted that "We especially love how the newspaper opened up its newsroom to residents, breaking down traditional barriers between reporters and readers."[16]

Another example of a great engagement project comes from The New York Times, with its Faces of Breast Cancer feature. The project ultimately included more than 200 stories, pictures, and videos about those living with or at risk of breast cancer, as well as their families (http://www.nytimes.com/projects/your-breast-cancer-stories).

What If Readers Chose the News?

In Chapter 2, we looked at how editors can make better choices in selecting content for their audiences. Following that advice can lead to publications that continuously engage readers. But might there be an even better way to choose stories that promote engagement?

NewsWhip decided to examine that question in early 2014. The company used its web app, Spike, which analyzes trending stories for publishers, marketers and others, to see how the readers of a number of online news sites might have ranked that day's top stories. The more social shares a story received, the more play it would get. Using that data, NewsWhip "remixed" the front pages of The Wall Street Journal, The New York Times, the Guardian and several other top news outlets.

The results – published at http://blog.newswhip.com/index.php/2014/03/people-powered-front-pages-rock – were interesting, to say the least. Although critics of popular opinion might expect the result to be front pages full of celebrities and cute kittens,[17] in many cases readers paid much more attention to health news, international issues and other serious matters than the journalists had. Of course, the cute kittens were not completely overlooked: The most-shared story on The Washington Post was about the birth of four lion clubs at the National Zoo.

Crafting and Using Social Media Guidelines

While the many forms of social media have proved to be essential tools in external engagement, those tools can backfire if not used correctly. Barely a week goes by without a story surfacing about someone embarrassing an employer (and usually losing a job) because of a stupid mistake on social media. The ease of composing and publishing tweets, updates and posts leads many to hit the Send button without thoroughly thinking matters through. Therefore, more publishers are developing guidelines to help their employees avoid problems.

If an organization already has a social media policy, every employee should be made aware of it and be expected to follow it. If no such policy exists, however, creating one is a worthwhile project. What follows are key ground rules for using social media. They are based on the policies of many journalistic publishers and in turn could form the basis for creating a new policy for any publisher looking to do that. The policies come from a Poynter.org article by Ellyn Angelotti titled "How to Create Effective Social-Media Guidelines."[18]

- Clearly state the publication's goals for social media use.
- Lay out the expectations for each employee (or, for larger organizations, department) in meeting those goals.
- Highlight legal concerns that employees need to pay special attention to, such as copyright, defamation and publication of confidential information and trade secrets.
- Offer a blend of guidelines so that some apply specifically to current popular social media platforms but others are broader and can apply to emerging technologies.
- Clearly indicate that employees need to take responsibility for their social media use, as well as what penalties they will face when violations occur.
- Strike the right tone, encouraging social media use, not scaring employees away from it. More guidelines should take the form of "do's" than "don't's."
- Encourage common sense and make clear that general journalist guidelines (for example, no campaign bumper stickers on cars) apply in the digital world, too (no political tweets).

CASE STUDY

When Tweets Break Bad

Perhaps because of its constant need to be "fed" and the shortness of its messages, Twitter seems to encourage users to do things they will soon regret. Within just a few weeks in fall 2013, two journalists drew a great deal of the wrong kind of attention for their ill-considered tweets.

First up was Philadelphia TV news anchor Joyce Evans. Following the series finale of "Breaking Bad," Evans tweeted, "Thought 'Breaking Bad' was hot last Sunday? See who's breaking bad in SW Philly, leavin' 6 people SHOT – Tonite at Ten!" Evans's followers immediately pounced on her flippant handling of an incident that killed one person and wounded five. Replies included, "This tweet sounds like it was written by a sociopath," "HAHAHAHAHHAHAHAHAHHAHA PEOPLE DIED. HAHAHAHAHHAHAHAHA" and "Worst local news tease ever?"[19]

While some news people likely learned to act a little more cautiously after Evans's incident, only a few weeks later Michelle R. Jones, breaking news director of Alabama Media Group, found herself at the center of a similar storm, this time over a poorly conceived hashtag. While hashtags are great tools for collecting tweets and responses on a topic, that was not Jones's intention when she used one in a tweet about a suicide. She tweeted, "Former FL Secretary of State Katherine Harris' husband dead of apparent suicide #hangingchad."

Thought "Breaking Bad" was hot last Sunday? @FOX29philly See who's breakin' bad in SW Philly leavin' 6 people SHOT - Tonite at Ten!

The hashtag was a reference to Harris's role in the 2000 U.S. presidential election. As secretary of state of Florida at the time, she supervised the counting of votes that ultimately went far in determining who was going to be the next president. One of the key questions in the count was how to handle ballots that had not been cleanly punched through to indicate a choice – ballots that were said to have "hanging chads."

Again, followers pounced on Jones, but she defended her tweet: "What kind [of] person thinks that is an attempt at humor? Get real." If Jones intended only to jog followers' memories about Harris, she is still guilty of not thinking how the hashtag could be taken – not as serious as intentionally trying to find humor in a person's death, but still a poor move. As one follower said, "What kind of person doesn't think about double meaning in what they put out in public? You need an editor."[20]

Former FL Secretary of State Katherine Harris' husband dead of apparent suicide #hangingchad talkingpointsmemo.com/news/police-fo...

Using Analytics to Learn More About Audience Usage and Preferences

In contrast to earlier times when editors essentially handed down pronouncements about what their audiences *should read*, today's editors and publishers are much more interested in what their audiences *are reading*. To grasp that, they rely on **analytics**. Simply put, analytics is the observation and interpretation of data patterns for effective decision-making. As Ian Hill, an online editor with 15 years of experience, notes:

When you're making decisions based on your analytics, you're typically rewarded with more readers, viewers or listeners. That's because you're creating content similar to that which you know your audience has actively consumed in the past. A good editor or journalist will learn how to comb through analytics for lessons that will help them create content that has a greater impact on their audience.[21]

Aron Pilhofer, editor of interactive news at The New York Times, echoes Hill's comment on the importance of using analytics, telling Poynter.org: "Engagement to us is very much about how people are participating in what we're doing. ... Engagement is one big step toward what we ultimately want to know, which is what kind of impact our journalism is having."[22]

Using analytics takes most of the guesswork out of content selection. Ian Hill explains how this is a revolution in journalism that was unprecedented in print and broadcast:

Online analytics are the most powerful tools the journalism industry's ever had for measuring its impact on the audience. Ratings only measure a sample of the audience and are inexact – you never know why a consumer turned the station at a specific time. Circulation is incredibly inexact – you can only speculate as to why more consumers buy a newspaper on certain days. Surveys, meanwhile, can't be trusted because of the respondents' tendency to lie to make themselves seem smarter/better educated/nicer. When it comes to online analytics, there are very few lies. That's because online analytics measure specific actions. We have metrics that can show who went to what piece of content on a website, how long they stayed, how much of the content they consumed, where they came from, where they went after, what device they used, and more. You might tell a survey that you read the Economist and you're interested in news about Syria. But online analytics will show that you actually came to our news site from BuzzFeed because you wanted to spend time with our photo gallery of corgis.[23]

Editors and publishers are typically interested in the following common metrics:

- *Unique visitors*. This refers to the specific IP addresses of those visiting a blog or website. No matter how many times a month the same IP address shows up in the logs or how many different parts of a site that user visits, it is still just one unique visitor.
- *Visits*. This refers to how many times in a given period a visitor or group of visitors come to the site. One unique visitor stopping by three times or three unique visitors stopping by once would both equal three visits.
- *Page views*. This tallies the number of different pages that visitors check out.
- *Referrers*. This shows where traffic is coming from. That information can be used to determine where to put more or less effort. If a blog post is sending large amounts of traffic, it's a good idea to visit the blog to say thanks.
- *Time spent*. As its name indicates, this metric tracks how long people stick around. Sites and stories with high time spent are doing something right in engaging their audiences.

While those metrics are tried and true, today they are taking somewhat of a backseat to others that look at how stories and posts travel through the social space. Richard Moynihan, social media and community manager at Metro Newspaper UK, told Journalism.co.uk that "Newsrooms might look at what sort of content social audiences are clicking through to, where they are arriving from and what devices they are using. ... At Metro, the social media team also look at how users interact with the content itself, such as 'whether they scroll all the way to the bottom, whether they watch the videos in it or just read the text ... and whether they engage below the article in the comments section.'"[24]

While all these measures come from online publications, their utility does not stop there. For publishers that also distribute print editions, the lessons from analytics can be applied there, as well. Chances are that staffers on the print side likely will need more help in interpreting the data and applying its lessons, since they are not as likely to be as familiar or comfortable with analytics as their online counterparts.

As the preceding might suggest, the bad news is that analytics involves using numbers, something many journalists are loath to do. But John Schlander, digital general manager for the Tampa Bay (Florida) Times, says that thinking about that aspect too much is not a good idea. Instead, he says, journalists need to think about what they know best: telling stories. The idea then is to look at the metrics to find what stories they tell, starting with useful questions.

In addition, a growing number of tools can help publishers understand what works and what doesn't. Commonly embraced tools include the following:

- Google Analytics (http://www.google.com/analytics), the best free tool available, which shows sources of traffic and where viewers go after they land on a page
- Twitter Analytics (https://analytics.twitter.com), another free tool, which shows the reach that tweets are getting
- Facebook Insights (https://www.facebook.com/help/search/?q=insights), another free tool that provides demographic data about the audience of Facebook pages and shows how the audience is discovering and responding to posts
- Fanpage Karma (http://www.fanpagekarma.com) and Alexa both offer free versions and are great for broad comparisons – you can see how you're doing versus your competitors
- SocialFlow (http://socialflow.com), which uses real-time data of audience interests, then places content where it will get the most attention
- Muck Rack (http://muckrack.com), which allows tracking of how colleagues and the competition are doing in gaining followers as well as tracks the social spread of stories (via a tool called Muck Rack Who Shared – http://muckrack.com/whoshared)
- A growing number of products such as Chartbeat (https://chartbeat.com) and Visual Revenue (http://visualrevenue.com) that allow real-time tracking of traffic, with the latter offering the possibility of changing headlines on the fly to see how the changes affect traffic
- Sprout Social (http://sproutsocial.com), recommended by Anthony DeRosa, editor-in-chief of Circa and former social media editor at Reuters, for its clean interface and ease of navigation – tracks all social networks, has a useful mobile app, and can limit access to specific departments or users[25]

No matter how the analytics are gathered and analyzed, it's important that they be shared. Inside the newsroom, all relevant team members should have access to the results so they can see what works and what doesn't and can ultimately work together. Some publishers go further than that, sharing some usage data with the *audience*. "BuzzFeed, for example, presents a 'social lift' figure on its stories, which, as described by executive editor Doree Shafrir … is 'the ratio of sharing' when comparing social referrals to arrivals via its own site. Those with a BuzzFeed account (which is free to sign up for) can also access a 'viral dashboard' for a more extensive breakdown of figures."[26] Even something as simple as displaying the number of Facebook shares a story has had can help a story take off.

Wrapping Up

In an age when people have endless demands on their time and distractions of all sorts, capturing and keeping an audience is more difficult than ever. Those who follow the rules of engagement can take satisfaction in knowing that they have succeeded where many have failed. As Michael Roston of the social media team at The New York Times has noted:

> Having a better understanding of data really helps you be a better storyteller as a journalist more than anything else. … It used to be that reporters were focused on satisfying editors, but I think a lot of reporters these days should be thinking more about how they're going to connect with an audience, and if you have a better idea of what does and doesn't work with that audience, ultimately you're going to do a better job of telling them stories.[27]

Key Points

- Engaging with the audience is increasingly important to build loyalty in the digital era.
- Social media are largely used to build engagement.
- Increasingly, mobile users are a vital focus of engagement.
- Efforts need to begin internally so that staff members all agree on the importance of engagement and are familiar with the tools available for it.
- External engagement can come in many forms and via an ever-expanding range of platforms. Facebook and Twitter are the two most widely used platforms today.
- Every publishing operation should have social media guidelines. Employees should be made aware of them. If no guidelines have yet been drawn up, they should be.
- Analytics offer vital insights into how audiences are engaging with content. A wide range of tools are available that cut across all kinds of digital media.

CHAPTER EXERCISE

Design an Engagement Project

Prepare for this exercise by reading Steve Buttry, "What Does 'Community Engagement' Mean?" The Buttry Diary, 3 June 2011, http://stevebuttry.wordpress.com/2011/06/03/what-does-community-engagement-mean/.

Next, choose an upcoming holiday or special event being held in your area. Using at least four of the different types of engagement that Buttry discusses in that article, come up with a variety of projects that a local news organization could undertake. Strive for as much variety as possible so that you can engage the maximum number of readers of all ages and interests. Write up two or three paragraphs explaining each one and what audience it would target.

 WRITE RIGHT

Untangling Words That Sound Like Each Other (Part 1)

Native English speakers should take pity on those new to the language. Not only does a spelling not guarantee a specific sound (see, for instance, *bough*, *cough*, *dough*, *hiccough*, *ought*, *rough* and *through*), but conversely many words that are spelled differently sound the same. It's no surprise that half of the Top 10 Common Word Errors listed in Chapter 1 are examples of this – that is, they are **homonyms**. Since the different spellings are all acceptable, they can pass right through spell-checking programs, even though the meaning is completely different from what was intended. What follows are more commonly confused examples. Part 2 of this list appears at the end of Chapter 10.

Aid: Something that provides help.

Aide: A person who plays a supporting role to another.

Allowed: That which is permitted.

Aloud: Spoken with use of the voice, not silently.

All together: Completely.

Altogether: This is not a word.

Altar: The platform on which a church service is held.

Alter: The verb meaning to change something, to adjust for a better fit, or spay or neuter an animal.

A part: Something that is one of the pieces of something else.

Apart: Away from others.

Bail: The action of securing someone's release from imprisonment or of removing water from a boat.

Bale: Gathering material into a large bundle; the resulting bundle.

Board: A piece of wood or a group of people who provide advice and direction to a company or organization.

Bored: Lacking interest.

Brake: The mechanism used for slowing or stopping a vehicle; the act of using that mechanism.

Break: A pause in the action; turning something into pieces.

Breach: To violate the terms of a contract; such a violation.

Breech: The rear of a human body, as in breech birth; also part of a firearm.

Capital: The seat of government; material wealth.

Capitol: The building in which a government does business. Only *U.S. Capitol* is capitalized.

Carat: A measurement of the weight of precious stones.

Caret: An editing symbol.

Carrot: The vegetable that supposedly helps night vision.

Karat: A measurement of the fineness of gold; 24 karat gold is pure.

Cereal: A breakfast food.

Serial: Happening in a sequence or a series.

Cite: To acknowledge the source of information; such an acknowledgment.

Sight: Vision; something seen or worth seeing.

Site: The place where something is occurring.

Click: A noise; the act of making that noise.

Clique: A small exclusive group.

(Continued)

(Continued)

Coarse: Rough or not refined.

Course: A forward movement; a part of a meal; a place where certain sports are played; and many others.

Complement: To add to something else; a person or thing that adds to something else.

Compliment: To praise; such praise.

Conceded: Acknowledged a loss.

Conceited: Having a high opinion of oneself.

Council: A group of people that provides advice or consultation or legislates.

Counsel: To advise; such advice, or a lawyer or group of lawyers.

Decent: Conforming to accepted standards.

Descent: A downward path or motion.

Discreet: Exercising caution.

Discrete: Separate from other pieces or parts.

Do: To perform or carry out an action.

Due: Expected to be paid or submitted.

Elicit: To draw out, as in eliciting a response.

Illicit: Illegal, unethical or shady.

Every day: A noun form that refers to a succession of days.

Everyday: An adjective meaning *routine*.

Faint: To pass out; slight (as in *a faint pink*).

Feint: A deceptive move, as in a game.

Fazed: Bothered, disturbed.

Phased: Brought into action in steps.

Foreword: Introductory matter in a book.

Forward: Toward the front; blunt.

Forth: Forward or onward.

Fourth: The one after the third.

Foul: An action that does not conform to the rules.

Fowl: Poultry.

Gait: A manner of walking.

Gate: An opening or passageway.

Gorilla: A large primate.

Guerrilla: A rebel fighter.

Hangar: Where airplanes are housed.

Hanger: What clothes are hung on.

Hear: To detect sounds.

Here: A current position.

Hoard: To obsessively collect; such a collection.

Horde: A large group.

Whored: Prostituted.

Humerus: The long bone in the upper arm.

Humorous: Amusing.

Incite: To bring one to action by provoking or urging.

Insight: A look into the hidden nature of something.

Jam: A jelly-like substance; a mess; a musical improvisation.

Jamb: The side of a door or window.

Juggler: A person who tosses balls or other items in the air in sequence.

Jugular: A large vein in the throat.

(Continued)

Knead: Working with the hands, as in making dough or giving a massage.

Need: To require.

Know: Having knowledge of something.

No: The opposite of *yes*.

Exercise

Choose the correct word in each sentence.

___ Red wine is a nice **a) complement b) compliment** to a steak dinner.

___ There are many reasons that some college students apply for financial **a) aid b) aide.**

___ My brother is an **a) altar b) alter** boy at church.

___ She had to **a) brake b) break** very hard when the driver in front of her stopped immediately.

___ His new book went into editing without a **a) foreword b) forward.**

___ The residents of the state **a) capital b) capitol** protested the development plans.

___ The reporter was unable to **a) elicit b) illicit** information from the police about

___ **a) illicit b) elicit** drug traffic.

___ She **a) cited b) sited c) sighted** the Great Gatsby in her paper.

___ The referee called a personal **a) foul b) fowl** on the linebacker for hitting the quarterback after the play was whistled dead.

___ After the horse hit his leg on the **a) gate b) gait**, his

___ **a) gate b) gait** was not normal.

___ The judge did not grant her **a) bail b) bale** after police found marijuana in her car.

___ Surprisingly, the employees were not **a) fazed b) phased** when they found out their top selling product would be

___ **a) fazed b) phased** out.

___ She was hoping for an engagement ring with at least a full **a) carat b) caret c) karat** diamond in it, although she would be happy no matter what the size.

EDITOR'S TOOLKIT

Organizations for Editors

In large measure, editing is a solitary pursuit. At even the largest organizations, editors mostly work autonomously and largely anonymously, at least until they slip up. Given that, it's no surprise that editors can feel isolated and crave conversation with like-minded professionals, as well as advice about changing standards and rules. Fortunately, a number of organizations offer that – and more.

The **American Copy Editors Society** (http://www.copydesk.org) has long served as the preeminent organization for editors in the United States. Members receive a quarterly newsletter, discounts on training opportunities, reduced registration fees for the annual national conference, and discounted registration fees for other organizations' conferences.

North of the United States, the **Editors Association of Canada** (http://www.editors.ca) offers connections to more than 1,500 other editors across the country as well as clients and employers, hosts an annual conference, and provides discounts on training and resources. The organization partnered with ACES in 2014.

For editors who work on their own, the **National Association of Independent Writers and Editors** (http://naiwe.com) deserves a look. The organization provides a wide range of services, including "marketing help, resources for writers and editors, discounts on writing software and freelance support services and more."

Any editor involved in the digital side should seriously consider joining the **Online News Association** (http://journalists.org). ONA offers a wide range of training, networking and professional development opportunities and hosts a yearly conference that draws upwards of 1,500 online journalists from around the world and culminates with the Online Journalism Awards.

Many editors and writers who focus on business find it worthwhile to join the **Society of American Business Editors and Writers** (http://sabew.org). Among other benefits, the group holds a yearly conference, hosts job boards and runs an annual Best in Business awards competition.

The **Society of Professional Journalists** (http://www.spj.org/index.asp) has a broader scope than the preceding organizations, but the more than 100-year-old organization offers a lot for any journalist. An annual conference covers some of the hottest issues in the field of journalism, and SPJ offers plenty of resources and training opportunities as well as a job board. The group is best known for its Code of Ethics, the most widely cited journalism ethics code.

Editors in the United Kingdom can find support from the local **Society for Editors and Proofreaders** (http://www.sfep.org.uk). The group provides training and professional resources, email discussion lists and a bimonthly magazine.

While the **Society for News Design** (http://www.snd.org) might not sound like a great fit for editors, the truth is that many editors also have to be designers, whether for print or online publications. SND offers training and employment resources, hosts an annual conference and sponsors an annual Best of News Design competition.

Student Study Site

Visit the Student Resource Site at **http://study.sagepub.com/lieb** to access:

- Chapter-by-chapter **web quizzes** for independent assessment of course material
- List of online web links and general resources

Chapter 10   Curation, Aggregation and Creation

S o far, we have looked at editing as the process of modifying, perfecting and displaying work typically created by another person. In the digital environment, however, editors also often act as creators themselves. At the simplest level, editors create collections of articles, photos or other items. But sometimes their work goes well beyond that, as they take an active role in creating maps, quizzes and other multimedia elements.

Curation and Aggregation

Before we jump into the ways editors create content, we first look at a task more closely associated with a primary part of the job of editing: selecting and packaging content. In an age of ever-expanding content, editors perform an essential task in separating the wheat from the chaff.

Doing that is often referred to as **curation**. While some people do not like using that word in this and other nontraditional contexts,[1] others feel it is appropriate for work that in some ways mirrors what museum curators do: selecting material, adding value to it and exhibiting it in the most useful and informative way.

While the use of curation to describe this process is new, the process itself has long been at the heart of journalism. In fact, what else is a general-interest newspaper except an example of the processes at work? Editors long have packaged original reporting by the paper's staff with national and international reporting, features, comics, horoscopes and much more from the wire services and syndicates – and of course, letters and guest columns from readers.

In a post on the Online Journalism Blog, Paul Bradshaw identifies three types of curation:

- Curation as distribution or relay
- Curation as aggregation or combination
- Curation as filter or distillation

In the following sections, we look at each of these in turn.

Curation as Distribution or Relay

Bradshaw notes this category is "curation at the platform level." That is, it most often can be found on certain platforms that make it easy to cut, paste and share links and other content.

Twitter lists are a prime example of this type of curation: Twitter users grouped together for a specific reason. Bradshaw cites three typical types of groupings:

- "Users who pass on information in a particular field (for example health journalists, workers and academics) or location
- "Users who share a particular quality (for example they are very funny, or fast)
- "Users who share a particular role (for example employers, or journalists)"[2]

One example is Sree Sreenivasan's list of social media editors, which groups more than 200 people working in that area (find it at https://twitter.com/sree/lists/socmedia-editors).

Blogrolls present another example of this type of curation. Simply put, they are lists created by bloggers to point their readers to other blogs they are likely to find interesting. For instance, The New York Times' "Blogs 101" (http://www.nytimes.com/ref/technology/blogs_101.html) is essentially an expanded blogroll about ... blogging, of course.

Tumblr blogs also exemplify this usage. For example, the Surviving College Tumblr (http://survivincollege.tumblr.com) collects animated GIFs, images, links and more into what its creators bill as "the ultimate guide to everything college – and beyond!"

Audio and video playlists are another form of curation via distribution. For instance, Spotify offers anyone the chance to "curate" a group of songs. Playlists.net is a list of lists of songs, grouped under a wide range of themes. Similar playlists can be found on YouTube, where users create groups of videos that play one after another. Playlists are typically arranged by subject or artist but can be grouped in any way imaginable.

Several forms of **image collections** also fall under this type of curation. Using Pinterest, Instagram and Flickr sets, millions of people group images together in a way that has meaning to them and, they hope, to others.

Twitter retweets provide another example of this type of curation. If a journalist is using them actively, simply looking at that journalist's Twitter stream will provide a good snapshot of what he or she is reading, thinking about, talking about and interested in.

Another example is **Flipboard**. While it began life as an app that let users pull together their own "news magazine," recent versions have also offered the option to create collections of articles to share with others. They do not even need to have a tablet or app; the collection is available on any standard browser. As Editor and Publisher noted, "Flipboard is becoming a player in a social media environment that has become an important source of traffic for most news organizations' websites."[3] A Flipboard magazine of The New York Times' "Notable Deaths of 2013" became the most-read collection ever on the platform.[4]

Curation as Aggregation or Combination

In a Q-and-A session with employees of The Washington Post shortly after his purchase of it, Amazon.com owner Jeff Bezos asked, "The problem is how do we get back to that glorious bundle that the paper did so well?" Bezos added, "That daily ritual is incredibly valuable, and I think on the Web so far, it's gotten blown up." But in a Post column shortly afterward, Timothy B. Lee noted that "That daily ritual got blown up for good reason. Trying to recreate the 'bundle' experience in Web or tablet form means working against the grain of how readers, especially younger readers, consume the news today."[5]

Lee's point is an important one, and it marks a substantial change not only from the pre-Web days but also from the earliest days of the Web. For a period in the 1990s, publishers would not even think about including links to outside sources for fear that readers would click them and disappear into cyberspace. Some publishers went so far as to file lawsuits against sites that linked to their material, claiming doing so was copyright infringement.

But clinging to old ideas of having a captive audience for a closed reading experience just was not a winning strategy in the age of the open Web. As Lee notes:

> No matter how good your news organization is, most of the best journalism is being done somewhere else. That's because no publication, even storied outlets such as The

New York Times or The Washington Post, can hope to hire a majority of the world's most talented journalists.[6]

Some would argue that this future has already arrived. But the practice of aggregation does not come without problems. Plenty of publishers have balked at the practice as it occurs on sites such as The Huffington Post and Business Insider, which often so fully summarize material from elsewhere that readers have little incentive to visit the originating sites, depriving them of revenue.

Generally speaking, whether aggregating material is ethical or not comes down to a few questions:

- Has the aggregator linked to the original source?
- Is the material clearly attributed to its owner or creator?
- Has the aggregator added value to the material?
- Has the aggregator used a reasonable amount of the material?

Only when the answer to all of these is a definite *yes* can aggregation be considered ethical.

Writers and editors can use multiple techniques to add value to aggregated material. Among those techniques:

- Complementing the material with original reporting and/or commentary or analysis
- Linking to existing stories on the same topic to provide context and background
- Packaging related stories to provide alternate takes and follow-up material
- Verifying material circulating via social media
- Analyzing data and presenting it in a form that makes it easier for the audience to understand[7]

Journalism Professor Mindy McAdams cites the feature "16 disturbing things [Edward] Snowden has taught us (so far)" from the GlobalPost (http://www.globalpost .com/dispatch/news/politics/130703/edward-snowden-leaks) as one example of ethical aggregation:

The (considerable) value added in this example is in the summary of a long and complex story. Each point has a link to an original source. Seven of the … links go to The Guardian, which broke the story; there are also links to other original news reports about this case. We could probably have a long discussion about whether this story is too derivative of Guardian reporting – I would argue that the value of the summary, and the "consequence" written for each of the … points, more than justifies the right of GlobalPost to publish this.[8]

At the opposite end of the spectrum, Ryan McCarthy of Reuters finds Business Insider often fails to add such value, citing this and other examples:

Business Insider wrote 112 words on a 182-word TMZ story on a former NFL running back who is now living with his parents. There are two quotes in the original piece, which TMZ says were obtained from court documents. Business Insider reprints both quotes wholesale, then lifts almost every other fact from the original article, including details on the player's contract and information about his child support obligations. … A minimum of effort could have added links to related stories on these pieces. With a little bit more effort the writer could have made observations about the larger context of the stories.[9]

A Mouse That Roars

Not long after RebelMouse hit the scene in 2012, users fell in love with its ability to pull together their social media feeds into a single, unified view available even to people who don't use social networks. But journalists saw something even more interesting than its ability to aggregate material: its ability to create pages with customized feeds and designs.

Some examples:

- The Wall Street Journal used RebelMouse to cover New York Fashion Week (http://blog.rebel-mouse.com/fashion_week_coverage_by_wsj_a-108829229.html).
- NPR Social Media used it to aggregate tweets from a list of member stations and reporters in the path of a blizzard (https://www.rebelmouse.com/nprstorms).
- Salon used RebelMouse to package its elections coverage (http://www.salon.com/category/elections).

Best of all, RebelMouse sites can be created almost instantaneously, and basic users pay no fee. Users can create multiple sites, each with its custom URL that makes it look like part of the news organization's site. Poynter offers a good overview at http://www.poynter.org/latest-news/top-stories/203595/how-news-orgs-are-using-rebelmouse-for-blizzard-fashion-week.

Curation as Filter or Distillation

The third type of curation involves repackaging conversations from other sources. Doing so is in fact one of the most helpful things an editor can do: Cut through all the noise to find the key points worth passing along. Bradshaw notes that BuzzFeed sometimes does this by distilling conversations from Reddit, a site in which community members submit content in multiple categories and vote submissions up or down, thereby determining their position on the site's pages. Despite Reddit's popularity with its registered users, the average Internet user might be put off by its format – which is where BuzzFeed comes in.

A great tool for distillation is Storify. Storify lets an editor monitor a wide range of social media to see how users are preparing for or reacting to an event, to gather reactions to an announcement or controversial topic, or for any of a wide range of other uses. The resulting distillation can combine photos, tweets, Facebook posts, YouTube videos and much more.

Many major news organizations use Storify to cover breaking stories or even to do retrospectives on them. For instance, NBC News created a Storify marking the first anniversary of Hurricane Sandy. The resulting Storify (http://storify.com/nbcnews/sandy-then-and-now) combined NBC News original content with that created by a wide range of others.

The Importance of Links

From the earliest days of the Web, one of its promises was that hypertext links could offer journalists the power to add context, background and depth to articles. As the Online Journalism Review advised readers in 2007, "Don't forget the Web's original interactive widget: hyperlinking, which can help enliven any news story by providing additional context and background, without interrupting its narrative flow."[10] Media guru Jeff Jarvis states it more succinctly: "Cover what you do best. Link to the rest."[11]

Writing for Nieman Journalism Lab, Jonathan Stray lists four main reasons to use links in online writing:

- *Links are good for storytelling.* Supporting documentation, other points of view and research materials all enrich the reading experience. But instead of cluttering articles with all that, links

(Continued)

(Continued)

help keep things streamlined by letting readers choose what additional information is worth pursuing. As Stray writes: "Readers who are already familiar with certain material, or simply not interested, can skip lightly over the story. Readers who want more can dive deeper at any point. That ability can open up new modes of storytelling unavailable in a linear, start-to-finish medium."

- *Links keep the audience informed.* Hyperlinks allow journalists to point readers to stories that their publication might not have covered. Stories that are scooped by one individual or organization have typically been re-reported by others. But links eliminate the need to do that. "A link is a magnificently efficient way for a journalist to pass a good story to the audience," Stray notes.
- *Links are a currency of collaboration.* As the previous point noted, no organization or individual can cover every interesting or important story. So links offer a way to "pay" others for their contributions, sending traffic to them and possibly enhancing their reputations.
- *Links enable transparency.* Attribution of information is a bedrock principle of journalism. As Stray notes: "I can't see any reason why readers shouldn't demand, and journalists shouldn't supply, links to all online resources used in writing a story. ... A link is the simplest, most comprehensive, and most transparent method of attribution."[12]

While some journalists have come only reluctantly to the use of links, there is wide consensus that they are here to stay. Of course, that raises issues when content appears in print as well as online. The Washington Post's policy on using links typifies how this potential problem is handled. "Links in Post stories," notes multiplatform editor Vince Rinehart, "are mostly placed on names and phrases to link to news stories, bios or profiles of newsmakers, or reports and such. They are invisible in print." Occasionally, however, links are useful in print, Rinehart notes, for example, "when we mention websites or Web addresses, such as at the end of a review when we are telling readers where they can go for more information about a theater and its productions. That works fine for print and online. We really don't have to worry about confusing wordings for print readers as a result."[13]

Creation

As mentioned at the beginning of this chapter, at times editors go well beyond repackaging the work of others and actually create elements on their own, or with the help of writers, designers and programmers. The list of items in this category changes regularly as technologies fall in and out of favor. But some things, like lists, photo galleries and maps, have become standard in publishing circles. As Business Insider founder, editor, and CEO Henry Blodget has noted, such elements reflect the reality that digital publishing offers many new opportunities for storytelling and information sharing. "There's a dramatically different way of storytelling on the Web," Blodget says. "You don't have to do something different – it's just there is a much bigger [pallete] in terms of storytelling tools."[14] Today's editors need to be familiar with those tools.

Listicles

We've already discussed a few types of lists in the preceding sections. But while things like Twitter lists merit attention, the listicle – a list-based article – has emerged as a common journalistic staple.

In one sense, there is nothing new about listicles. Many magazines have long relied on them for major features: "The 10 Best Cities for Artists," "The Top Brunch Spots in Town," "10 Ways to Drive Your Partner Wild in Bed," and so on. In fact, U.S. News & World Report is known widely for its list of top universities. But in another sense, listicles are a perfect creation for the moment, as they strike younger readers – the so-called *digital natives* who do a good deal of their reading via short Facebook updates and Twitter posts – as a perfect delivery vehicle for information.

The trend also has been driven partly by the increase in mobile news consumption. In fact, in a 2013 survey of news reading habits, "News syndication company Mobiles Republic found news reading to have been replaced by 'news snacking'; checking news content far more frequently, for short, sharp bursts of attention."[15] In that environment, listicles make a great deal of sense.

Undoubtedly, no site has done more to promote the use of listicles than BuzzFeed. As BuzzFeed's editorial director Jack Shepherd has noted: "At their best, lists are just scaffolding for stories: The list format grabs the attention because it's an easy way for people to process information and for readers to know what they're getting, but that's not even close to half the battle. A great list that people share everywhere has to be an experience."[16]

And with the passage of time, BuzzFeed has begun using listsicles for serious journalism. As one example, Luke Lewis, editor of BuzzFeed UK, cites a "viral news story" from Venezuela based on a series of images. The piece, "29 Heartbreaking Images From the Protests in Venezuela" (http://www.buzzfeed.com/conzpreti/29-heartbreaking-images-from-the-protests-in-venezuela), shows that listicles work "very well for explaining serious topics and giving it impact," Lewis says. Readers likely agree, as it attracted more than half a million views in its first 40 days online.[17]

While there are doubters,[18] many believe that great listicles will become a regular source of serious journalism. "Any editor can tell you that listicles typically draw more pageviews than stories written in the standard narrative format. That has led some data-driven publications, even outside of BuzzFeed, to go nearly full listicle," Jack Marshall of Digiday writes.[19]

Some psychologists would tend to agree. In 2011, the psychologists Claude Messner and Michaela Wänke investigated what, if anything, could alleviate the so-called "paradox of choice" – the phenomenon that the more information and options we have, the worse we feel. They concluded that we feel better when the amount of conscious work we have to do in order to process something is reduced; the faster we decide on something, whether it's what we're going to eat or what we're going to read, the happier we become.[20] Given that, lists appeal to readers because they offer a finite number of choices that are apparent from the outset. That increases the odds that readers will be able to completely read the lists, increasing their sense of satisfaction. And that satisfaction in turn makes readers likely to click on other lists.

In addition to being well-written, many of the most popular listicles share another trait: They are often targeted to specific demographics. For instance, BuzzFeed's "40 Signs You Went to Berkeley" (http://www.buzzfeed.com/louispeitzman/signs-you-went-to-berkeley) would likely be meaningless to most readers. But it offers a feeling of being in on a secret to its targeted group – who are highly likely to share it with other Berkeley grads.[21]

Photo Galleries and Slide Shows

In one sense, photo galleries and slide shows (photo galleries with accompanying audio) are just another form of list: one item – in this case, each an image – after another. And like listicles, they have gained prominence and importance in the digital world.

In fact, in some ways photo galleries and slide shows are one of the purest examples of Web journalism, as there was no equivalent in prior media. And their popularity is without question. By the mid-2000s, The New York Times reported that about 10 percent of its online page views came from photo galleries. And MSNBC.com's "The Clarks: An American story of wealth, scandal, mystery" (http://www.msnbc.msn.com/id/35266269/ns/business-picture_stories) drew nearly 80 million page views, from more than 2 million unique visitors, who on average spent a whopping 13 minutes lingering on the package of photos and text.[22]

While there may not seem to be many differences between photo galleries and slide shows, there are some important ones:

A photo gallery enables the user to click through the photos one by one [and] is good for things like awards ceremony arrival pictures, where users want to stop and stare at

CASE STUDY

Creating Lists at BuzzFeed

Mention lists and BuzzFeed likely comes to mind. The site is home to countless lists like "10 Things Dogs Probably Think About When They're Dreaming" and "10 Signs You Might Actually Be an Adult." While both of those examples use the common "Top 10" structure – long ago made a key part of American culture by David Letterman – that number is in no way magical.

In fact, in an analysis of BuzzFeed lists, Knight-Mozilla fellow Noah Veltman found that the most common list sizes also included 15, 21 and 25. But many BuzzFeed lists topped 30 items, and there was, as one of Veltman's collaborators found, "a slight correlation between list length and how many tweets the list gets—the longer the list, the more tweets."

But the numbers tell only part of the story. A review of BuzzFeed lists by Nieman Journalism Lab staff writer Caroline O'Donovan also found that lists fall into three main categories:

1. The listicle, which is just a grouping of pictures, gifs or other material with nothing to tie them together, like "109 Cats in Sweaters."

2. The definitive list, which tries to be the final word on a topic, like "The 50 Cutest Things that Ever Happened." When done well – which involves a good deal of work – such lists have a strong tendency to go viral.

3. The framework list, which is used to structure a narrative, like "54 Reasons You Should Go to a Dog Surfing Competition Before You Die."

Speaking of a framework list, O'Donovan notes: "This is the most important kind of list for BuzzFeed, the one that helped it get past its reputation for creating Internet drivel and begin building a broader audience. This kind of list has the best content, but also the most arbitrary length – there are as many items as it takes for the story to be done." And sometimes that number of items changes after a list is posted. "We've looked at it in real time, which specific items on a list people were sharing the most, and started cutting out the ones that weren't getting shares," Jack Shepherd told O'Donovan. So what is the best length for a list? The one that perfectly complements the material in it.[23]

each image in their own time, or when the order/timing of the pictures is not important. A photo gallery is also good when the situation does not have good audio possibilities.

On the other hand, the sounds of an audio slideshow create a multimedia experience that can transport the viewer into the time and place shown in the images. Audio slideshows are plotted out in a cinematic way, meaning the timing and order of the images and sounds can be adjusted to heighten the effect of the storytelling.[24]

Typically, creating a photo gallery or slide show is not a one-person operation. But editors can play many roles in pulling them together. In fact, an editor might be assigned to handle all but the first step of reporting and gathering multimedia:

- "reporting/gathering the photos and audio;
- "deciding on a storytelling form and/or narrative thread for the piece;
- "selecting photos and audio clips that best convey the story;
- "editing the audio together into a soundtrack; and
- "making choices about the order in which the photos appear; the duration of time each photo stays onscreen; and the relationship between what is seen and heard at any given moment. This could be referred to as the 'cinematics.'"[25]

For those who have not worked on photo galleries or slide shows, the following sites offer plenty of good advice on what to do and not to do:

- "What makes a good audio slideshow: the dos and don'ts" (http://themultimediajour nalist.wordpress.com/2013/03/15/what-makes-a-good-audio-slideshow-the-dos-and-donts)
- "What makes a good audio slideshow?" (http://audiojournalism.wordpress.com/2011/03/29/ what-makes-a-good-audio-slideshow)
- "5 Common photo slideshow mistakes" (http://www.mediabistro.com/10000words/5-common-photo-slideshow-mistakes_b303)

And lots of great examples can be found in "Advanced Online Media–Audio Slideshows": http://journalismatwestminster.wordpress.com/2013/01/25/advanced-web-journalism-audio-slideshows.

Quizzes

While long a standard of magazines, quizzes have only recently made a big splash on the digital scene, showing up with regularity only in 2014. And just as with listicles, the most fertile breeding ground was BuzzFeed. As Slate noted, "You've seen them – the BuzzFeed quizzes filling up your Facebook timeline, purporting to tell you which city you should live in, which Muppet you are, or which food matches your personality."[26] Quizzes took on a much more pronounced role at BuzzFeed when editors realized that one published in 2013 was shared online more than anything else BuzzFeed had published that year. Subsequent quizzes such as "What city should you actually live in?" got as many as 20 million views.

Summer Anne Burton, BuzzFeed's managing editorial director, explains the popularity of quizzes: "People really like to have organization and structure – it's just appealing. There's something reassuring about it. Quizzes have that in common with lists – they make content accessible."

While many would argue that the quizzes popularized by BuzzFeed cannot be considered journalism, they often offer real content. As Burton says: "At the end of the day, while quizzes are formally comprised of questions and answers, what you're getting is content that interests you disguised as a narrative about yourself. It's like the plate you serve your food on. You don't talk about the plate – you talk about the food."[27]

Readily shareable quiz results go a long way to explain the popularity of this format. People can easily post their results on Facebook and Twitter, where friends are motivated to comment and take the quiz themselves.

Not surprisingly, traditional journalistic operations have tried their hand at quizzes. The Baltimore Sun's "Which Character Are You from 'The Wire'?" (http://data.baltimoresun .com/quizzes/the-wire) gave local readers and far-flung fans a chance to see who they most resembled in the hit show. And The New York Times' dialect quiz "How Y'all, Youse and You Guys Talk" was the news site's most popular "article" of 2013, for a time reigning as the most emailed, the most blogged, and the most tweeted feature on the site.[28]

While an intern created The New York Times' quiz, this type of interactive typically requires a certain level of technical skill that most editors will not have. It's likely just a matter of time, however, until the tools for creating them are readily available.

Timelines and Chronologies

Two tools that are sometimes confused, timelines and chronologies, are good for showing how events played out over time. As journalism educator Mindy McAdams notes: "A timeline shows actual spans of time, with proportional measurements for decades, years, days or hours, depending on the total time involved. … A chronology, on the other hand, shows the momentum of a

series of events. It might be more effective if presented as a list, or as an illustrated slideshow."
McAdams suggests several questions to guide editors in creating timelines and chronologies:

- "Will people like it?
- "Is it helpful, easy to understand?
- "Is it confusing?
- "Hard to use?
- "Does it add something that text alone would not convey?
- "Does the graphic need to be a timeline – or would a regular slideshow (or map, or whatever) be equally effective?"[29]

While the most impressive timelines and chronologies are the result of collaborations of writers, artists, coders and others, several free tools can help an editor create one quickly. While new tools arrive regularly, some well-known examples include Timeline JS (http://timeline .verite.co/#hero-unit), Tiki-Toki (http://www.tiki-toki.com), Dipity (http://www.dipity .com) and Timeline-Setter (https://github.com/propublica/timeline-setter).

Maps

Maps have long played an important role in journalism. From showing where disasters and battles occurred to showing how a sequence of events played out, maps long have allowed journalists to present some information visually that is much easier for readers to comprehend than words alone would be.

In the digital environment, maps become even more powerful players when combined with databases. Instead of readers having to sift through loads of textual data, they can get a quick visual overview, then drill down into the data. For a good example of presenting data visually, check out the Baltimore Homicide map at http://data.baltimoresun.com/bing-maps/homicides/. For comparison, the raw data can be viewed at http://data.baltimoresun .com/bing-maps/homicides/recenthundred.php.

Two other features make online maps appealing. First, virtually anyone can create one. Unlike some other elements, no coding or graphics expertise is required. Second, they can be automated so that as information is added to the database, the map is immediately updated. That makes them particularly useful for breaking news stories such as election results, natural disasters, and so on. A few good sources of information on producing these types of maps are "Data Visualization DIY: Our Top Tools" (http://datajournalismhandbook.org/1.0/en/ delivering_data_7.html) and "KDMC Maps Tutorials" (http://multimedia.journalism.berkeley .edu/tutorials/cat/maps). A tutorial on using Fusion Tables, a common tool for such map making, can be found at https://sites.google.com/site/fusiontablestalks/talks/fusion-tables-where-2-0-workshop.

Maps even can be used to enlist readers to research and report a story. A year after Hurricane Sandy struck the eastern United States, Al Jazeera America created an interactive map that let people affected by the storm share their stories. Users could submit text, photos and video. Submissions were then plotted on a map, allowing readers to find others near them. To view Al Jazeera's map, please see http://america.aljazeera.com/multimedia/ 2013/10/map-reliving-hurricanesandyoneyearlater.html.

Another online-only type of map is what's referred to as a *mashup*. These combine maps with user comments, video, audio, pictures, news reports and more. One example was posted during the 2009 London G20 summit (http://news.bbc.co.uk/2/hi/uk_news/7975220 .stm). As engaging as these types of maps are, they are also by nature more complex to create, so an individual editor will not likely successfully create one.

Animated GIFs

Early on in the life of the Web, users were shocked and amused to find a new type of moving graphics – sort of like miniature movies. These animated GIFs were essentially a digital version of the old-fashioned paper flipbook. It didn't take long for the interest in them to wane, however, as real video soon found its way onto the Web.

But fast-forward 15 years, and animated GIFs were back with a vengeance. While most were as devoid of content as the dancing Calvin and Hobbes had been in the late 1990s, the format found many admirers in news circles, and they set about using them to augment their storytelling. As a Poynter report from 2012 noted, "More compelling than a static photo and more immediate than Web video, the animated GIF ... is a uniquely digital mode of conveying ideas and emotion. ... the animated GIF has gone from a simple file type to its own mode of expression. GIFs have grown up, and they are everywhere right now."[30]

Not everyone is happy about that, at least when it comes to their use on journalistic sites. "There are a limited number of contexts in which GIF illustration is appropriate for news reportage," notes a piece on the Parse.ly blog. "For example, it would be in extremely poor taste to illustrate a disaster with GIFs. Saturating a text article with GIFs harms the user experience, too, because GIF heavy pages typically load slowly and may fail to load at all on mobile platforms."[31]

Nevertheless, successful – and tasteful – examples do pop up. The Atlantic did an interesting job with "The Case Against Cars in 1 Utterly Entrancing GIF" (http://www.theatlantic .com/business/archive/2013/11/the-case-against-cars-in-1-utterly-entrancing-gif/281615). The Wire.com broke down Olympic gymnastics champion Gabby Douglas's "Awesome Night" (http://www.thewire.com/global/2012/08/gabby-douglass-amazing-night-gif-guide/55370). And part of the coverage of the Coachella festival by The New Yorker took the form of GIFs (http://www.newyorker.com/online/blogs/photobooth/2013/04/slide-show-gifs-from-coachella.html#slide_ss_0=1).

When it seems like an animated GIF might advance a story, it doesn't take much time or effort to make one. Poynter offers a useful tutorial at http://www.poynter.org/how-tos/ newsgathering-storytelling/183802/what-journalists-need-to-know-about-animated-gifs-really. Or for even simpler and faster results, they can be created online at sites like http:// makeagif.com/video-to-gif.

Other Possibilities

Mention presentations and most people think of the boring PowerPoints they have been forced to sit through in school or work meetings. But online presentations are another tool that might have a place in news stories. A PowerPoint deck explaining how Netflix's leaders shaped the culture and motivated performance at the company – 127 slides with no music or animation – was viewed more than 5 million times, and a Harvard Business Review article based on it proved extremely popular.[32]

Other presentation tools are also worth exploring. As Steve Buttry, former digital transformation editor for Digital First Media, has written: "Prezi might help you explain a process that's key to your story. Or ThingLink could turn a key image into an interactive element: In a photo of the key characters in your story, you could embed links about their backgrounds or their roles in the story."[33] More information on those two tools can be found at their respective websites, https://prezi.com and https://www .thinglink.com.

Wrapping Up

In the digital environment, the role of an editor is an expansive one. Researching and packaging others' material as well as creating engaging content of his or her own is all part of the process that once involved little more than correcting grammar and style and checking facts. As a result, editors today play an even more important role in the journalistic process than they have in the past.

Key Points

- While the term *curation* has only recently become widespread in describing some roles of editors, the process goes to the heart of what they have long done in their jobs.
- Curation can generally be seen as falling into one of three types: distribution or relay, aggregation or combination, and filter and distillation.
- The practice of aggregation raises ethical issues when editors fail to put their own stamp on the material they are using or borrow so heavily that readers might not visit the originating sites of the content they are using.
- Hyperlinks are a key element in online content, as they offer many benefits to readers that would be impossible to deliver without them.
- The emerging online content forms of listicles and quizzes offer new ways to engage audiences and spread the word about a publication's offerings as users share them via social media.
- Photo galleries, slide shows, timelines, chronologies, maps, animated GIFs and other devices can be used to clarify and amplify information for the audience.

CHAPTER EXERCISE

Brainstorming Multimedia

Using a local newspaper, find an interesting local story.

Using that story, come up with a list of at least five multimedia enhancements such as those discussed in this chapter or others that you can imagine: photo galleries, quizzes, GIFs, lists, maps, timelines, etc. If you have access to the necessary hardware and software, create at least two of those items to share with your classmates.

For the final step, look up the story online. What, if any, multimedia elements were used there? How do they compare in terms of telling the story with the ideas that you created?

 # WRITE RIGHT

Untangling Words That Sound Like Each Other (Part 2)

In Chapter 9, we began looking at commonly confused homonyms. In this section, we work our way through the rest of the alphabet.

Lead: To take the front position; a toxic metal.

Led: The past tense of the verb *lead*.

Lean: To tilt in one direction.

Lien: The legal right to take possession of another's property until a debt is paid.

Lessen: To lower, as in the amount or severity.

Lesson: That which is learned.

Lets: Allows.

Let's: Contraction for *let us*.

Lightening: Removing weight from.

Lightning: An electrical discharge in the sky.

Loan: To give something to another with the expectation of having it returned; such a transaction.

Lone: Solitary or sole.

Loose: Not tight.

Lose: To misplace.

Manner: The way in which something is done.

Manor: An estate.

Mantel: A shelf above a fireplace.

Mantle: A cloak or robe.

Marshal: A military or law enforcement officer; to gather up, as in *marshal the forces*.

Marshall: A proper name.

Martial: Pertaining to the military.

Miner: One who works in mines.

Minor: Of lower ranking; a person not yet of legal age.

Moral: A lesson of a story; having high principles.

Morale: Spirits.

Naval: Pertaining to the navy.

Navel: Belly button or similar mark (as in *navel oranges*).

Overdo: To make too much of a fuss about.

Overdue: Past deadline.

Pair: Two things that go together.

Pare: To cut down.

(Continued)

(Continued)

Pear: A tasty fall fruit.

Patience: The quality of being able to wait.

Patients: People seeking medical treatment.

Peak: The top or the ultimate; to reach a final stage.

Peek: To look at.

Pique: To arouse curiosity.

Pedal: A device to propel a bike or make a vehicle go or stop; turning such a device, as on a bicycle.

Peddle: To sell.

Plain: Not fancy or ornate.

Plane: Airplane; a mathematical term.

Poor: Lacking wealth or resources.

Pore: To examine carefully; a small opening in the skin.

Pour: To dispense a liquid.

Presence: The state of being present; the way a person carries himself or herself.

Presents: To deliver; gifts.

Principal: The person in charge of a school; the main one, as in *the principal lesson.*

Principle: A rule.

Profit: Money made on a transaction.

Prophet: A person through whom a god speaks.

Rack: A structure for hanging items; to cause to suffer.

Wrack: Ruin.

Rain: A form of precipitation.

Reign: To rule over.

Rein: A device for controlling an animal.

Raise: To increase.

Rays: Beams of sound or light.

Raze: To demolish.

Reek: To stink of.

Wreak: To cause or inflict.

Right: Opposite of left; proper; a legal claim.

Rite: A ritual.

Wright: One who creates something, as in a playwright.

Write: To put words on paper or screen.

Road: A surface designed for traveling upon.

Rode: Past tense of *ride*.

Rowed: Past tense of *row*.

Root: The bottom part of a plant.

Route: A road; the plan for getting from one point to another.

Scene: The basic component of a play or movie; something seen by a person; a place where an event occurs.

Seen: The past perfect of *see*.

Seam: The joint of two pieces of fabric or other material.

Seem: Appear.

Stationary: Set in place.

Stationery: Materials used for writing notes or letters.

Summary: A conclusion.

Summery: Feeling like or reminiscent of the warm season.

(Continued)

(Continued)

To: Preposition meaning the opposite of *from*.

Too: Also.

Two: One plus one.

Trooper: A military or police officer.

Trouper: An actor in a company; a hardworking person.

Vain: Without purpose.

Vane: A blade, as on a windmill.

Vein: An organ for carrying blood.

Waiver: A release of a right or responsibility.

Waver: To be unsteady or unsure.

Weather: Atmospheric conditions.

Whether: A conjunction that indicates an alternative or alternatives. Rarely is it necessary to add *or not*.

Who's: Contraction for *who is*.

Whose: Possessive form of *who*.

Yoke: A harness for an animal.

Yolk: The yellow part of an egg.

For many more, check out Alan Cooper's Homonyms at http://www.cooper.com/alan/homonym_list.html. While the list is dated, it covers just about every homonym imaginable.

Exercise

Choose the correct word in each sentence.

___ The student's parents thought that they had instilled stronger **a) moral b) morale**

___ **a) principals b) principles** in their son.

___ We printed the letters on company **a) stationery b) stationary.**

___ She was excited when her friend said her good example had **a) lead b) led** her to apply for college.

___ The patient's commitment began to **a) waiver b) waver** as he looked at the

___ **a) waiver b) waver** he was supposed to sign before surgery.

___ The boys wanted to **a) reek b) wreak** havoc on the town after finding out what happened.

___ The theatrical company enlisted one of the **a) troopers b) troupers** to play the lead in the show.

___ One day baby Prince George of Cambridge will **a) reign b) rein** over England after his father.

___ When the AP Stylebook changed Web site to website, such panic broke out in newsrooms across the country that **a) martial b) marshal c) marshall** law was declared.

EDITOR'S TOOLKIT

Creating an Engaging Storify

As pointed out earlier in this chapter, Storify is a popular and useful tool for distilling social conversations. The interface makes it easy for anyone to create a project in little time.

But for good user engagement, it's important to create the best Storify possible. To do so, it's helpful to begin with the definition of a Storify. In the company's own words: "Storify lets you curate social networks to build social stories, bringing together media scattered across the Web into a coherent narrative. We are building the story layer above social networks, to amplify the voices that matter and create a new media format that is interactive, dynamic and social."[34]

So in a nutshell, a Storify lets the creator gather social media nuggets – many of which will disappear quickly – and package them together to tell a story. It's that last word, *story*, that's most important. A Storify is *not* just a collection of social media tidbits; it needs to be an actual story.

And like other journalistic stories, every Storify should have a title, a summary, a lead, transitions and an ending. In fact, the best way to create a good Storify is to start by putting together an outline of what the creator wants to say, and then find the pieces to support the point. Along the way, it's possible that contradictory information or additional ideas will pop up. That's fine; just as in reporting any story, it's important to be flexible to deal with new information.

Before getting to that stage, however, it's a good idea to visit the Storify.com home page and check out the featured examples. A range of different types of stories are featured there, offering good ideas about how to structure a Storify. This is also a good time to review "Meta! Here's how Storify looks telling the story of Storify" (http://www.niemanlab.org/2010/09/meta-heres-how-storify-looks-telling-the-story-of-storify).

Now it's time to create the Storify.

1. Write a headline that demonstrates good SEO (search engine optimization). Here is a good example from Mother Jones magazine: *Hacking For The FBI: A Timeline Of How An Informant Sold Out Anonymous.*

2. Write a summary of 50 to 100 words to give the reader a fuller idea of what your Storify is about. Here's an example from Purdue University: *Hundreds of people in the Purdue community gathered at McCutcheon Hall to march to Hovde Hall in memory of Trayvon Martin, an unarmed Florida teen that was shot and killed last month.*

3. Write a lead. Sometimes, the summary is sufficient without a lead. But in many cases a strong lead will help get a reader interested in the Storify. Here's an example of the headline, summary and lead working together, created by Storify user Jake Nelson:

(Continued)

(Continued)

Social Media Keeps Tornado-Stricken Town Connected

Residents of a Michigan town hit by a tornado were able to keep in touch and disseminate information via social networks on Thursday.

When a tornado with wind speeds over 135 mph touched down in the village of Dexter, Michigan, on March 15, 2012, those in the affected area were able to communicate and exchange information about the storm using Twitter and Facebook.

4. Use Storify to find and embed several pieces of social media of at least three different types to tell the story, interspersing hyperlinks and original narrative along the way.

5. Every Storify needs an ending. The ending does not have to be a huge production, just something that lets the reader know it is done. Here's the ending from the tornado Storify: *The storm destroyed more than 100 homes, but thanks to effective tornado warnings, nobody was killed.*

6. Review the Storify (checking for spelling, style, etc.), then save it and embed it on the site.

Student Study Site

Visit the Student Resource Site at **http://study.sagepub.com/lieb** to access:

- Chapter-by-chapter **web quizzes** for independent assessment of course material
- List of online web links and general resources

Chapter 11   **Editorial Triage**

In many emergency rooms, patients' initial contact is with a triage station. That is the point where workers assess the urgency of their injuries or illnesses. Those in more serious condition get moved to the head of the line, while others get to read decades-old magazines for hours on end.

While it's rare – but not unheard of – for an editor to receive copy in critical condition, another form of triage is often mentioned in newsrooms. In this case, **editorial triage** refers to the fact that in some cases material arrives so close to deadline that the editor cannot possibly do a thorough job. So the editor has to use a strategy designed to catch the most serious problems in the least amount of time.

"In an ideal world, you'd look at every piece of copy three times: once to clean up the easy stuff, once to give it a thorough edit, and once to double-check everything," notes Wendalyn Nichols, the past editor of Copyediting.com. "But who lives in that world these days? You need to know how to make the best difference to a document in the time you have."[1]

Shani Hilton, BuzzFeed deputy editor in chief, would seem to agree. "We often will publish things and have copy editors look through it afterward," she says, "the idea being that we don't want our copy editing to hold up things from getting on the website. Ultimately, with breaking news, if there's a typo in the head or a typo in the lead, it's not that big of a deal. We'll fix it when we can."[2] This practice, known as **back-editing**, has become increasingly common in the digital environment. Even well-regarded publications like Slate, which edits all its news articles before publication, does not edit its blog posts in advance.[3]

As we have seen throughout this book, however, publishing without editing can be very risky. So every editor should have a triage checklist ready for those occasions when there just is not enough time to do everything. As Eric Brenner writes:

> It's better to plan ahead. In a calm moment, create your triage list. Decide ahead of time whether, say, it's more important to your publication to spell a TV show's character names correctly than to follow your serial comma rule. Then when it's time to triage, you know to skim the content for the character names rather than for commas.[4]

Such a checklist should balance thoroughness with efficiency. As editor Pam Nelson noted in her blog: "Thousands of words can fly by a copy editor's eyes in a single shift, and myriad things need to be checked and checked off on pages. If I were in charge of copy editors, I would tell them to focus on the most important things (and the list would be short), and worry less about some things."

Nelson is among many editors who have shared their triage lists.[5] Wendalyn Nichols offers a different take on a checklist, one focusing more on the mechanics of writing than on fact-checking.[6] And Nick Jungman, former managing editor of the Wichita Business Journal, has probably created the easiest-to-remember list: Take care of the headACHES.

That acronym stands for Accuracy, Clarity, Headlines, Efficiency and Style, his ranking of tasks from most to least important.[7]

For our purposes, it is most useful to look back over the topics covered in this book and to consider how to deal with them when time is of the essence. The following triage checklist attempts to do that.

1. Does the lead quickly make apparent what's in this for the reader? If not, there's little reason to worry about anything else, as readers will quickly become nonreaders.

2. Are names, titles and businesses spelled correctly? When time is extremely limited, focus particularly on names connected with any defamatory charges, foreign names and names that can be used for either gender.

3. Do names in text match those in headlines and captions? One editor recalls overlooking a photo caption identifying Count Basie as Louis Armstrong. "I was proofreading the words and just glancing at the pictures," she explained.[8]

4. Do numbers add up? Add or subtract figures, check ages against birth years, make sure *millions* are not *billions*, etc.

5. Are there any major holes? The purpose of journalism is to inform readers, not to leave them with unanswered questions. Sometimes stylistic problems and verbosity can lead to confusion. (For example, *A chef cannot add too much salt to this recipe* either means that a chef *can* or *cannot* do so.)

6. Does the headline accurately reflect the main point and latest news in the story? Are all words spelled correctly? Are any words repeated?

7. Is all potential defamatory material covered by one of the defenses? Has the writer given those accused of or criticized for something a chance to respond?

8. Are there any potential copyright violations, particularly in multimedia elements? Vince Rinehart of The Washington Post stresses the importance of making sure that photo sources are correct in order to avoid copyright issues.[9]

9. Finally, are there any glaring style or word usage errors? As Nick Jungman notes: "Too often copy editors like to indulge their OCD over simple style points. But I argue those are usually the least of our worries."[10] (See the Write Right sections at the ends of Chapters 1, 9, 10 and 11 for the most common word usage errors.)

An editor who goes by the handle Copy Curmudgeon agrees with the placement of style and usage errors at the end of the process:

I'd a million times rather let through a hideous typo than a factual error of any importance, rather allow a greengrocer's apostrophe than have a writer's meaning be lost or confused, rather permit a sea of ugly jargon (with definitions, of course) than replace it with one ambiguous layman's term. In my line of work, the beauty of the language is always firmly secondary to its accuracy, though of course we aim for both.[11]

Other editors offer succinct ideas for providing the most help to copy in the least amount of time. One good suggestion is to always check the first sentence and the last paragraph, the places where many mistakes occur.

Perhaps the most extreme triage model comes from Brian Baresch, whose Twitter handle of @Editer hints that he might not be entirely serious: "Extreme efficiency on deadline: 'Is the headline in English? Is the f-word in the lede?' If Y+N, respectively, hit Send."[12]

Of course, virtually every editor would agree that the single most important element in triage editing is to avoid introducing any errors. Editors are only human, and the pressure of impending deadlines can lead them to slip up. When that occurs, it is far worse than if they had done nothing at all.

Wrapping Up

As we have seen through the course of this book, the job of editing is a very broad one that requires attention to a wide range of factors. Unfortunately, time does not always permit a thorough edit. In such cases, triage editing is the best solution: focusing on the things most likely to undermine reader confidence and cause legal problems. A checklist that guides editors through the process of triage is an important resource that every news organization should develop to make sure that when time is tight, the staff can do the best job possible.

Key Points

- Time does not always permit a thorough edit of material before publishing. In those situations, triage editing is the solution: catching the most serious problems in the least amount of time.
- Triage editing works best when it is based on a checklist that balances thoroughness with efficiency.
- Important checklist items include names, numbers, and potential defamation.
- Nick Jungman's headACHES model provides a helpful means of remembering key points to check.

CHAPTER EXERCISE

Creating a Triage Checklist

Using the information presented in this chapter, come up with a 10-point triage checklist for a publication assigned by your instructor. Keep in mind that this list should be able to be handled in a minimal amount of time, as an editor is at deadline.

Next, use this checklist to review an article assigned by your instructor. Take no more than 15 minutes for this. Save that edited version.

Finally, using an original version of that same article, do a thorough edit on it, taking as much time as you need. Compare the results with the version of the article you edited in the previous step. How do they differ? Is there anything your list omitted that you now think should be included, and conversely is there anything in your list that could possibly be omitted?

 ## WRITE RIGHT

Other Confusing Words

In the previous two installments of this section, we looked at words that are commonly confused because they sound so similar. In addition to them, there are many other words that trip up writers and editors. This list contains many of the most common ones.

Aggravate: To make a condition worse.

Irritate: To incite or provoke.

(Continued)

(Continued)

Allusion: A hint or an indirect reference. To allude to something is not to name the thing specifically or to refer to names specifically.

Delusion: A false belief, especially a psychotic one.

Illusion: An unreal impression, misconception or image perception.

Alumnus: A graduate of a school. An alumnus can be either gender but is typically male.

Alumna: A female graduate.

Alumnae: A group of female graduates.

Alumni: A group of male graduates, or a group of graduates of both genders.

Bad: An adjective that should be used to describe the subject of a sentence following verbs such as *is*, *feel* and *taste*.

Badly: An adverb that should modify a verb or adjective.

Between: Refers to two.

Among: Refers to more than two.

Burglary: The act of breaking into a building to commit a crime.

Robbery: Taking something from another person through the use of violence or intimidation.

Theft: A general term for taking another's property without consent.

Collision: A violent contact between moving bodies. A car cannot collide with a tree, a lamppost or any other stationary body.

Compose: To make up.

Comprise: To include. *Comprised of* is always wrong.

Convince: To satisfy someone by proof.

Persuade: To plead with or urge a person so he or she will do or believe something.

Dais: A platform that can hold several people.

Lectern: A slanted table (either floor standing or desktop) on which speakers place their notes.

Podium: A raised platform on which a speaker or conductor stands.

Dilemma: A choice between two equally unfavorable or disagreeable alternatives.

Disinterested: Impartial.

Uninterested: Lacking interest.

Drowned: It is proper to say someone was drowned only when another person held his or her head under water.

Famous: Widely known, usually in a positive light.

Infamous: To have a bad reputation.

Healthful: Something that improves health.

Healthy: In good health.

Ironically: Saying something ironically is saying the contrary of what is expressed. Irony is a form of sarcasm. With apologies to Alanis Morissette, ironically does not mean by coincidence.

Jail: A facility normally used to confine persons awaiting trial or sentencing on misdemeanors or felonies, persons serving sentences for misdemeanors, and persons confined for civil matters, such as failure to pay alimony.

Prison: A maximum security facility for persons convicted of felonies.

Mean, Average: The sum of the units divided by the number of units.

Median: The number in the middle (such as the middle score or income): Half lie above, half below.

Mode: The most commonly occurring number.

Nauseated: Feeling or becoming sick.

Nauseous: Causing disgust.

Parole: Release of a person who is serving a sentence that is still in effect. If the person violates parole, he or she will return to jail or prison.

Probation: A suspended sentence.

Percentage: A figure derived by dividing one number by another.

Percentage point: A figure derived by subtracting one number from another.

Prostate: A gland that can cause problems for men late in life.

Prostrate: Lying face down to show submission or adoration, or overcome by heat.

(Continued)

(Continued)

Ravage: To destroy or ruin.

Ravish: To fill with joy, carry away forcibly or rape.

Ravishing: Unusually striking.

Ravenous: Extremely hungry.

Record: To use the phrases *new record, all time record* or *record first* is to be redundant.

Regime: A political or ruling system. Usually has a negative connotation.

Regimen: A system of diet and exercise for improving health.

Regiment: A military unit consisting of two or more battalions.

Ship: A large vessel.

Boat: A small vessel propelled by oars, sails or outboard motor.

Tall: Used to describe something attached to the ground.

High: Used to describe something not attached to the ground.

Temperature: A measurement of how warm or cool it is, temperature can move only up or down. **Weather** can become warmer or cooler.

Unique: One of a kind. The word never takes qualifiers.

Exercise

Choose the correct word in each sentence.

1. ___ Shakespeare makes a number of biblical **a) illusions b) allusions** in his plays.

2. ___ The burger shop near campus is the site of frequent armed **a) thefts b) robberies c) burglaries**.

3. ___ The core for the Mass Communications major is **a) comprised b) composed** of several upper-level courses.

4. ___ The thought of never having to take another editing class left the students **a) nauseous b) nauseated**.

5. ___ A good copy editor serves as a(n) **a) disinterested b) uninterested** spectator.

6. ___ The guest speaker looked around in vain trying to locate a **a) lectern b) podium** on which she could place her notes.

7. ___ In order to get ready for summer on the beach, he adopted a new **a) regime b) regimen c) regiment** of diet and exercise.

8. ___ The forecast is calling for the **a) temperature b) weather** to be warmer in a few days.

9. ___ As a former junk food fanatic, she initially did not like the idea, but now she is happy to eat only **a) healthful b) healthy** foods.

10. ___ The constant changes in the work schedule **a) aggravated b) irritated** him so much that he finally decided it was time to find a more stable job.

EDITOR'S TOOLKIT

Automated Editing Tools

Sometimes deadlines leave editors with barely enough time to even glance at a piece of copy before hitting the Publish button. While it's always a good idea to check for things that could cause legal problems as well as checking major facts, on some occasions that is all an editor can do.

Fortunately, new tools have hit the market in recent years that promise to help weed out misspellings, style errors and other lesser problems. While that is obviously only part of the process – and some would argue, the least important part – advocates say the software is useful. Editing consultant Merrill Perlman notes that copy editing software can allow copy editors to focus on bigger-picture issues such as factual errors. Perlman groups grammar software with dictionaries and thesauruses – all valuable tools, but none can handle the entire job by itself.[13]

Among the tools:

- **AP StyleGuard** (https://www.apstylebook.com/?do=product&pid=APGSG-917360–1) is a subscription service that integrates with Microsoft Word to automatically check documents for AP style.
- **Grammarly** (http://www.grammarly.com) offers a free seven-day trial and is then available via paid subscription. It scans text

"for proper use of more than 250 advanced grammar rules, spanning everything from subject-verb agreement to article use to modifier placement." In addition, it can check for plagiarism.

- **Lingofy** (http://www.apstylebook.com/?do=product&pid=APL-917360) is also a subscription service, available to subscribers via a Web browser plug-in powered by Tansa Systems' proofing engine. Lingofy corrects errors in spelling, AP style and usage. In addition, it offers a personal dictionary in which users can enter and maintain their own terms, such as proper names not found in The AP Stylebook.
- **PerfectIt** (http://www.intelligentediting.com) is available as a limited-feature free online checker, a free limited-feature plug-in for Word and Google Docs, and downloadable software. It checks for consistent hyphenation and capitalization, international spelling variations and other matters that standard spell checkers do not handle.
- **Tansa** (http://www.tansasystems.com/index.cfm) is available as enterprise-based software or via the Web. The software is designed to correct spelling errors, word usage problems and AP style issues, as well as checking the spelling of proper names, places and punctuation.

Student Study Site

Visit the Student Resource Site at **http://study.sagepub.com/lieb** to access:

- Chapter-by-chapter **web quizzes** for independent assessment of course material
- List of online web links and general resources

NOTES

Chapter 1

1. "Total Number of Websites," InternetLiveStats, 6 May 2014, http://www.internetlivestats.com/total-number-of-websites.
2. "Buzz in the Blogosphere: Millions More Bloggers and Blog Readers," 8 March 2012, http://blog.nielsen.com/nielsenwire/online_mobile/buzz-in-the-blogosphere-millions-more-bloggers-and-blog-readers.
3. "How We Will Read: Clay Shirky," 5 April 2012, http://blog.findings.com/post/20527246081/how-we-will-read-clay-shirky.
4. Michael King, "Will Automated Copy Editors Replace Human Ones?" American Journalism Review, 15 April 2014, http://ajr.org/2014/04/15/copy-editors-in-digital-world.
5. "Copy editing: It's taught me a lot, but it has to change," The Buttry Diary, 25 May 2012, http://stevebuttry.wordpress.com/2012/05/25/copy-editing-its-taught-me-a-lot-but-it-has-to-change.
6. "The Empty Copy Desk," The Baltimore Sun, 23 May 2012, http://www.baltimoresun.com/news/language-blog/bal-the-empty-copy-desk-20120523,0,1491312.story.
7. John Nicosia, "NBC News Confuses 'Harvest Moon' Singer Neil Young With Moon Walker Neil Armstrong," Mediaite, 25 August 2012, http://www.mediaite.com/tv/nbc-news-confuses-harvest-moon-singer-neil-young-with-moon-walker-neil-armstrong; Tim Graham, "NY Times Messes Up the Dakotas On a Map," Newsbusters.org, 5 January 2014, http://newsbusters.org/blogs/tim-graham/2014/01/05/ny-times-messes-dakotas-map#ixzz30xwPy04m; "BBC News, Halo and the Slight Image Search Error," The Guardian, 28 May 2012, http://www.theguardian.com/technology/gamesblog/2012/may/28/bbc-halo-image-news; Brian Stelter, "CNN and Fox Trip Up in Rush to Get the News on the Air," 28 June 2012, http://www.nytimes.com/2012/06/29/us/cnn-and-foxs-supreme-court-mistake.html?_r=0; "Regret the Error," Poynter.org, 25 June 2012, http://www.poynter.org/latest-news/regret-the-error/178451/new-york-times-confuses-gremlins-with-boys-anthony-hopkins-with-anthony-perkins.
8. Adam Liptak, "Blogger Giving Advice Resists a State's: Get a License," The New York Times, 6 August 2012, http://www.nytimes.com/2012/08/07/us/nutrition-blogger-fights-north-carolina-licensing-rebuke.html.

Chapter 2

1. "Top 15 Most Popular News Websites," http://www.ebizmba.com/articles/news-websites.
2. Hamilton Nolan, "Online Paywalls and the Future of Media: A Few Hard Truths," Gawker.com, 7 December 2012, http://gawker.com/5966560/online-paywalls-and-the-future-of-media-a-few-hard-truths.
3. Adrianne Glowski, "5 Critical Tips For Identifying Your Target Audience," Tchnori.com, http://technori.com/2013/02/3122-5-critical-tips-for-identifying-your-target-audience.
4. Melissa Culbertson, "How To Conduct a Reader Survey For Your Blog (and Why You Really Need To Do One!)," Blog Clarity, 14 November 2013, http://www.blogclarity.com/how-to-conduct-a-reader-survey-for-your-blog-and-why-you-really-need-to-do-one.
5. Ramsay Taplin, "The Essential Guide to Creating a Survey Your Readers Will Love," Blog Tyrant, n.d., http://www.blogtyrant.com/blog-survey.
6. Louise Lee, "How to Conduct a Focus Group," Businessweek.com, 8 October 2009, http://www.businessweek.com/stories/2009-10-08/how-to-conduct-a-focus-group.
7. "Online Focus Groups," 2020Research.com, n.d., http://www.2020research.com/online-focus-groups-two-better-ways-to-insights.

8. Debbie Bates-Schrott, "Magazine Mission Statements," BatesCreative.com, 28 April 2009, http://batescreative.com/blog/strategy/magazine-mission-statements.

9. Susan West, "Clarify Your Magazine's Mission Statement," WestGoldEditorial.com, 24 February 2005, http://westgoldeditorial.com/2005/02/clarify-your-magazines-mission-statement. Reprinted with permission, West Gold Editorial.

10. John Benditt, "Case Study: The Scientist," DrivingWheel Consulting, n.d., http://www.drivingwheelconsulting.com/DrivingWheel_Case_Study_-_The_Scientist.html.

11. Steven Greenhouse, "Clothiers Act to Inspect Bangladeshi Factories," The New York Times, 7 July 2013, http://www.nytimes.com/2013/07/08/business/global/clothiers-in-deal-for-inspecting-bangladeshi-factories.html.

12. An interesting discussion of the design of Hotwired.com can be found in this article: Jeffrey Veen, "Looking back at Hotwired," Veen.com, 12 July 2006, http://www.veen.com/jeff/archives/000903.html.

13. Ian Hill, "4 Keys to Online Success for News Organizations," IanHillMedia.tumblr.com, 15 May 2013, http://ianhillmedia.tumblr.com/post/50493732410/4-keys-to-online-success-for-news-organizations.

14. Scott Laningham, "James Mathewson on audience, relevance, and search," IBM.com, 12 January 2011, http://www.ibm.com/developerworks/podcast/dwi/cm-int011211-mathewson.html.

15. "What Is Content Marketing?" Content Marketing Institute, n.d., http://contentmarketinginstitute.com/what-is-content-marketing.

16. Shane Snow, "What journalists need to know about 'content marketing,'" Poynter.org, 28 September 2012, http://www.poynter.org/how-tos/digital-strategies/187229/what-journalists-need-to-know-about-content-marketing.

17. Matthew Ingram, "Why newspapers need to lose the 'view from nowhere,'" 22 May 2012, GigaOm.com, http://gigaom.com/2012/05/22/why-newspapers-need-to-lose-the-view-from-nowhere.

18. Jay Rosen, "The View from Nowhere: Questions and Answers," 10 November 2010, http://pressthink.org/2010/11/the-view-from-nowhere-questions-and-answers.

19. Debbie Williams, "How to Create a Successful Blog Editorial Strategy in Just Six Steps," MarketingProfs.com, 18 June 2012, http://www.marketingprofs.com/articles/2012/8183/how-to-create-a-successful-blog-editorial-strategy-in-just-six-steps#ixzz2Ygd9qb6X.

20. Carrie Morgan, "The Blog Editorial Calendar: Taking Your Client's Blog From Blah to Incredible," SocialMediaToday.com, 21 March 2013, http://socialmediatoday.com/carriemorgan/1316241/blog-editorial-calendar-taking-your-client-s-blog-blah-incredible.

Chapter 3

1. Jay Forman, "Monkeyfishing," Slate.com, 8 June 2001, http://www.slate.com/articles/news_and_politics/vice/2001/06/monkeyfishing.html.

2. See Alex Kuczynski, "Tortured Tale Of Journalism And Monkeys," The New York Times," 25 June 2001, http://www.nytimes.com/2001/06/25/business/tortured-tale-of-journalism-and-monkeys.html, and James Taranto, "Best of the Web Today," The Wall Street Journal, 7 February 2007, http://online.wsj.com/article/SB123196759339682829.html.

3. Michael Kinsley, "Monkeyfishing: Slate Apologizes," Slate.com, 25 June 2001, http://www.slate.com/articles/news_and_politics/slate_fare/2001/06/monkeyfishing_slate_apologizes.html.

4. Jack Shafer, "Slate's author of 'Monkeyfishing' now says none of his story was true," Slate.com, 6 February 2007, http://www.slate.com/articles/news_and_politics/press_box/2007/02/jay_forman_redux.html.

5. Craig Silverman, "AP Issues Correction for Stories Citing Manti Te'o's Fake Girlfriend," Poynter.org, 11 February 2013, http://www.poynter.org/latest-news/regret-the-error/203803/ap-issues-correction-for-stories-citing-manti-teos-fake-girlfriend.

6. Timothy Burke and Jack Dickey, "Manti Te'o's Dead Girlfriend, The Most Heartbreaking And Inspirational Story Of The College Football Season, Is A Hoax," Deadspin.com, 1 January 2013, http://deadspin.com/5976517/manti-teos-dead-girlfriend-the-most-heartbreaking-and-inspirational-story-of-the-college-football-season-is-a-hoax.

7. Craig Silverman, "'Abraham Lincoln Invented Facebook' Tale Was the Perfect Shareable Story," Poynter.org, 10 May 2012, http://www.poynter.org/latest-news/regret-the-error/173523/why-the-fake-abraham-lincoln-invented-facebook-story-was-too-good-to-check.

8. Nate St. Pierre, "Anatomy of a Hoax: How Abraham Lincoln Invented Facebook," Natestpierre. me, 10 May 2012, http://natestpierre.me/2012/05/10/hoax-abraham-lincoln-invented-facebook. Reprinted by permission of Nate St. Pierre.

9. Craig Silverman, "New Research Details How Journalists Verify Information," Poynter.org, 27 February 2013, http://www.poynter.org/latest-news/regret-the-error/203728/new-research-details-how-journalists-verify-information.

10. Margaret Sullivan, "The Times's Work in Progress," The New York Times, 23 March 2013, http://www.nytimes.com/2013/03/24/opinion/sunday/the-timess-work-in-progress.html?pagewanted=all&_r=0.

11. Full story can be found at http://floost.com/reuters.news-post-dreamliner-fire-probe-focuses-on-beacon-boeing-shares-rise-5309685.

12. Beth Braccio Hering, "22 Commonly confused job titles: What do these workers actually do?" CareerBuilder.com, 12 July 2010, http://www.careerbuilder.com/Article/CB-1963-The-Workplace-22-Commonly-confused-job-titles-What-do-these-workers-actually-do.

13. "Most Misspelled Cities in America," EPodunk.com, n.d., http://www.epodunk.com/top10/misspelled/index.html.

14. Timothy Stenovec, "Mitt Romney iPhone App, 'With Mitt,' Misspells 'America,'" The Huffington Post, 30 May 2012, http://www.huffingtonpost.com/2012/05/30/mitt-romney-iphone-app-with-mitt-america-amercia_n_1555714.html.

15. Andre Natta, "Associated Press correction suggests art museum's the size of a doghouse," Poynter.org, 25 June 2013, http://www.poynter.org/latest-news/regret-the-error/216836/associated-press-correction-suggests-art-museums-the-size-of-a-dollhouse.

16. "Anniversary leads to some Titanic mistakes," The Toronto Star, 13 April 2012, http://www.thestar.com/news/insight/2012/04/13/anniversary_leads_to_some_titanic_mistakes.html.

17. Robert Lee Hotz, "Mars Probe Lost Due to Simple Math Error," The Los Angeles Times, 1 October 1999, http://articles.latimes.com/1999/oct/01/news/mn-17288.

18. Richard Witkins, "Jet's Fuel Ran Out After Metric Conversion Errors," The New York Times, 30 July 1983, http://www.nytimes.com/1983/07/30/us/jet-s-fuel-ran-out-after-metric-conversion-errors.html.

19. "Space Mountain Accident Report Released," MouseInfo.com, 21 January 2004, http://www.mouseinfo.com/forums/tokyo-disney-resort/13134-olc-space-mountain-accident-report-released.html.

20. Herb Weisbaum, "Urban legends outlawed ... April Fools'!" MSNBC.com, 1 April 2007, http://www.nbcnews.com/id/17798063/#.UUNBfhyG2So.

21. See, for instance Jonathan Dube, "April Fool's in the News," Cyberjournalist.net, n.d., http://www.cyberjournalist.net/features/aprilfools.htm.

22. "17 Times 'The Onion' Fooled People Who Should Know Better," The Huffington Post, 25 September 2012, http://www.huffingtonpost.com/2012/09/25/fooled-by-the-onion_n_1912413.html.

23. National Gallery of Art (news release), "First Major Exhibition Devoted to History of Manipulated Photography through the 1980s Opens at National Gallery of Art February 17," 16 January 2013, http://www.nga.gov/content/ngaweb/press/exh/3506.html.

24. Ray Richmond, "Fox News Channel Finds Itself Outfoxed," The Los Angeles Times, 9 March 2002, http://articles.latimes.com/2002/mar/09/entertainment/et-richmond9.

25. "The Accidental Tourist," Snopes.com, 20 August 2007, http://www.snopes.com/rumors/photos/tourist.asp.

26. "The Accidental Tourist."

27. "Hurricane Sandy Photographs," Snopes.com, 26 November 2012, http://www.snopes.com/photos/natural/sandy.asp.

28. Craig Silverman, "How Journalists Can Avoid Getting Fooled by Fake Hurricane Sandy Photos," Poynter.org, 29 October 2012, http://www.poynter.org/latest-news/regret-the-error/193470/how-journalists-can-avoid-getting-fooled-by-fake-hurricane-sandy-photos.

29. Craig Silverman, "Three Ways to Spot If an Image Has Been Manipulated," Poynter.org, 22 June 2012, http://www.poynter.org/latest-news/regret-the-error/173387/three-ways-to-spot-if-an-image-has-been-manipulated.

30. Andrew Fitzgerald, "Verifying Tweets when news breaks: Q&A with the NYT's Jennifer Preston," Twitter Blogs, 18 October 2013, https://blog.twitter.com/2013/verifying-tweets-when-news-breaks-qa-with-the-nyts-jennifer-preston-0.

31. David Itzkoff, "Really Cute, But Totally Fake," The New York Times, 26 February 2013, http://www.nytimes.com/2013/02/27/arts/television/pig-rescues-goat-and-the-video-is-really-cute-but-totally-faked.html.

32. Itzkoff.

33. Itzkoff.

34. Jeff Yang, "Anatomy of a meme: The real story behind the Swedish mannequins that looked like 'real women,'" Quartz, 19 March 2013, http://qz.com/64251/anatomy-of-a-meme-the-real-story-behind-the-swedish-mannequins-that-looked-like-real-women.

35. Delia Lloyd, "What an Unusual Swedish Mannequin Reveals About Body Image," The Washington Post, 16 March 2013, http://www.washingtonpost.com/blogs/she-the-people/wp/2013/03/16/what-a-swedish-mannequin-hoax-reveals-about-body-image.

36. Yang, "Anatomy of a meme."

37. Vince Rinehart, personal communication, 8 May 2014.

38. Dan Steinberg, "GW Offers Strong Performance During Virginia's Perfect Game," The Washington Post, 30 March 2011, http://www.washingtonpost.com/blogs/dc-sports-bog/post/gw-offers-strong-performance-during-virginias-perfect-game/2011/03/30/AFhbPg2B_blog.html.

39. Elianna Lev, "Researcher Warns More Prevention Needed to Fight Fetal Alcohol Syndrome," CBC News, 27 June 2006, http://list.web.net/archives/apolnet-l.bak/msg01609.html; originally published at http://www.cbc.ca/cp/health/060625/x062508.html.

40. Curt Hazlett, "Copy Editors: Act as the readers' advocate," American Press Institute, 29 January 2004, http://www.americanpressinstitute.org/rt/hazlett012904 (no longer online).

41. Bill Bickel, "Badly-Written Article of the Week," Crime, Justice & America, 23 July 2012, http://crimejusticeandamerica.com/badly-written-article-of-the-week. Original article at http://abcnews.go.com/US/york-police-captain-mistakenly-shoots-son/story?id=16837822#.UVHJaRyG2Sr.

42. Cecilia Kang, "Verizon, Cablevision emerge as unlikely allies of cable-TV customers fed up with bundling," The Washington Post, 19 March 2013, http://www.washingtonpost.com/business/technology/verizon-cablevision-emerge-as-unlikely-allies-of-cable-customers-fed-up-with-bundling/2013/03/19/11fe0dac-900d-11e2-9cfd-36d6c9b5d7ad_story.html.

43. Megan McArdle, "Why Can't We Unbundle Cable?" The Atlantic, 3 June 2011, http://www.theatlantic.com/business/archive/2011/06/why-cant-we-unbundle-cable/239849.

44. Justin Green, "The Classic Case of a Buried Lede," The Daily Beast, 25 October 2012, http://www.thedailybeast.com/articles/2012/10/25/the-classic-case-of-a-buried-lede.html. Original article at http://www.theatlantic.com/international/archive/2012/10/what-are-the-odds-that-israel-just-attacked-sudan/264082.

45. Lisa Power and William Kelly, "How a teen's iPod can tell you if they will be trouble," The Courier-Mail, 4 February 2013, http://www.couriermail.com.au/news/national/how-a-teens-ipod-can-tell-you-if-they-will-be-trouble/story-fndo1uez-1226570321479.

46. Tim Byron, "According To Study: Does Listening To Deviant Music Actually Lead To Delinquent Behaviour?" The Vine, 18 February 2013, http://www.thevine.com.au/life/news/according-to-study-does-teens-listening-to-deviant-music-lead-to-delinquent-behaviour.

47. "French Scuba Team Finds Parts from Saint-Exupery's Missing Plane," USA Today, 7 April 2004, http://usatoday30.usatoday.com/news/world/2004-04-07-france-plane-parts_x.htm.

48. Virginia Cook, "More Than Thoughtless" (letter to the editor), The Washington Post, 30 April 2005, pg. A-17.

49. Craig Silverman, "Slate's Good Strategy for Correcting Errors on Twitter, Elsewhere," Poynter.org, 4 March 2014, http://www.poynter.org/latest-news/regret-the-error/235681/slates-good-strategy-for-correcting-errors-on-twitter-elsewhere.

50. Craig Silverman, keynote speech to Breakfast of Editing Champions, Association for Education in Journalism and Mass Communication annual conference, 8 August 2014, Montreal, Canada.

51. Craig Silverman, "Since Twitter Hasn't Built a Correction Feature, Here Are 3 Things Journalists Can Do Instead," 29 May 2013, Poynter.org, http://www.poynter.org/latest-news/regret-the-error/214484/since-twitter-hasnt-built-a-correction-feature-here-are-3-things-journalists-can-do-instead.

52. Deborah Howell, "Quote, Unquote," The Washington Post, 12 August 2007, http://www.washingtonpost.com/wp-dyn/content/article/2007/08/10/AR2007081001922.html.

53. Fred Vultee, "Audience Perceptions of Editing Quality: An Experimental Study of the Effects of News Processing," Paper presented to the Newspaper Division, Association for Education in Journalism and Mass Communication, August 2011.

54. Andrew Beaujon, "AP Removes Distinction Between 'Over' and 'More Than,'" Poynter.org, 20 March 2014, http://www.poynter.org/latest-news/mediawire/244240/ap-removes-distinction-between-over-and-more-than.

Chapter 4

1. John E. McIntyre, "No One Right Way," The Baltimore Sun, 16 July 2013, http://articles.baltimoresun.com/2013-07-16/news/bal-no-one-right-way-20130716_1_journalism-course-editing-copy.

2. Christian Cajochensend email, Songül Altanay-Ekici, Mirjam Münch, Sylvia Frey, Vera Knoblauch, Anna Wirz-Justice, "Evidence that the Lunar Cycle Influences Human Sleep," Current Biology, 25 July 2013, http://www.cell.com/current-biology/retrieve/pii/S0960982213007549.

3. "Study Links Lunar Cycles and Human Sleep Patterns," The Washington Post, 29 July 2013, http://www.washingtonpost.com/national/health-science/study-links-lunar-cycles-and-human-sleep-patterns/2013/07/29/a0d06238-f55b-11e2-a2f1-a7acf9bd5d3a_story.html.

4. "Consider Your Voice, Tone and Persona," WritingCommons.org, n.d., http://writingcommons.org/open-text/writing-processes/think-rhetorically/716-consider-your-voice-tone-and-persona.

5. David A. Sarro, commenting on Erin Brenner, "Three Steps to Protecting the Author's Voice," Copyediting.com, 25 June 2013, http://copyediting.com/three-steps-protecting-author-s-voice.

6. Brenner, "Three Steps to Protecting the Author's Voice."

7. Leslie Kaufman, "Self-Taught Cook, Best-Selling Cookbook," The New York Times, 12 December 2012, http://www.nytimes.com/2012/12/13/books/a-cooking-blog-yields-a-franchise-and-a-husband.html?_r=0.

8. Deb Perelman, "Roasted Pear and Chocolate Chunk Scones," SmittenKitchen.com, 26 October 2012, http://smittenkitchen.com/blog/2012/10/roasted-pear-and-chocolate-chunk-scones.

9. Kaufman, "Self-Taught Cook, Best-Selling Cookbook."

10. Brenner, "Three Steps to Protecting the Author's Voice."

11. Scott Laningham, "James Mathewson on Audience, Relevance and Search," IBM.com, 12 January 2011, http://www.ibm.com/developerworks/podcast/dwi/cm-int011211-mathewson.html.

12. Carlos Lozada, "Confessions of an editor: A review of 'How to Write Short' by Roy Peter Clark," The Washington Post, 22 August 2013, http://www.washingtonpost.com/opinions/confessions-of-an-editor-a-review-of-how-to-write-short-by-roy-peter-clark/2013/08/22/cfcaf1e4-0068-11e3-9711-3708310f6f4d_story.html.

13. Jonathan Crossfield, "Resisting Extravagant Verbosity," 20 November 2008, JonathanCrossfield.com, http://www.jonathancrossfield.com/blog/2008/11/resisting-extravagant-verbosity.html.

14. Crossfield.

15. "Style Guide," The Economist, n.d., http://www.economist.com/styleguide/introduction. Full essay can be found at https://www.mtholyoke.edu/acad/intrel/orwell46.htm.

16. "Cure My Verbosity," Ask.com, 3 February 2010, http://ask.metafilter.com/144987/Cure-My-Verbosity.

17. "Paramedic Method: A Lesson in Writing Concisely," Purdue Owl, n.d., http://owl.english.pur due.edu/owl/owlprint/635.

18. This is one of many good practice examples available at "Revising Sentences Using the Paramedic Method," Lirvin.net, n.d., http://www.lirvin.net/WGuides/Pmethod.htm.

19. "Wordiness Made Spare," Plain Language.gov, n.d., http://www.plainlanguage.gov/examples/before_after/wordiness.cfm.

20. List retrieved from "Conjunctions," Capital Community College, n.d., http://grammar.ccc.com mnet.edu/grammar/conjunctions.htm.

21. Geoff Nunberg, "The Word 'Hopefully' Is Here To Stay, Hopefully," NPR.com, 30 May 2012, http://www.npr.org/2012/05/30/153709651/the-word-hopefully-is-here-to-stay-hopefully.

Chapter 5

1. Brian Clark, "How to Write Magnetic Headlines," Copyblogger, n.d., http://www.copyblogger.com/magnetic-headlines.

2. Found at http://www.dailymail.co.uk/news/article-2300604/David-Phelps-son-Westboro-Baptist-Church-leader-attacked-naked-35-STONE-man-hilarious-publicity-stunt-video.html.

3. Michael Roston, "If a Tweet Worked Once, Send It Again – and Other Lessons from The New York Times' Social Media Desk," Nieman Lab, 6 January 2014, http://www.niemanlab.org/2014/01/if-a-tweet-worked-once-send-it-again-and-other-lessons-from-the-new-york-times-social-media-desk.

4. Shelley Kramer, "Blogging Best Practices: Subheads Matter," V3im.com, 29 March 2013, http://www.v3im.com/2013/03/blogging-best-practices-subheads-matter/#axzz2TrLLgwDu.

5. Shawn Smith, "Headline writing: How web and print headlines differ," New Media Bytes, 25 March 2008, http://www.newmediabytes.com/2008/03/25/differences-between-web-online-print-headlines.

6. Brian Clark, "Do Keywords in Post Titles Really Matter?" Copyblogger, n.d., http://www.copyblogger.com/do-keywords-in-post-titles-really-matter.

7. Tracy Gold, "Content Strategy: 9 Secrets for Awesome Blog Post Titles," Content Marketing Institute, 23 January 2013, http://contentmarketinginstitute.com/2013/01/content-strategy-best-blog-post-titles.

8. "About Us," Upworthy, n.d., http://www.upworthy.com/about.

9. Jeff Bercovici, "These Five Astonishing Headline Writing Secrets Will Make You Cry, Or At Least Click," Forbes, 1 March 2013, http://www.forbes.com/sites/jeffbercovici/2013/03/01/these-five-astonishing-headline-writing-secrets-will-make-you-cry.

10. Steve Buttry, "Susan Steade's SEO headline tips: Business up front, party in the back," The Buttry Diary, 1 November 2013, http://stevebuttry.wordpress.com/2013/11/01/susan-steades-seo-headline-tips-business-up-front-party-in-the-back.

11. Bercovici, "These Five Astonishing Headline Writing Secrets."

12. "Case Study: How a Headline Made the Difference Between 100 and 5000 Visits," Pick The Brain, 31 January 2007, http://www.pickthebrain.com/blog/case-study-how-a-headline-made-the-difference-between-100-and-5000-visits.

13. Choire Sicha, "Take A Minute To Watch The New Way We Make Web Headlines Now," The Awl, 17 January 2013, http://www.theawl.com/2013/01/take-a-minute-to-watch-the-new-way-we-make-web-headlines-now.

14. Bercovici, "These Five Astonishing Headline Writing Secrets."

15. Sicha, "Take A Minute."

16. "The Funniest Headline Fails Of All Time," The Huffington Post, 26 April 2010, http://www.huffingtonpost.com/2010/02/24/the-funniest-headline-fai_n_474212.html#s70487&title=TIgers_Not_So.

17. "Headline Writing: Punctuation and Splits," KUEditing.com, n.d., http://www.kuediting.com/headlines/punctuation-and-splits.

18. Brian Clark, "One Big Way to Avoid a Headline Fail," Copyblogger.com, n.d., http://www.copyblogger.com/headline-fail.

19. Monica Moses, "Sell Stories! Write Great Cutlines," Poynter.org, 27 July 2002, http://www
.poynter.org/how-tos/newsgathering-storytelling/eyes-on-the-news/1419/sell-stories-write-
great-cutlines.

20. Sydney Smith, Rhonda Roland Shearer, "Super Hero Firefighter? NBC News Caption Said 'Fireman
Holds Up a Fire Truck' in Sinkhole," 5 March 2013 http://www.imediaethics.org/News/3797/
Super_hero_firefighter_nbc_news_caption_said_fireman_holds_up_a_fire_truck_in_sinkhole.php.

Chapter 6

1. "Legal Guide for Bloggers," Electronic Frontier Foundation, n.d., https://www.eff.org/issues/
bloggers/legal.

2. For more on this, see Mark Goodman, "Legal Issues for Publishing Online," National Scholastic
Press Association, n.d., http://www.studentpress.org/nspa/pdf/wheel_legalissuesonline.pdf.

3. Douglas E. Lee, "Prior Restraint," First Amendment Center, 13 September 2002, http://www
.firstamendmentcenter.org/prior-restraint.

4. Campbell Robertson, "Blogger's Incarceration Raises First Amendment Questions," The New York
Times, 11 January 2014, http://www.nytimes.com/2014/01/12/us/bloggers-incarceration-raises-
first-amendment-questions.html.

5. Jamie Schuman, "Alabama Blogger Jailed After Violating Prior Restraint over Articles that Alleged
High-Profile Affair," Reporters Committee for Freedom of the Press, 25 October 2013, http://www
.rcfp.org/browse-media-law-resources/news/alabama-blogger-jailed-after-violating-prior-
restraint-over-articles.

6. Nicole Flatow, "Alabama Blogger Released After Five Months In Jail," ThinkProgress.org, 3 April
2014, http://thinkprogress.org/justice/2014/04/03/3422592/alabama-blogger-released-after-
five-months-in-jail.

7. Michael Rooney, "Blogger Roger Shuler Released after Five Months in Jail," Reporters Committee
on Freedom of the Press, 2 April 2014, http://www.rcfp.org/browse-media-law-resources/news/
blogger-roger-shuler-released-after-five-months-jail.

8. Jonathan Friendly, "Settlement Due in Alton Telegraph Libel Case," The New York Times, 15 April
1982, http://www.nytimes.com/1982/04/15/us/settlement-due-in-alton-telegraph-libel-case.
html.

9. New York Times Co. v. Sullivan, CaseBriefs, n.d., http://www.casebriefs.com/blog/law/torts/
torts-keyed-to-epstein/defamation/new-york-times-co-v-sullivan.

10. See, for example, "Lawsuit claims CLTV used wrong photo in story," the Chicago Tribune, 1
February 2012, http://www.chicagotribune.com/news/local/breaking/chi-lawsuit-claims-cltv-
used-wrong-photo-in-story-20120201,0,3108313.story.

11. Hustler Magazine v. Falwell, CaseBriefs, n.d., http://www.casebriefs.com/blog/law/torts/torts-
keyed-to-epstein/privacy/hustler-magazine-v-falwell.

12. "When Omission of Material Facts May Constitute Defamation," Reporters Committee for
Freedom of the Press, n.d., http://www.rcfp.org/browse-media-law-resources/digital-journalists-
legal-guide/when-omission-material-facts-may-constitu.

13. David Carr, "Judge Clarifies That Bloggers Can Be Journalists (Just Not One in Particular)," The
New York Times, 2 April 2012, http://mediadecoder.blogs.nytimes.com/2012/04/02/judge-
clarifies-that-bloggers-can-be-journalists-just-not-one-in-particular.

14. "Judge rules, again, that blogger Crystal Cox is not a journalist. You know why? Because she ISN'T
a journalist," The Legal Satyricon, 30 March 2012, http://randazza.wordpress.com/2012/03/30/
judge-rules-again-that-blogger-crystal-cox-is-not-a-journalist-you-know-why-because-she-isnt-a-
journalist.

15. Carr.

16. Sean Hollister, "Bloggers Get the Same Libel Protection as Traditional Journalists, Federal Court
Rules," The Verge, 18 January 2014, http://www.theverge.com/2014/1/18/5320828/bloggers-
get-the-same-libel-protection-as-traditional-journalists.

17. "Defamation Law: Guide to Libel and Slander Law," HG.org, n.d., http://www.hg.org/
defamation.html.

18. Adam Liptak, "Serving You Tonight Will Be Our Lawyer," The New York Times, 7 March 2007, http://www.nytimes.com/2007/03/07/dining/07lega.html.

19. Bose Corp. v. Consumers Union of United States, Inc., CaseBriefs, n.d., http://www.casebriefs.com/blog/law/civil-procedure/civil-procedure-keyed-to-marcus/appeals/bose-corporation-v-consumers-union-of-united-states-inc.

20. "Texas Cattlemen vs. Howard Lyman and Oprah Winfrey," Howard Lyman: Mad Cowboy, n.d., http://www.madcowboy.com/01_BookOP.000.html.

21. Kristi Eaton and Grant Schulte, "Pink Slime Maker Sues ABC News For $1.2 Billion: Lawsuit Accuses Network Of Defamation," The Huffington Post, 13 September 2012, http://www.huffingtonpost.com/2012/09/13/pink-slime-abc-news-lawsuit-defamation_n_1880709.html.

22. Abby Simon, "Jury: Blogger Johnny Northside must pay $60,000 to fired community leader," StarTribune.com, 12 March 2011, http://www.startribune.com/local/117805398.html?refer=y.

23. Abby Simon, "Verdict Stands Against Blogger in Firing at U," StarTribune.com, 29 August 2011, http://www.startribune.com/local/minneapolis/128638308.html?refer=y.

24. "$60,000 Verdict for Blogging the Truth About A Person Intending to Get Him Fired—Reversed," The Volokh Conspiracy, 20 August 2012, http://www.volokh.com/2012/08/20/60000-verdict-for-blogging-the-truth-about-a-person-intending-to-get-him-fired-reversed.

25. For more on this, see "Opinion and Fair Comment Privileges," Digital Media Law Project, 22 July 2008, http://www.dmlp.org/legal-guide/opinion-and-fair-comment-privileges.

26. "Fair Report Privilege," Digital Media Law Project, 22 July 2008, http://www.dmlp.org/legal-guide/fair-report-privilege.

27. "Neutral Report Privilege," Digital Media Law Project, 22 July 2008, http://www.dmlp.org/legal-guide/neutral-report-privilege.

28. "Neutral Report Privilege."

29. "Opinion and Fair Comment Privileges," Digital Media Law Project, 22 July 2008, http://www.dmlp.org/legal-guide/opinion-and-fair-comment-privileges.

30. Matthew Belloni, "Courtney Love to Pay $430,000 to Settle Twitter Defamation Case," The Hollywood Reporter, 3 March 2011, http://www.hollywoodreporter.com/blogs/thr-esq/courtney-love-pay-430000-settle-163919.

31. Devon Maloney, "Courtney Love, Professional Defendant: Breaking Down 5 Recent Legal Snafus," Spin, 11 July 2012, http://www.spin.com/articles/courtney-love-professional-defendant-breaking-down-5-recent-legal-snafus.

32. Pamela Chen, "Courtney Love Found Not Liable in Landmark Twitter Defamation Case," Spin, 24 January 2014, http://www.spin.com/articles/courtney-love-twitter-defamation-lawsuit-verdict-guilty.

33. Susan H. Aprill, "Defamation and the Media," The Florida Bar Media & Communications Law Committee, 1 September 2004, http://www.floridabar.org/DIVCOM/PI/RHandbook01.nsf/1119bd38ae090a748525676f0053b606/f4f331f77edc8784852569cb004cb22c.

34. The Digital Media Law Project offers summaries of defamation laws in several states at http://www.dmlp.org/legal-guide/state-law-defamation.

35. "Proving Fault: Actual Malice and Negligence," Digital Media Law Project, 7 August 2008, http://www.dmlp.org/legal-guide/proving-fault-actual-malice-and-negligence.

36. "Are YOU a Public Figure?" National Academy of Television Arts and Sciences, New York, 6 April 2009, http://www.nyemmys.org/en/art/36.

37. Jonathan D. Hart, "Internet Law: A Field Guide," Sixth Edition, BNA Books, 2008, p. 320.

38. "Online Defamation Law," Electronic Frontier Foundation, https://www.eff.org/issues/bloggers/legal/liability/defamation.

39. "Proving Fault: Actual Malice and Negligence."

40. "Libel and Slander Per Se vs Per Quod," Dancing with Lawyers, n.d., http://www.dancingwithlawyers.com/freeinfo/libel-slander-per-se.shtml.

41. Hart, p. 361.

42. "Publishing the Statements and Content of Others," Digital Media Law Project, 25 August 2009, http://www.dmlp.org/legal-guide/publishing-statements-and-content-others.

43. "Section 230 Protections," Electronic Frontier Foundation, n.d., https://www.eff.org/issues/bloggers/legal/liability/230.

44. "Protection for satire and parody," Reporters Committee for Freedom of the Press, n.d., http://www.rcfp.org/browse-media-law-resources/digital-journalists-legal-guide/protection-satire-and-parody.

45. "Protection for satire and parody."

46. Hart, p. 325.

47. "Anonymous speech online: When must the identity of a masked commenter be revealed?" Reporters Committee for Freedom of the Press, n.d., http://www.rcfp.org/browse-media-law-resources/digital-journalists-legal-guide/anonymous-speech-online-when-must-identit.

48. "Guarding Against the Chill: A Survival Guide for SLAPP Victims," The First Amendment Project, n.d., http://www.thefirstamendment.org/slapp.html.

49. "Vogel v. Felice," Digital Media Law Project, 11 September 2008, http://www.dmlp.org/threats/vogel-v-felice.

50. Hart, p. 326.

51. "Correcting or clarifying published mistakes," Reporters Committee for Freedom of the Press, n.d., http://www.rcfp.org/browse-media-law-resources/digital-journalists-legal-guide/correcting-or-clarifying-published-mistak.

52. Hart, p. 333.

53. Hart, p. 341.

54. "Citizen Media Law Project Launches Legal Assistance Network for Online Journalists," 19 November 2009, http://cyber.law.harvard.edu/newsroom/Online_Media_Legal_Network.

Chapter 7

1. Priscilla M. Regan, "Legislating Privacy: Technology, social values and public policy" 46 (1995), 111 supra note 20 cited in Daniel J. Solove, "A Brief History of Information Privacy Law," in PROSKAUER ON PRIVACY §§ 1.1-.6 (Christopher Wolf, ed., 2006). Available at SSRN: http://ssrn.com/abstract=914271.

2. The topic was addressed in the landmark 1890 decision. Samuel D. Warren & Louis D. Brandeis, The Right to Privacy, 4 HARV. L. REV. 193 (1890), cited in Daniel J. Solove, "A Brief History of Information Privacy Law," in PROSKAUER ON PRIVACY §§ 1.1-.6 (Christopher Wolf, ed., 2006). Available at SSRN: http://ssrn.com/abstract=914271.

3. Restatement (Second) of Torts, available at http://www.tomwbell.com/NetLaw/Ch05/R2ndTorts.html.

4. "Getting It Right, But in a 'False Light,'" Reporters Committee for Freedom of the Press, n.d., http://www.rcfp.org/browse-media-law-resources/digital-journalists-legal-guide/getting-it-right-false-light-0.

5. "Getting It Right, But in a 'False Light.'"

6. "Getting It Right, But in a 'False Light.'"

7. Restatement (Second) of Torts.

8. "Publishing Highly Personal and Embarrassing Information About Another, Even if Completely True," Reporters Committee for Freedom of the Press, n.d., http://www.rcfp.org/browse-media-law-resources/digital-journalists-legal-guide/publishing-highly-personal-and-embarrassi.

9. "Publishing Highly Personal and Embarrassing Information About Another, Even if Completely True."

10. "Publishing Highly Personal and Embarrassing Information About Another, Even if Completely True."

11. "Intrusion Upon Seclusion," IT Law Wiki, n.d., http://itlaw.wikia.com/wiki/Intrusion_upon_seclusion#cite_ref-11.

12. "Liability for Intrusive or Harassing Newsgathering Activities," Reporters Committee for Freedom of the Press, n.d., http://www.rcfp.org/browse-media-law-resources/digital-journalists-legal-guide/liability-intrusive-or-harassing-newsgath#sthash.5jd9WVlp.dpuf.

13. Restatement (Second) of Torts.

14. "Liability for Intrusive or Harassing Newsgathering Activities."

15. A full account of the case can be found in Don Van Natta Jr., Jo Becker and Graham Bowley, "Tabloid Hack Attack on Royals, and Beyond," The New York Times, 1 September 2010, http://www.nytimes.com/2010/09/05/magazine/05hacking-t.html?ref=newsoftheworld.

16. More on the case can be found at Daniel Fisher, "Can Katherine Heigl Win Lawsuit Over Unauthorized Tweet Of Her Face? Probably," Forbes, 15 April 2014, http://www.forbes.com/sites/danielfisher/2014/04/15/can-katherine-heigl-win-for-unauthorized-use-of-her-face-probably/; and Nate Raymond, "Katherine Heigl, Duane Reade end lawsuit over actress' photo," Reuters, 27 August 2014, http://www.reuters.com/article/2014/08/27/us-people-katherineheigl-idUSKBN0GR2BD20140827.

17. "Using Another Person's Name or Photograph," Reporters Committee for Freedom of the Press, n.d., http://www.rcfp.org/browse-media-law-resources/digital-journalists-legal-guide/using-another-persons-name-or-photograph.

18. "Brief History of RoP," Right of Publicity, n.d., http://rightofpublicity.com/brief-history-of-rop.

19. Tim Barribeau, "Getty, AFP Appeal $1.2 Million Ruling on Daniel Morel Case," 14 January 2014, http://www.americanphotomag.com/article/2014/01/getty-afp-appeal-12-million-ruling-daniel-morel-case.

20. "Fair Use," Digital Media Law Project, n.d., http://www.dmlp.org/legal-guide/fair-use.

21. From Section 107 of the U.S. Copyright Act, as cited in "Fair Use."

22. Andrew Beaujon, "Washington Post Aggregates Nearly Entire Putin Op-ed," Poynter.org, 12 September 2013, http://www.poynter.org/latest-news/mediawire/223525/washington-post-aggregates-nearly-entire-putin-op-ed/#.UjIDUKi7aKQ.twitter.

23. "Protecting Yourself Against Copyright Claims Based on User Content," Digital Media Law Project, n.d., http://www.dmlp.org/legal-guide/protecting-yourself-against-copyright-claims-based-user-content.

24. "Publishing Product or Service Endorsements," Digital Media Law Project, n.d., http://www.dmlp.org/legal-guide/publishing-product-or-service-endorsements.

25. "Panel on the FTC's New Endorsement and Testimonial Guides," Rebecca Tushnet's 43(B)log, 1 December 2009, http://tushnet.blogspot.com/2009/12/panel-on-ftcs-new-endorsement-and.html.

26. "Avoiding Misleading and Unsubstantiated Claims," Digital Media Law Project, n.d., http://www.dmlp.org/legal-guide/avoiding-misleading-and-unsubstantiated-claims.

27. "Using the Name or Likeness of Another," Digital Media Law Project, n.d., http://www.dmlp.org/legal-guide/using-name-or-likeness-another. The original legal complaint is well worth reading at http://www.dmlp.org/sites/citmedialaw.org/files/2007-09-00-Alison%20Chang%20Complaint_0.pdf.

28. "Massachusetts," Reporters Committee for Freedom of the Press, 1 August 2012, http://www.rcfp.org/reporters-recording-guide/state-state-guide/massachusetts#sthash.fkcQlFye.dpuf.

29. Louise Roug, "Eye in the Sky," Columbia Journalism Review, 1 May 2014, http://www.cjr.org/cover_story/eye_in_the_sky.php.

30. Roug.

31. Gene Ely, "Rachel, I'm Thinking of Writing a Blog," Medialife Magazine, 5 October 2012, http://www.medialifemagazine.com/rachel-im-thinking-of-writing-a-blog.

32. Peter Lattman, "Apple Fan Site Shuts Down As Part Of Lawsuit Settlement," 20 December 2007, The Wall Street Journal, http://blogs.wsj.com/law/2007/12/20/apple-fan-site-shuts-down-as-part-of-lawsuit-settlement.

33. Lindsay Goldwert, "Cash-strapped Philly: Bloggers must pay for business license," New York Daily News, 23 August 2010, http://www.nydailynews.com/money/cash-strapped-philly-bloggers-pay-business-license-article-1.205909#ixzz2hMJ76zH9.

34. See, for instance, Steve Green, "Righthaven Extends Copyright Lawsuit Campaign to Individual Web Posters," VegasInc, 12 January 2011, http://www.vegasinc.com/news/2011/jan/12/righthaven-extends-copyright-lawsuit-campaign-indi.

35. Jody Vandergriff, "The True Cost of Copyright Infringement," WebDAM, 10 March 2011, http://www.webdamsolutions.com/digital-asset-management/true-costs-of-copyright-infringement.

36. The decision can be found at http://supreme.justia.com/cases/federal/us/443/97/case.html.

37. Sydney Smith, "Should Journalists Name Juveniles in Crime Stories?" iMediaEthics, 2 July 2011, http://www.imediaethics.org/News/1544/Should_journalists_name_juveniles_in_crime_stories.php.

38. Neal Ungerleider, "Saudi Arabia Now Forcing News Bloggers to Obtain Licenses, Promote Islam," Fast Company, 12 January 2011, http://www.fastcompany.com/1716303/saudi-arabia-now-forcing-news-bloggers-obtain-licenses-promote-islam.

39. Alex Au Waipang, "Singapore Bloggers Wary of News Site License Scheme," Committee to Protect Journalists, 4 June 2013, http://www.cpj.org/internet/2013/06/singapores-news-site-license-plan-raises-questions.php.

40. Declan McCullagh, "Dow Jones Settles Net Defamation Suit," CNET.com, 15 November 2004, http://www.zdnet.com/news/dow-jones-settles-net-defamation-suit/139780.

41. The material in this section is based on "Dealing with Foreign Legal Threats," Digital Media Law Project, n.d., http://www.dmlp.org/legal-guide/dealing-foreign-legal-threats.

42. Declan McCullagh and Evan Hansen, "Libel without frontiers shakes the Net," CNET.com, 11 December 2002, http://news.cnet.com/Libel-without-frontiers-shakes-the-Net/2100-1028_3-976988.html.

43. The bill creating the SPEECH Act can be found at http://www.gpo.gov/fdsys/pkg/PLAW-111publ223/html/PLAW-111publ223.htm.

44. David Ardia, "Libel Tourism: A First Amendment Holiday," Digital Media Law Project, 16 September 2008, http://www.dmlp.org/blog/2008/libel-tourism-first-amendment-holiday.

Chapter 8

1. "Registering Reporters: How Licensing of Journalists Threatens Independent Media," Center for International Media Assistance, n.d., http://cima.ned.org/publications/research-reports/registering-reporters-how-licensing-journalists-threatens-independent.

2. "Congress and the Justice Dept's Dangerous Attempts to Define 'Journalist' Threaten to Exclude Bloggers," Electronic Frontier Foundation, 23 July 2013, https://www.eff.org/deeplinks/2013/07/congress-and-justice-depts-dangerous-attempts-define-journalist-threaten-exclude.

3. "CORRECTING THE RECORD; Times Reporter Who Resigned Leaves Long Trail of Deception," The New York Times, 11 May 2003, http://www.nytimes.com/2003/05/11/us/correcting-the-record-times-reporter-who-resigned-leaves-long-trail-of-deception.html.

4. Ann O'Neill and Beth Karas, "Trust Me, an Infamous Serial Liar Says," CNN.com, 19 December 2011, http://www.cnn.com/2011/12/16/justice/stephen-glass/index.html.

5. Steve Buttry, "Our cheating culture: Plagiarism and fabrication are unacceptable in journalism," The Buttry Diary, 31 October 2011, http://stevebuttry.wordpress.com/2011/10/31/our-cheating-culture-plagiarism-and-fabrication-are-unacceptable-in-journalism.

6. Sara Jean Green and Ian Ith, "Ethics of Paper's Fake Arson Story Debated," The Seattle Times, 18 April 2003, http://community.seattletimes.nwsource.com/archive/?date=20030418&slug=sherer18e.

7. Buttry, "Our cheating culture."

8. Howard Kurtz, "Sun Columnist Dismissed; Attribution Issues Cited," The Washington Post, 5 January 2006, http://www.washingtonpost.com/wp-dyn/content/article/2006/01/04/AR2006010402179.html.

9. Kathy English, "A clear case of in-house plagiarism: Public Editor," The Toronto Star, 4 October 2013, http://www.thestar.com/opinion/public_editor/2013/10/04/a_clear_case_of_inhouse_plagiarism_public_editor.html.

10. Mark Ellison, "Professional Harikari," marcellison.com, 4 October 2013, http://www.marcellison.com/blog/?p=2845.

11. Erik Wemple, "CNN Fires News Editor Marie-Louise Gumuchian for Plagiarism," The Washington Post, 16 May 2014, http://www.washingtonpost.com/blogs/erik-wemple/wp/2014/05/16/cnn-fires-news-editor-marie-louise-gumuchian-for-plagiarism.

12. "NPAA Code of Ethics," National Press Photographers Association, n.d., https://nppa.org/code_of_ethics.

13. Jim Goldstein, "Ethics of Photography: Career Suicide by Photoshop," JMG Galleries, 17 April 2007, http://www.jmg-galleries.com/blog/2007/04/17/ethics-of-photography-career-suicide-by-photoshop.

14. Steve Myers, "AP Drops Freelance Photographer Who Photoshopped His Shadow Out of Image," Poynter.org, 11 July 2011, http://www.poynter.org/latest-news/mediawire/138728/ap-drops-freelance-photographer-who-photoshopped-his-shadow-out-of-image.

15. Jack Shafer, "The Lying Game," Columbia Journalism Review, 24 September 2012, http://www.cjr.org/review/the_lying_game.php?page=all.

16. For more on this topic, see J.D. Lasica, "Taking Ethics to the Net," Quill, July/August 2001, p. 42.

17. Bob Steele, "Lying in the Name of Truth: When Is It Justified for Journalists?" Poynter.org, 5 July 2007, http://www.poynter.org/latest-news/everyday-ethics/83268/lying-in-the-name-of-truth when-is-it-justified-for-journalists.

18. Bob Steele, "Deception/Hidden Cameras Checklist," Poynter.org, 5 July 2002, http://www.poynter.org/uncategorized/744/deceptionhidden-cameras-checklist.

19. Gene Foreman, "Journalism Ethics in a Digital Age," University of Arkansas, 10 April 2013, http://journalism.uark.edu/wp/?p=2723.

20. For more on this story, see Julie Moos, "The Atlantic publishes then pulls sponsored content from Church of Scientology," Poynter.org, 15 January 2013, http://www.poynter.org/latest-news/mediawire/200593/the-atlantic-pulls-sponsored-content-from-church-of-scientology.

21. Foreman.

22. Gabriel Sherman, "Sulzberger Swings the Axe Again: Why the Times Publisher and Jill Abramson Were Doomed From the Start," New York Magazine, 15 May 2014, http://nymag.com/daily/intelligencer/2014/05/sulzberger-swings-the-axe-why-he-fired-abramson.html.

23. For a good discussion of this issue, see Robert I. Berkman and Christopher A. Shumway, "Digital dilemmas: Ethical issues for online media professionals," Iowa State Press, 2003, pp. 276–279.

24. Kira Goldenberg, "Journalism Ethics in a Digital Age," Columbia Journalism Review, 26 October 2012, http://www.cjr.org/behind_the_news/journalism_ethics_in_a_digital.php?page=all.

25. J.D. Lasica, "Transparency Begets Trust in the Ever-Expanding Blog-o-Sphere," Online Journalism Review, 12 August 2004, http://ojr.org/ojr/technology/1092267863.php.

26. Greg Marx, "Darts and Laurels," Columbia Journalism Review, 17 September 2009, http://www.cjr.org/darts_and_laurels/news_outlets_in_connecticut_gr.php. A follow-up can be found at http://usnews.nbcnews.com/_news/2012/01/04/9951141-former-ad-exec-sentenced-to-70-years-for-kidnapping-wife?lite.

27. David Carnoy, "Top 40 must-have Blu-ray discs," CNET, 22 December 2013, http://reviews.cnet.com/8301-18438_7-10207170-82/top-40-must-have-blu-ray-discs.

28. Joe Strupp, "The Inside Story: Newspapers go 'transparent,'" Editor and Publisher, 28 January 2007, http://www.editorandpublisher.com/PrintArticle/THE-INSIDE-STORY-Newspapers-Go-Transparent-.

29. Sarah Knapton, "BBC Staff Told to Stop Inviting Cranks on to Science Programmes," The Telegraph, 4 July 2014, http://www.telegraph.co.uk/culture/tvandradio/bbc/10944629/BBC-staff-told-to-stop-inviting-cranks-on-to-science-programmes.html.

30. Foreman.

31. Erik Wemple, "New York Post: 'Bag Men' headline was an 'attention-getter,'" The Washington Post, 4 November 2013, http://www.washingtonpost.com/blogs/erik-wemple/wp/2013/11/04/new-york-post-bag-men-headline-was-an-attention-getter.

32. Claire Cain Miller, "Tech Blogger Parts With AOL," The New York Times, 12 September 2011, http://www.nytimes.com/2011/09/13/technology/michael-arrington-and-aol-part-company.html?_r=0.

33. Amy Webb, Google Plus, 6 September 2011, https://plus.google.com/112609956355138553458/posts/RSoukUZfAZm.

34. Antony Loewenstein, "My Wishlist for Journalism in 2014," The Guardian, 26 December 2013, http://www.theguardian.com/commentisfree/2013/dec/27/my-wishlist-for-journalism-in-2014.

35. "Anonymous Sources," Society of Professional Journalists, n.d., http://www.spj.org/ethics-papers-anonymity.asp.

36. "Anonymous Sourcing > Fairness," NPR Ethics Handbook, n.d., http://ethics.npr.org/tag/anonymity.

37. Lindsay Gsell, "Comments Anonymous," American Journalism Review, February/March 2009, http://ajrarchive.org/article.asp?id=4681.

38. Barb Darrow, "Huffington Post to End Anonymous Comments," Gigaom, 21 August 2013, http://gigaom.com/2013/08/21/huffington-post-to-end-anonymous-comments.

39. Joshua Benton, "Tough Love: Gawker finds making it harder for comments to be seen leads to more (and better) comments," Neiman Journalism Lab, 13 April 2010, http://www.niemanlab.org/2010/04/tough-love-gawker-finds-making-it-harder-for-comments-to-be-seen-leads-to-more-and-better-comments.

40. Gregory Ferenstein, "Surprisingly Good Evidence That Real Name Policies Fail To Improve Comments," TechCrunch, 29 July 2012, http://techcrunch.com/2012/07/29/surprisingly-good-evidence-that-real-name-policies-fail-to-improve-comments.

41. Cynthia Tucker, "Why Don't We Name Victims of Rape?" The Atlanta Journal-Constitution, 13 July 2011, http://blogs.ajc.com/cynthia-tucker/2011/07/13/why-dont-we-name-victims-of-rape.

42. Frank Smyth, "Do News Blackouts Help Journalists Held Captive?" Committee to Protect Journalists, 26 February 2013, http://www.cpj.org/security/2013/02/do-news-blackouts-help-journalists-held-captive.php.

43. Dan Murphy, "Richard Engel Freed, But News Blackout Debate Remains," Christian Science Monitor, 13 December 2012, http://www.csmonitor.com/World/Security-Watch/Backchannels/2012/1218/Richard-Engel-freed-but-news-blackout-debate-remains.

44. Smyth.

45. Glenn Greenwald, "The NYT's Journalistic Obedience," The New York Times, 21 February 2011, http://www.salon.com/2011/02/21/nyt_16.

46. Kevin Drum, "Political Animal," Washington Monthly, 24 June 2004, http://www.washington-monthly.com/archives/individual/2004_06/004216.php.

47. See, for instance, "Photos of the Boston Marathon Bombing," The Atlantic, 15 April 2013, http://www.theatlantic.com/infocus/2013/04/photos-of-the-boston-marathon-bombing/100495.

48. David Carr, "Train Wreck: The New York Post's Subway Cover," 5 December 2012, http://mediadecoder.blogs.nytimes.com/2012/12/05/train-wreck-the-new-york-posts-subway-cover/?_php=true&_type=blogs&smid=tw-share&_r=0.

49. Adam Martin, "New York Times: Graphic Empire State shooting photo was newsworthy," The Atlantic Wire, 24 August 2012, http://www.thewire.com/national/2012/08/new-york-times-says-graphic-empire-state-shooting-photo-was-newsworthy/56186.

50. For an overview, see Stephen J.A. Ward, "Ethics in a Nutshell," University of Wisconsin Center for Journalism Ethics, n.d., http://ethics.journalism.wisc.edu/resources/ethics-in-a-nutshell.

51. Thomas H. Bivins, "A Worksheet for Ethics Instruction and Exercises in Reason." Journalism Educator, June 1993 48: pp. 4–16.

52. Stephen J.A. Ward, "Digital Media Ethics," University of Wisconsin Center for Journalism Ethics, n.d., http://ethics.journalism.wisc.edu/resources/digital-media-ethics.

53. Melissa McEwan, "Careless, Cruel, and Unaccountable," Shakesville.com, 17 January 2014, http://www.shakesville.com/2014/01/careless-cruel-and-unaccountable.html.

54. Bill Simmons, "The Dr. V Story: A Letter From the Editor," Grantland.com, 14 January 2014, http://grantland.com/features/the-dr-v-story-a-letter-from-the-editor.

55. Goldenberg, "Journalism Ethics in a Digital Age."

56. Alfred Hermida, "Social Media Poses Digital Dilemma for Journalists," Journalism Ethics for the Global Citizen, 8 June 2007, http://www.journalismethics.ca/feature_articles/social_media_poses_digital_dilemmas.htm, cited in "The Facebook Conundrum: The New Haven Independent and the Annie Le Murder," Knight Case Studies Initiative, The Journalism School, Columbia University, n.d., https://casestudies.jrn.columbia.edu/casestudy/www/layout/standard.asp?case_id=53&id=539.

57. Patrick Barkham and Jeff Jarvis, "Were Reporters Right to Solicit Information from Students' Web Pages?" The Guardian, 23 April 2007, http://www.theguardian.com/media/2007/apr/23/mondaymediasection.

58. For more on this, see Chip Stewart, "Can I Use a Facebook Photo in a News Story Without Permission?" Texas Center for Community Journalism, n.d., http://digital.community-journalism.net/askanexpert/answers/can-i-use-facebook-photo-news-story-with.

59. "The Facebook Conundrum: The New Haven Independent and the Annie Le Murder," Knight Case Studies Initiative, The Journalism School, Columbia University, n.d., https://casestudies.jrn.columbia.edu/casestudy/www/layout/standard.asp?case_id=53&id=538&pid=0.

60. "The Facebook Conundrum: The New Haven Independent and the Annie Le Murder," Knight Case Studies Initiative, The Journalism School, Columbia University, n.d., https://casestudies.jrn.columbia.edu/casestudy/www/layout/standard.asp?case_id=53&id=540&pid=0.

Chapter 9

1. Josh Stearns, "Journalism Will Rise and Fall With Its Communities," Freepress.net, 4 February 2014, http://www.freepress.net/blog/2014/02/04/journalism-will-rise-and-fall-its-communities?utm_content=bufferc5e07.

2. Mallory Jean Tenore, "Social media editor role is 'more about an evolution than a contraction,'" Poynter.org, 30 May 2013, http://www.poynter.org/latest-news/mediawire/214781/social-media-editor-role-is-more-about-an-evolution-than-a-contraction.

3. Steve Buttry, "Engagement editors: an emerging, important job in Digital First newsrooms," The Buttry Diary, 22 March 2012, http://stevebuttry.wordpress.com/2012/03/22/engagement-editors-an-emerging-important-job-in-digital-first-newsrooms.

4. Buttry, "Engagement editors."

5. Mary Hartney Nahorniak, private communication, 3 January 2014.

6. Buffy Andrews, "So Many New Ways to Connect With Readers," YorkBlog.com, 16 January 2011, http://www.yorkblog.com/buffy/2011/01/16/so-many-new-ways-to-connect-with-readers.

7. Katherine Viner, "The rise of the reader: journalism in the age of the open web," The Guardian, 9 October 2013, http://www.theguardian.com/commentisfree/2013/oct/09/the-rise-of-the-reader-katharine-viner-an-smith-lecture.

8. Steve Buttry, "What Does 'Community Engagement' Mean?" The Buttry Diary, 3 June 2011, http://stevebuttry.wordpress.com/2011/06/03/what-does-community-engagement-mean.

9. Buttry, "What Does 'Community Engagement' Mean?"

10. Abigail Edge, "Five Social Media Tips from The Wall Street Journal," Journalism.co.uk, 4 February 2014, http://www.journalism.co.uk/news/five-tips-for-social-media-success-from-the-wall-street-journal/s2/a555772.

11. Nahorniak.

12. Michael Roston, "If a Tweet Worked Once, Send It Again – and Other Lessons from The New York Times' Social Media Desk," Nieman Lab, 6 January 2014, http://www.niemanlab.org/2014/01/if-a-tweet-worked-once-send-it-again-and-other-lessons-from-the-new-york-times-social-media-desk.

13. Brian Anthony Hernandezian, "The Grammys Social Team Is Just 1 Woman: This Is How She Does it All," Mashable, 26 January 2014, http://mashable.com/2014/01/26/grammys-social-media-lindsay-gabler.

14. Nahorniak.

15. Steve Buttry, "Vote for Your Favorite Winter Engagement Project," The Buttry Diary, 27 December 2013, http://stevebuttry.wordpress.com/2013/12/27/vote-for-your-favorite-winter-engagement-project.

16. Steve Buttry, "Jessica Keating wins Community Engagement DFMie for 'Beyond Bankruptcy,'" Inside Thunderdome, 27 March 2014, http://insidethunderdome.com/2014/03/27/jessica-keating-wins-community-engagement-dfmie-beyond-bankruptcy.

17. See, for instance, Derek Thompson, "The Facebook Effect on the News," The Atlantic, 12 February 2014, http://www.theatlantic.com/business/archive/2014/02/the-facebook-effect-on-the-news/283746.

18. Ellyn Angelotti, "How to Create Effective Social-Media Guidelines," Poynter.org, 2 July 2013, http://www.poynter.org/how-tos/digital-strategies/217139/how-to-create-effective-social-media-guidelines.

19. "Philadelphia Anchor Compares Horrible Shooting To 'Breaking Bad' In Tweet," The Huffington Post, 7 October 2013, http://www.huffingtonpost.com/2013/10/07/joyce-evans-breaking-bad-shooting-tweet-philadelphia_n_4056522.html.

20. Jim Romenesko, "Inappropriate Hashtag?" JimRomenesko.com, 21 November 2013, http://jimromenesko.com/2013/11/21/inappropriate-hashtag.

21. Ian Hill, email to author, 10 December 2013.

22. Meena Thiruvengadam, "How Journalists Can Measure Engagement," Poynter.org, 9 April 2013, http://www.poynter.org/how-tos/digital-strategies/209695/how-journalists-can-measure-engagement.

23. Hill.

24. Rachel Bartlett, "How Newsrooms Can Use Social Analytics to Guide Editorial Strategy," Journalism.co.uk, 19 June 2013, http://www.journalism.co.uk/news/how-newsrooms-can-use-social-analytics-to-guide-editorial-strategy/s2/a553295.

25. Rachel Bartlett, "#Tip: Analytics Tools for Journalists," Journalism.co.uk, 6 June 2013, http://www.journalism.co.uk/tip-of-the-day/-tip-analytics-tools-for-journalists/s419/a562015/.

26. Bartlett, "How Newsrooms."

27. Bartlett, "How Newsrooms."

Chapter 10

1. See, for instance, Scott Simon, "Go On, 'Curate' This Commentary, Too," NPR.com, 8 September 2012, http://www.npr.org/2012/09/08/160771957/go-on-curate-this-commentary-too.

2. Paul Bradshaw, "Journalism *Is* Curation: Tips on curation tools and techniques," Online Journalism Blog, 30 September 2013, http://onlinejournalismblog.com/2013/09/30/curation-tools-tips-advice-journalism/.

3. Rob Tornoe, "Digital Publishing: Flipping for Flipboard," Editor and Publisher, 17 September 2013, http://www.editorandpublisher.com/Columns/Article/Digital-Publishing2013-08-29T12-49-53.

4. Joshua Benton, "The Leaked New York Times Innovation Report is One of the Key Documents of This Media Age," Nieman Lab, 15 May 2014, http://www.niemanlab.org/2014/05/the-leaked-new-york-times-innovation-report-is-one-of-the-key-documents-of-this-media-age.

5. Timothy B. Lee, "Sorry, Jeff Bezos, the News Bundle Isn't Coming Back," The Washington Post, 5 September 2013, http://www.washingtonpost.com/blogs/the-switch/wp/2013/09/05/sorry-jeff-bezos-the-news-bundle-isnt-coming-back.

6. Lee.

7. More on these techniques can be found at Steve Buttry, "Aggregation guidelines: Link, attribute, add value," The Buttry Diary, 16 May 2012, http://stevebuttry.wordpress.com/2012/05/16/aggregation-guidelines-link-attribute-add-value.

8. Mindy McAdams, "Aggregation and curation in journalism," Teaching Online Journalism, 7 September 2013, http://mindymcadams.com/tojou/2013/aggregation-and-curation-in-journalism/.

9. Ryan McCarthy, "Business Insider, Over-aggregation, and the Mad Grab for Traffic," Reuters.com, 22 September 2011, http://blogs.reuters.com/felix-salmon/2011/09/22/business-insider-over-aggregation-and-the-mad-grab-for-traffic.

10. Robert Niles, "Five Lessons from 2007," Online Journalism Review, 21 December 2007, http://www.ojr.org/071220niles.

11. Jeff Jarvis, "Cover What You Do Best. Link to the Rest," Buzzmachine, 22 February 2007, http://buzzmachine.com/2007/02/22/new-rule-cover-what-you-do-best-link-to-the-rest.

12. Jonathan Stray, "Why link out? Four journalistic purposes of the noble hyperlink," Nieman Journalism Lab, 8 June 2010, http://www.niemanlab.org/2010/06/why-link-out-four-journalistic-purposes-of-the-noble-hyperlink.

13. Vince Rinehart, personal communication, 16 May 2014.

14. Hamish McKenzie, "Business Insider CEO Henry Blodget Defends Slideshow Journalism: 'It's native digital storytelling,'" PandoDaily, 14 November 2013, http://pando.com/2013/11/14/business-insider-henry-blodget-defends-slideshow-journalism-its-native-digital-storytelling.

15. Anna Lawlor, "5 Ways the Listicle Is Changing Journalism," The Guardian, 12 August 2013, http://www.theguardian.com/media-network/media-network-blog/2013/aug/12/5-ways-listicle-changing-journalism.

16. Aneya Fernando, "Why Listicles Are Here to Stay," 10,000 Words, 14 October 2013, https://www.mediabistro.com/10000words/why-listicles-are-here-to-stay_b23198.

17. Rachel Bartlett, "How BuzzFeed Uses Lists to Make News More Accessible," Journalism.co.uk, 31 March 2014, http://www.journalism.co.uk/news/how-buzzfeed-uses-lists-to-make-news-more-accessible/s2/a556291.

18. See, for example, Max Kalehoff, "Six Undeniable Reasons Why Listicles Have Jumped The Shark," MediaPost, 29 October 2013, http://www.mediapost.com/publications/article/212284/six-undeniable-reasons-why-listicles-have-jumped-t.html.

19. Jack Marshall, "The Listicle Era is (Sadly) Here to Stay," Digiday, 15 August 2013, http://digiday.com/publishers/listicle-era.

20. Maria Konnikova, "A List of Reasons Why Our Brains Love Lists," The New Yorker, 2 December 2013, http://www.newyorker.com/tech/elements/a-list-of-reasons-why-our-brains-love-lists.

21. Katie Tschopp, "How the Listicle is Reshaping Journalism," Zazoom Blog, 24 September 2013, http://www.zazoomvideo.com/how-the-listicle-is-reshaping-journalism.

22. Paul Grabowicz, "The Transition to Digital Journalism," UC Berkeley Graduate School of Journalism, 16 February 2014, http://multimedia.journalism.berkeley.edu/tutorials/digital-transform/photos-and-photo-slideshows.

23. Caroline O'Donovan, "The 3 Key Types of BuzzFeed Lists To Learn Before You Die," Nieman Journalism Lab, 11 October 2013, http://www.niemanlab.org/2013/10/the-3-key-types-of-buzzfeed-lists-to-learn-before-you-die.

24. Reuben Stern, "Tips for Making Good Audio Slideshows," Convergence Journalism, 21 March 2012, http://convergence.journalism.missouri.edu/?p=556.

25. Stern.

26. Dan Kois and Chris Kirk, "Which BuzzFeed Quiz Are You?" Slate, January 2014, http://www.slate.com/articles/technology/low_concept/2014/01/which_buzzfeed_quiz_are_you_quiz.html.

27. Caroline O'Donovan, "Are quizzes the new lists? What BuzzFeed's latest viral success means for publishing," Nieman Journalism Lab, 19 February 2014, http://www.niemanlab.org/2014/02/are-quizzes-the-new-lists-what-buzzfeeds-latest-viral-success-means-for-publishing.

28. Robinson Meyer, "The New York Times' Most Popular Story of 2013 Was Not an Article," The Atlantic, 17 January 2014, http://www.theatlantic.com/technology/archive/2014/01/-em-the-new-york-times-em-most-popular-story-of-2013-was-not-an-article/283167 and Allahpundit, "Resistance Is Futile: Everyone in America must take the NYT's dialect quiz," Hot Air, 24 December 2013, http://hotair.com/archives/2013/12/24/resistance-is-futile-everyone-in-america-must-take-the-nyts-dialect-quiz.

29. Mindy McAdams, "Timelines in journalism: A closer look." Teaching Online Journalism, 1 April 2011, http://mindymcadams.com/tojou/2011/timelines-in-journalism-a-closer-look/.

30. Ann Friedman, "What journalists need to know about animated GIFs – really," Poynter.org, 8 August 2012, http://www.poynter.org/how-tos/newsgathering-storytelling/183802/what-journalists-need-to-know-about-animated-gifs-really.

31. "Do Journalists Need to Know About GIFs?" Parse.ly, 9 August 2012, http://blog.parsely.com/post/70/do-journalists-need-to-know-about-gifs.

32. Patty McCord, "How Netflix Reinvented HR," Harvard Business Review, January-February 2014, http://hbr.org/2014/01/how-netflix-reinvented-hr/ar/1.

33. Steve Buttry, The Buttry Diary, "Organizing a Complex Story," 25 January 2014, http://stevebuttry.wordpress.com/2014/01/25/organizing-a-complex-story.

34. "Guided Tour," Storify.com, n.d., http://storify.com/tour.

Chapter 11

1. Wendalyn Nichols, "When You're On Deadline: Editorial Triage," Copyediting.com, n.d., http://www.copyediting.com/when-youre-deadline-editorial-triage-0#sthash.BNxMmAKF.dosD8upk.dpuf.

2. Michael King, "Will Automated Copy Editors Replace Human Ones?" American Journalism Review, 15 April 2014, http://ajr.org/2014/04/15/copy-editors-in-digital-world.

3. Dan Appenfeller, "Copy Editors Carve Niche in Digital Media Landscape," American Journalism Review, 13 May 2014, http://ajr.org/2014/05/13/copy-editors-digital-media.

4. Eric Brenner, "The Need for Guidelines," Copyediting.com, 22 January 2013, http://www.copyediting.com/need-guidelines#sthash.rYMckd25.dpuf.

5. Pam Nelson, "Copy editing in a hub: You're your own QA," American Copy Editors Society, 16 September 2013, http://grammarguide.copydesk.org/2013/09/16/copy-editing-in-a-hub-youre-your-own-qa/#more-2155.

6. Wendalyn Nichols, "Tip of the Week: Setting Editing Expectations," Copyediting.com, 3 April 2012, http://www.copyediting.com/tip-week-setting-editing-expectations#sthash.gWczfFBU.dpuf.

7. Eric Cummings, "Triage for the Copy Desk," ACES 2012 NOLA (coverage of the 16th National Conference of the American Copy Editors Society), 13 April 2012, http://nola.copydesk.org/blog/triage-for-the-copy-desk.

8. Jennifer Boynton, commenting on Carol Fisher Saller, "Copyeditor Confessions: Me First," Subversive Copy Editor Blog, 25 March 2013, http://www.subversivecopyeditor.com/blog/2013/03/copyeditor-confessions-me-first.html.

9. Vince Rinehart, personal communication, 29 April 2014.

10. Gerri Berendzen, "#ACESchat No. 7: Copy Editing Triage," Storify.com, 5 March 2013, http://storify.com/gerrrib/aceschat-no-7-copy-editing-triage.

11. Copy Curmudgeon, "Triage," Ask Copy Curmudgeon, 28 September 2012, http://askcopycurmudgeon.com/2012/09/28/triage.

12. Berendzen.

13. King.

INDEX

Abbasi, R. Umar, 115
Abramson, Jill, 109
Active sentences, 68
Actual malice, 80
Adjectival clauses, 86
Adjectives, 87
Advertising, 10
Advertorials, 109
Agence France-Presse, 92
Ages, as factual errors, 27–28
Aggregation, curation as, 139–141
Albom, Mitch, 104
"Allegedly," 80–81
Amazon.com, 139
American Copy Editors Society, 136
American Journalism Review, 113
Analytics, 129–131
Andrews, Buffy, 125–126
Angelotti, Ellyn, 128
Animated GIFs, 146–147
Anonymity, 112–113
Anonymous online comments, 113
Anonymous publishing
  defamation and, 82
  in workplace, 96
AOL, 112
AP Stylebook, 41–42
AP StyleGuard, 161
Apostrophes, 101–102
Apple, 96–97
Archives, defamation in, 84
Aristotle, 116
Arrington, Michael, 112
Asking questions, in headlines, 65
Associated Press, 106 (photo)
Atlanta Journal-Constitution, The, 113
Atlantic, The, 34, 147
Atlantic Monthly, The, 109
Attribution, of quotations, 40
Audience
  analytics used to learn about, 129–131
  content focused on, 43
  demographic traits of, 11–12
  ideas developed from, 19–20
  keeping of, 11
  psychographic traits of, 11–12
  target, 11–13
  writing style for, 44–45
Audio playlists, 139
Audio recordings, 95
Automated editing tools, 161

Back-editing, 155
Balance, 110–111
Baltimore Sun, The, 105, 145
Baquet, Dean, 116
Baresch, Brian, 156
Bartering, 11
Bezos, Jeff, 139
Bing, 35–36, 102
Bivins, Thomas, 116–117
Blair, Jayson, 104
Blodget, Henry, 142
Blog(s), 54–56
Bloggers
  business license for, 97
  deadlines and, 23
  foreign licensing of, 98
  imprisonment of, 72
  as journalists, 74, 76
  publishing of product or service
    endorsements, 94
Blogging, in workplace, 96–97
Blogrolls, 139
Bradshaw, Paul, 138, 141
Brainstorming of ideas, 19
Brand journalism, 20
Brenner, Erin, 45, 155
Buried leads, 33
Burton, Anne, 145
Business license, 97
Businesses, defamation effects on, 75
Buttry, Steve, 2, 104, 125–126, 132, 147
BuzzFeed, 131, 141, 143–145, 155

Caption, 66
Carr, David, 116
Center for International Media Assistance, 103
Chang, Alison, 95
Chartbeat, 131
Cheney, Dick, 114
Chicago Tribune, 37
Chronologies, 145–146
Chronology, as factual errors, 28
Ciarelli, Nicholas, 97
Cinematics, 144
Clarity, 46–51
Clark, Roy Peter, 47
Classified advertising, 10
Clauses, 22
Code of ethics, 103, 107, 116–117, 123
Coll, Steve, 96
Colloquial language, 44

Colons, 59
Columbia Journalism Review, 109
Commas, 86–87
Communications Decency Act, 80, 94
Community engagement, 126
Compound subjects, 21
Confidentiality, 112–113
Conflict, 18
Conflicts of interest, 111–112
Conjunctions, 53–54, 86
Content
    audience-centered, 43
    of others, responsibility for publishing, 94
    traditional news values for, 14–15. *See also*
        News values
    writer-centered, 43
Content marketing, 20
Content Marketing Institute, 20
Context, facts versus opinions determined by,
    76–77
Conversions, as factual errors, 28
Cooke, Janet, 104
Coordinating conjunctions, 54, 86
Copy. *See* Content
Copy editors, 2
Copyediting.com, 155
Copyright
    borrowing of information, 97–98
    infringement of, 92–94
    privacy and, 95
Corrections, 37, 83–84
Cox, Crystal, 74
Creation
    of animated GIFs, 146–147
    of chronologies, 145–146
    of listicles, 142–143
    of maps, 146
    of photo galleries, 143–145
    of quizzes, 145
    of slide shows, 143–145
    of timelines, 145–146
Creative Commons license, 93, 95
Crossfield, Jonathan, 47
Curation
    as aggregation or combination, 139–141
    definition of, 138
    as distribution or relay, 138–139
    as filter or distillation, 141
Curiosity gap, 64
Currency, 18–19
Custom content, 20
Cutlines, 66–67

Dangling modifiers, 121–122
Dashes, 59
Dates, as factual errors, 28
Davis, Raymond, 114
Deadlines, 23
Deadspin, 10, 24
Deception, 107–108

Defamation
    anonymous publishing and, 82
    in archive material, 84
    businesses affected by, 75
    corrections and clarifications for, 83–84
    definition of, 71, 73
    facts versus opinions, 75–77
    factual allegations and, 73
    false light versus, 90
    falsity and, 73
    global differences in, 99
    harming a person's reputation and, 73, 75
    libel, 72
    by omission, 73
    parody and, 81–82
    private figures, 78
    public figures, 78–80
    public officials, 78–80
    publication and, 73
    satire and, 81–82
    slander, 72
    status differences and, 77–82
Demographic traits, 11–12
Dependent clause, 53, 86
Detrich, Allan, 107
Detroit Free Press, 104
Dictionary, 7–8
Digital First Media, 2, 104, 125, 127, 147
Digital Media Law Project, 77–78, 80, 88, 92,
    94, 99
Digital Millennium Copyright Act, 94
Digital natives, 142
Digital publishing
    challenges associated with, 3
    deadlines in, 23
    instantaneous nature of, 71
    niche in, 10–11
Disclosure, of company relationships, 94
Disfluencies, 40
Display advertising, 10
Diversity, 117–118
Downstyle, of headlines, 58
Drones, 95–96
Duane Reade, 91

Eastside Journal, 105
Editing
    automated tools for, 161
    back-editing, 155
    online sites for practice in, 102
    overzealous, holes caused by, 34–35
    for voice, 46
Editor(s)
    blogs for, 54–56
    function of, 2
    organizations for, 136–137
    social media, 125
    traditional roles of, 2–3
    writers versus, 1
Editorial calendar, 23

Editorial triage
    checklist for, 156
    definition of, 155
    error prevention in, 156
Editors Association of Canada, 136
EditTeach.org, 102
EFF. *See* Electronic Frontier Foundation
Electronic Frontier Foundation, 71, 103
Embarrassing-facts tort, 90
Emotion, 44, 64
Empathy, 44
Employment, 96–97
Engagement
    analytics used to learn about audience, 129–131
    community, 126
    external, 125–127
    internal, 124–125
    Storify for, 153
    tools for, 131
Engagement editor, 125
Errors
    corrections for, 37
    factual. *See* Factual errors
    prevention of, 156
    in publishing, 2–3
    summary of, 37–38
Ethics/ethical issues
    anonymity, 112–113
    balance, 110–111
    code of, 103, 116–117, 123
    confidentiality, 112–113
    conflicts of interest, 111–112
    deceptive practices used to obtain
        information, 107–108
    diversity as concern of, 117–118
    fabrication, 104
    fairness, 110–111
    funding, 108–109
    image manipulation, 106–107
    overview of, 103
    plagiarism, 104–106
    sensitivity, 114–116
    taste, 114–116
    transparency, 109–110
    withholding information that could lead to
        harm, 113–114
Existing publications
    demographic information gathering, 12
    psychographic information gathering, 12
External engagement, 125–127

Fabrication, 104
Facebook, 13, 32, 37, 73, 91, 108, 119, 124, 126,
    131, 141–142, 145
Facebook Insights, 131
Facts
    contextual test for, 76–77
    opinion versus, 75–77
    private, public disclosure of, 90
Factual allegations, defamation and, 73

Factual errors
    common types of, 25–28
    corrections for, 37
    defamation and, 80
    definition of, 25
    names, 26
    numbers, 27–28
    place names, 26–27
    titles, 26
Fair report privilege, 77
Fair use, of copyrighted material, 92–94
Fairness, 110–111
Fake images, 31
False light, 90
Falsity, defamation and, 73
Fanpage Karma, 131
Filling holes, 31–35
First Amendment, 96
Fisher, Max, 93
Flesch-Kincaid Grade Level test, 51
Flickr, 93, 119
Flipboard, 139
Focus groups, 12–13
Fogel, Jeremy, 99
Forbes.com, 109
Foreign legal issues, 98–99
Foreman, Gene, 108–109, 111
Formal writing style, 44
Forman, Jay, 24
Fourth Amendment, 96
Fox News Channel, 30
Fragment, 53–54
Freepress.net, 124
Funding, 108–109
Fused sentence, 54

Gabler, Lindsay, 126
Gawker Media, 10
General-interest news publications, 9
George, 104
Getty Images, 92, 98
GIFS, animated, 146–147
Gizmodo, 10
Glass, Stephen, 104
GlobalPost, 140
Google, 11, 35–36, 61, 92, 98, 102, 106, 127
Google Analytics, 131
Google Glass, 95
Google News, 70
Google Trends, 63
Government, 97–98
Grammarly, 161
Grannis, Paul, 83
Grantland.com, 118
Greenwald, Glenn, 114
Gross negligence, 78
Group nouns, 21

Harming a person's reputation, 73, 75
Hazlett, Curt, 33

Headlines
    asking questions in, 65
    curiosity gap in, 64
    downstyle of, 58
    emotion conveyed in, 64
    importance of, 64
    latest news included in, 60
    lead and, 58
    length of, 60–61
    mullet model for, 63
    multiple-line, 59
    online, 62–65
    overpromise and overdeliver in, 64
    present tense of, 59
    print, 62
    punctuation with, 58–59
    resources for writing of, 70
    rewriting of, 64
    search engine optimization and, 62–63
    sexually suggestive, 65
    simplicity of, 57–59
    size of, 60–61
    specificity of, 59–60
    style rules for, 58–59
    subheads with, 61–62
    subject-verb-object format for, 57–58
    time element of, 59
    tips for creating, 60
    trends in, 63–65
    Twitter, 61
    type size of, 60
    upstyle of, 58
    word repetition in, 59
Headlinese, 59, 70
Heigl, Katherine, 91
Hermida, Alfred, 118
Hernandez, Marco A., 74
Heron, Liz, 124, 126
Hill, Ian, 19, 129–130
Hilton, Shani, 155
Hoaxes, 24–25, 28–29
Hochberg, Adam, 109
Hoff, John, 76
Hoffman, Dustin, 92
Holes
    buried leads as cause of, 33
    definition of, 25
    filling, 31–35
    lack of information as cause of, 33–34
    looking for, 32
    misunderstanding of reports as cause of, 34
    overzealous editing as cause of, 34–35
    source credibility problems as cause of, 34
HollywoodPulse.com, 30
Homonyms, 132–136, 148–153
Huffington, Arianna, 113
Huffington Post, The, 113
Human interest, 18
Hustler Magazine v. Falwell, 73

Ideas
    audience used to develop, 19–20
    brainstorming of, 19
    in sentences, 50–52
Identities, 67
Images. See also Photographs
    collections of, 139
    fake, 31
    manipulation of, 29–32, 106–107
    retouching of, 106
    taste and sensitivity of, 114–115
IMDB.com, 35
Impact, 15–16
Indefinite pronouns, 22
Independent clause, 53, 86
Informal writing style, 44–45
Information
    deceptive methods used to obtain, 107–108
    illegally obtained, disclosing or publishing
        of, 95
    lack of, holes caused by, 33–34
    online resources used to find and verify,
        35–36
    from public record, 90
    subject-verb-object format for reading of, 58
    withholding of, harm caused by, 113–114
Information gathering
    for existing publications, 12
    for new publications, 12
Interactive Telecommunications Program, 1
Interests, 10–11
"Internet Law: A Field Guide," 82–83
Interrupters, 40
Intrusion into seclusion, 91
Invisibility, of demographic groups, 118
Involuntary limited purpose public figures, 79
io9, 10

Jalopnik, 10
Jargon, 44
Jarvis, Jeff, 109, 141
Jezebel, 10
Journalistic privileges
    fair report, 77
    neutral report, 77
    opinion and fair comment, 75–77
Journalists, bloggers as, 74, 76
Jumping to conclusions, 111
Jungman, Nick, 155

Kant, Immanuel, 116
Kaplan, Jeremy, 88
Katz, Andrew, 30
Keating, Jessica, 127
Kennedy, John F., 114
Koechley, Peter, 63–64
Kolb, Joseph J., 98
Korean Communications Commission, 113
Kotaku, 10

Lack of information, holes caused by, 33–34
Language, colloquial, 44
Lanham, Richard, 48
Leads, 58
Leahy, Patrick, 114
Lee, Timothy B., 139
Legal hotlines, 88
Legal issues
   copyright infringement, 92–94
   defamation. *See* Defamation
   drones, 95–96
   foreign, 98–99
   new technologies, 95–96
   overview of, 71
   privacy. *See* Privacy
   pro bono programs, 88
   product endorsements, 94
   recordings, 95
   resources for, 87–88
   responsibility for publishing the statements
     and content of others, 94
   service endorsements, 94
Legal Schnauzer, 72
Lewis, Luke, 143
Libel, 72
Libel tourism, 99
License, 97–98
Lifehacker, 10
Limited purpose public figures, 79
Lingofy, 161
Links, 141–142
Listicles, 142–143
Loewenstein, Antony, 112
Long sentences, 49–50

Magazines
   deadlines for, 23
   headlines used in, 62
   niche for, 10–11
   writers for, 2
Mailer, Norman, 50
Main descriptive sentence, of cutline, 66
Malice, actual, 80
Manipulation of images, 29–32
Maps, 146
Marketer content, 109
Mashup, 146
Mathewson, James, 19–20, 46
Mayer, Joy, 126
McAdams, Mindy, 140, 145
McBride, Kelly, 31
McCarthy, Ryan, 140
McIntyre, John, 2, 43
Mentation presentations, 147
Mentoring, 125
Messner, Claude, 143
Metro Newspaper UK, 130
Microsoft Word, 51
Minor, 97–98

Misappropriation, 91–92
Mission statement, 13–14
Misunderstanding of reports, holes caused
   by, 34
Modifiers, dangling, 121–122
Moore, Jerry, 76
Morel, Daniel, 92
Moynihan, Richard, 130
Muck Rack, 131
Mullet model, 63
Multiple-line headlines, 59
MySpace, 119
Myths, 28–29

Nahorniak, Mary Hartney, 125–127
Names
   consent to use, 92
   as factual errors, 26, 67
   of minors, 97–98
   misappropriation of, 91
National Association of Independent Writers
   and Editors, 136
National Geographic, 107
National Press Photographers Association, 107
National security, 97
Negligence, 78–79
Neutral report privilege, 77
New publication
   information gathering for, 12
   niche for, 10–11
New Republic, The, 104
New York Post, 16 (photo), 107, 111, 115
New York Times, The, 3, 16 (photo), 31, 37, 93,
   104, 115 (photo), 116, 126, 130, 143
New York Times Co. v. Sullivan, 73, 80
News stories. *See* Stories
News values
   conflict, 18
   currency, 18–19
   human interest, 18
   impact, 15–16
   prominence, 17
   proximity, 17–18
   timeliness, 17
   traditional list of, 14–15
   unusualness, 17
   visual impact, 19
News websites, 9
Newseum, 70
Newspapers
   decline of, 9
   description of, 1–2
   headlines used in, 62
   online, 9
   writers for, 2
Newsroom 101, 102
Newsweek, 107
NewsWhip, 128
Newsworthiness, 90

Niche, 10–11
Nichols, Wendalyn, 155
Nolan, Hamilton, 10
Nominalization, 48
Numbers, as factual errors, 27–28

Objectivity, 20
Obsidian Finance Group, 74
O'Donovan, Caroline, 144
Olesker, Michael, 105
Omission, defamation by, 73
Onion, The, 29–30, 81
Online comments, anonymous, 113
Online headlines, 62–65
Online Journalism Blog, 138
Online Media Legal Network, 88
Online News Association, 137
Online newspapers, 9
Online publications, 71
Online resources, for finding and verifying
    information, 35–36
Online Writing Lab (Purdue), 102, 121
Opinion
    contextual test for, 76–77
    disclosing of, 111
    facts versus, 75–77
    false underlying facts and, 75
Opinion and fair comment privilege, 75–77
Original work, copyright infringement issues
    for, 93
Orwell, George, 48
Oswald, Lee Harvey, 114
Overholser, Geneva, 113
Overzealous editing, 34–35
Oxford English Dictionary, 8

Padrick, Kevin, 74
Paradox of choice, 143
"Paramedic Method, The," 48
Parody, 81–82
Passive sentences, 68–69
Passive voice, 68–69
Percentage, 28
Perelman, Deb, 46
PerfectIt, 161
Pervasive public figures, 78–79
Philebrity.com, 97
Photo galleries, 143–145
Photographs. See also Images
    captions for, 66
    cutlines for, 66–67
    manipulation of, 29–31
    metadata embedded in, 98
Photoshop, 107
Pick The Brain blog, 64
Pilhofer, Aron, 130
Place names, as factual errors, 26–27
Plagiarism, 104–106
PlainLanguage.gov, 49
Plato, 116

Plotz, David, 37
Plural form nouns, 22
Posts, social media, 118–119
Poundstone, Paula, 30
PowerPoint, 147
Poynter Institute, 31, 37, 66, 93, 108, 130, 147
Prepositional phrases, 22
Present tense
    of cutlines, 67
    of headlines, 59
Preston, Jennifer, 31
Print media
    headlines in, 60, 62
    subheads in, 62
Prior restraint, 72
Privacy
    aspects of, 89–90
    copyright and, 95
    false light, 90
    global differences in, 99
    historical description of, 89
    intrusion into seclusion, 91
    misappropriation, 91–92
    public disclosure of private facts, 90
    right of publicity, 92
Private figures, 78, 119
Private-facts tort, 90
Privileges
    fair report, 77
    neutral report, 77
    opinion and fair comment, 75–77
Pro bono programs, 88
Product endorsements, 94
Prominence, 17
Proximity, 17–18
Psychographic traits, 11–12
Public disclosure of private facts, 90
Public figures
    defamation of, 78–80
    misappropriation of, 91
    overzealous surveillance of, 91
Public officials, 78–80
Public record, information from, 90
Publication
    in defamation definition, 73
    existing. See Existing publications
    new. See New publication
Publicity, right of, 92
Publishing
    digital. See Digital publishing
    errors in, 2–3
    newspapers, 1–2
    traditional types of, 1–2
    trends that affected, 1
Punctuation, with headlines, 58–59
Purdue Online Writing Lab, 102, 121
Putin, Vladimir, 93

Questions, in headlines, 65
Quizzes, 145

Quotations, 39–40
Quotes (punctuation), 59

Rawls, John, 116
Reader survey, 12–13
"Reader's Guide to Headlinese, A," 70
RebelMouse, 141
Recordings, 95
Reddit, 141
Redundancies, 47
Reporters Committee on Freedom of the Press,
    81–83, 88, 90, 92, 95
Reputation, harming a person's, 73, 75
Retouching of images, 106
Reuters, 140
Richmond, Ray, 30
Right of publicity, 92
Righthaven LLC, 97–98
Rihanna, 91
Riley, Robert Jr., 72
Rinehart, Vince, 32, 142
Rivera, Pedro, 96
Rolling Stone, 104
Romney, Mitt, 95
Rosen, Jay, 88
Roston, Michael, 131
Run-on, 54

Safe harbor provisions, 94
San Jose Mercury News, 63
Satire, 81–82
Saudi Arabia, 98
Schlander, John, 131
Search engine optimization, 62–63
Securing the Protection of our Enduring and
    Established Constitutional Heritage Act, 99
Self-censorship, 109
Semicolons, 59
Sensitivity, 114–116
Sentence(s)
  active, 68
  clarity in, 46–51
  fused, 54
  length of, 49–50
  passive, 68–69
  redundancies in, 47
  single idea in, 50–52
  wordiness in, 48
Sentence fragment, 53–54
Separation of church and state, 109
Service endorsements, 94
Sexually suggestive headlines, 65
Shepherd, Jack, 143–144
Shirky, Clay, 1
Short sentences, 49–50
Shuler, Roger, 72
Silverman, Craig, 31, 37
Simple negligence, 78
Simpson, O.J., 107
Singapore, 98–99

Singular-meaning nouns, 22
Slander, 72
SLAPP suits, 82–83
Slate, 37, 145
Slide shows, 143–145
SmittenKitchen.com, 46
Snopes.com, 29–30
Snowden, Edward, 97
Social media
  guidelines for using, 128
  posts, 118–119
Social media editor, 125
SocialFlow, 131
Society for Editors and Proofreaders, 137
Society for News Design, 137
Society of American Business Editors and
    Writers, 137
Society of Journalists' Journalist's Toolbox, 102
Society of Professional Journalists, 88, 112, 137
Source credibility problems, holes caused by, 34
Sources, confidentiality of, 112–113
SPEECH Act. See Securing the Protection of our
    Enduring and Established Constitutional
    Heritage Act
Sprout Social, 131
Sreenivasan, Sree, 139
St. Pierre, Nate, 25
Stahl, Jeremy, 37
Stanford University's Copyright & Fair Use
    website, 94
Statements of others, responsibility for
    publishing, 94
Status differences, defamation affected by, 77–82
Steade, Susan, 63
Stearns, Josh, 124
Steele, Bob, 108
Stereotyping, 118
Stewart, Martha, 107
Stories
  indirect effects of, 16
  proximity used in selection of, 18
Storify, 141, 153–154
Stray, Jonathan, 141
Student Press Law Center, 88
Stylebook, 41–42
Subheads, with headlines, 61–62
Subject-verb agreement, 21–22
Subject-verb-object format, for headlines, 57–58
Subordinating conjunctions, 53
Surveys, 12–13
Sweeney, Joey, 97
Synonyms, 59

Tansa, 161
Target audience, 11–13
Taste, 114–116
"Telling the Truth and Nothing But," 106
Think Secret, 96
Third person, 44
Time, 107

Timeline(s), 145–146
Timeliness, 17
Titles, as factual errors, 26
Toledo Blade, 107
Toronto Star, 37, 105
Tovar, Miguel, 106 (photo)
Trade secrets, 96–97
Transformative work, 93
Transparency, 109–110
Tumblr, 13
Tumblr blogs, 139
Tweets, 129
Twitter, 13, 31, 37, 47, 61, 91, 108, 116, 119,
   126–127, 129, 142, 145, 156
Twitter Analytics, 131
Twitter lists, 139
Twitter retweets, 139

Unusualness, 17
Upstyle, of headlines, 58
Upworthy.com, 63
Urban legends, 28–29

Values. *See* News values
Veltman, Noah, 144
Verbosity, 46–50
Verbs
   passive voice and, 68
   subject-verb agreement, 21–22
VerificationJunkie.com, 36
Video manipulation, 29–31
Video playlists, 139
Video recordings, 95
Viner, Katherine, 126
Visual impact, 19

Vogel, John, 83
Voice
   description of, 45–46
   passive, 68–69

Wall Street Journal, The, 124
Wänke, Michaela, 143
Ward, Stephen J.A., 117
Washington Post, The, 3, 32, 37, 40, 104, 139
Webb, Amy, 112
Webster's Third New International
   Dictionary, 8
Weisbaum, Herb, 28–29
Whyld, Lewis, 96
WikiLeaks, 97
Wikipedia, 35–36
Wind-ups, 49
Wired, 18
Wise, Mike, 40
Wong, Justin, 95
Wordiness, 48
Workplace, blogging in, 96–97
World Wide Web
   birth of, 1
   links, 141–142
Writers
   challenges for, 3
   editors versus, 1
   voice of, 45–46
Writing
   styles of, 44–45
   subject-verb-object format for, 58

York Daily Record, 125
YouTube, 31, 139, 141

ABOUT THE AUTHOR

Thom Lieb is a professor of Journalism and New Media at Towson University in Maryland. He has taught the News Editing course there since he joined the faculty in 1990, and additionally has taught it at four other universities. The two editions of his previous editing text, *Editing for Clear Communication,* have been used in classrooms for more than 15 years.

Lieb has been involved with digital media since its inception. His "Editing for the Web" online project was used for training in schools and newsrooms around the world. For several years, he served as a columnist for the Journal of Electronic Publishing, and he is a longtime member of the Online News Association.

In addition, Lieb has worked as a writer and editor for newspapers, newsletters, magazines and online media. He is the author of "Building Basic News Sites" and "All the News: Writing and Reporting for Convergent Media."

Lieb earned his bachelor's degree in Journalism and Communication from Point Park University in Pittsburgh, his master's in Magazine Journalism from Syracuse University, and his doctorate in Public Communication/Journalism from the University of Maryland at College Park.

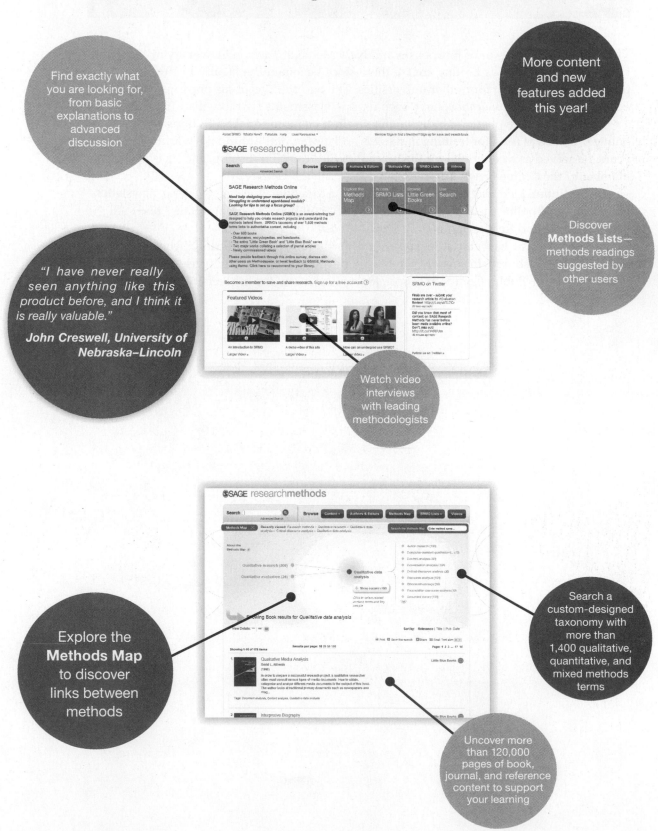

SAGE researchmethods

The essential online tool for researchers from the world's leading methods publisher

Find exactly what you are looking for, from basic explanations to advanced discussion

More content and new features added this year!

"I have never really seen anything like this product before, and I think it is really valuable."

John Creswell, University of Nebraska–Lincoln

Discover **Methods Lists**— methods readings suggested by other users

Watch video interviews with leading methodologists

Explore the **Methods Map** to discover links between methods

Search a custom-designed taxonomy with more than 1,400 qualitative, quantitative, and mixed methods terms

Uncover more than 120,000 pages of book, journal, and reference content to support your learning

Find out more at
www.sageresearchmethods.com